Quest for the *Real* Samoa

Samoan values are strongly situational rather than individualistic

Quest for the *Real* Samoa

The Mead/Freeman CONTROVERSY
& Beyond

LOWELL D. HOLMES

Postscript by Eleanor Leacock

Bergin & Garvey Publishers, Inc.
MASSACHUSETTS

First published in 1987 by
Bergin & Garvey Publishers, Inc.
670 Amherst Road
South Hadley, Massachusetts 01075

89   98765432

Manufactured in the United States of America.

Library of Congress Cataloging-in-Publication Data

Holmes, Lowell Don, 1925–
   Quest for the real Samoa.

   Bibliography: p.
   Includes index.
   1. Ethnology—Samoan Islands. 2. Mead, Margaret,
1901–1978. 3. Freeman, Derek. 4. Samoans—Social
life and customs. I. Title.
GN671.S2H64 1987   306'.0996   86-8317
ISBN 0-89789-110-4

All photographs courtesy of the author.

Contents

Preface

Why have I written this book? Is it because I so greatly revered Margaret Mead that I do not wish to have her memory tarnished? Is it because I am an American and therefore feel committed to support the theoretical framework of Franz Boas, the "Father of American Anthropology?" Or is it because my career as a cultural anthropologist has been so productive and so distinguished that I now want to share my special knowledge with the scientific world?

To begin with I owe nothing special to Margaret Mead.

I left Northwestern University in 1954 to begin fieldwork in Pago Pago. Although I wrote to Margaret Mead as soon as I arrived in Pago Pago, my response from her could hardly be described as friendly. Apparently, Mead thought that her former classmate at Columbia, Melville Herskovits, had put me up to some mischief. She maintained that I should have come to New York and spent time with her and her field notes, and this would have been an indication of my sincerity and good faith. After her initial letter I did not hear from her again until I wrote requesting some special information.

One day while reading *Coming of Age in Samoa* I turned to the appendix and studied the case histories of the teenage girls Mead had worked with in Ta'ū village. Some of the girls appeared to be deviants while others were quite conventional in their behavior. It occurred to me that it might be interesting to follow up on these people and see how the life histories of the deviants might have differed from those of the conventionals over 28 years. I wrote Mead about my ideas and asked for the real names of the girls, since those in *Coming of Age in Samoa* were obviously fictitious. She wrote back to say that she had to protect the identity of the girls for ethical reasons but that if I would reconstruct the composition of all the households in Ta'ū village for the period of 1925 that she would reveal the households in which the girls lived. This was never done because, after taking a census of the village and comparing it with one taken by the government four years earlier, I found that discrepancies were numerous and in some households as much as 50 percent of its composition was different. The task of reconstruction would have been almost, if not completely, impossible and would have taken much more time than the findings would have been worth.

During my time in the field Mead was helpful, however, and she often sent me photocopies of unpublished documents, such as William Churchill's *Fa'alupega i Manu'a*, which was important in understanding village political structure. I never thought at the time that my restudy of Margaret Mead's work would in 1983 become vitally important in sorting out the facts in anthropology's greatest controversy in 100 years, the debate brought on by the publication of Derek Freeman's *Margaret Mead and Samoa: the Making and UnMaking of an Anthropological Myth.*

Upon my return from Samoa in 1954 my relationship with Mead was one of storm and stress at best. My first book, *Ta'ū: Stability and Change in A Samoan Village* (1958), was given a terrible review by her in the *American Anthropologist.* Some years later Margaret mellowed a bit toward me, and I frequently had the opportunity to sit down and carry on a friendly discussion about what we shared in common—a knowledge of Samoa and Samoans. We occasionally appeared on panels together discussing Polynesian issues, but I was hardly a protégé of this eminent anthropologist, although she often sent me copies of letters she had written to people about Samoan matters. On one occasion she recommended me to someone as a consultant on Samoa, and she even directed one scholar to me with the recommendation that I was more informed about the recent cultural developments in Samoa than she.

While I was educated in the Boasian tradition by a student of Boas, Melville Herskovits, it was a theoretical tradition which I saw as embracing both cultural and biological aspects of the nature of the human animal and one which rejected all forms of deterministic thinking. I could not have accepted anything less.

The importance of culture in the lives of human beings is for me an important given, not just a loose variable in an otherwise stolid theory. The influence of culture as a vital force in human behavior has been a major ingredient in the scientific thought of most recognized anthropologists, from Edward Tylor to Franz Boas to Alfred Kroeber to Leslie White to Gregory Bateson. Even the British who tend to talk about "society," "structure," and "function" but rarely "culture," see human behavior as a product of both traditional mores and biological needs.

My career in anthropology has hardly been so extraordinary that I feel compelled to pass on a series of "truths" about the nature of mankind, although my experience in Samoa and other cultures has provided me with some insights into human behavior that armchair anthropologists never learn. I believe I have learned a few things about how to study a society that is not my own and I am aware of the major pitfalls in field research. I must admit that I owe a great deal to Derek Freeman, as do most Samoan specialists these days, for rescuing all of our careers from obscurity. With all the mayhem going on in the world today people tend to forget about a peaceful little spot like Samoa.

Much of what I have included in this book has appeared in other articles and books that I have written during my thirty-year career as an anthropologist. The volume is therefore somewhat of a compilation; some sections have undergone major rewriting and other parts have been used with only minor revision. Therefore I would like to note the particular materials I have drawn upon and thank the original publishers for the reuse of the data. I would like to thank the Polynesian Society who originally published my book *Ta'ū: Stability and Change in a Samoan Village*, Holt, Rinehart, and Winston for use of sections from *Samoan Village*, and I would like to acknowledge the fact that I have drawn upon data from my doctoral dissertation at Northwestern University (1957) and from the following periodicals: *Journal of American Folklore, Current Anthropology, American Anthropologist, The Sciences, Quarterly Review of Biology, Canberra Anthropology, Journal of Psychological Anthropology, Anthropologica, Journal of Missiology* and *Anthropological Quarterly*. I have also drawn upon material previously published by me in the Oxford University Press volume *Land Tenure in the Pacific* and the Wiley and Sons book *Anthropology, An Introduction*. To my wife, Ellen, for her services as a dedicated editor and proof reader and to my secretary, Georgia Ellis, who spent long hours at the word processor, I offer my sincere thanks.

LOWELL D. HOLMES,
Wichita State University

SAMOAN PRONUNCIATION GUIDE

While a few exceptions exist, vowels, dipthongs and consonants are generally pronounced as follows:

a is pronounced as *a* in f*a*ther.

e is pronounced as *a* in c*a*dence.

i is pronounced as *ee* in s*ee*.

o is pronounced as *o* in s*o*.

u is pronounced as *oo* in s*oo*n.

ae and ai are distinct dipthongs, but both approximate *ie* in v*ie*.

ao and au are distinct dipthongs, but both approximate *ow* in n*ow*.

ei is pronounced as *ay* in s*ay*.

ou is pronounced as *ow* in l*ow*.

All consonants approximate those in English except g which is pronounced *ng* as in lo*ng*.

' indicates glottal stop.

¯ indicates long vowel.

Quest for the *Real* Samoa

American Samoan village

ONE

Mead's *Coming of Age* Research

In 1911 Franz Boas, Margaret Mead's future mentor and role model, wrote a book titled *The Mind of Primitive Man*. The edition published in Germany carried the title *Kultur und Rasse*. This book which has been called the "Magna Carta of self-respect for the lower races" (Swanton 1930), put forward the idea that there were no lower races (or higher races) at all. Boas was skeptical of any purported "demonstration" of innate racial differences that supported explanations of racial inferiority or superiority. In his book, Boas advanced the idea that

> historical events appear to have been much more potent in leading races to civilization than their faculty, and it follows that achievements of races do not warrant us in assuming that one race is more highly gifted than the other. [1911:17]

While urging that considerable attention be given to the nature of particular historical events in the explanations of levels of cultural achievement, he did not (as Derek Freeman now charges; 1983: 31–33, 40) completely reject the possibility that biological differences could influence some types of behavior or that it was scientifically valid to disregard completely the biological nature of the human animal and dwell exclusively on culture as the sole determinant of human behavior. In 1910 Boas wrote:

> Anatomical observations on the various races suggest that differences in the form of the nervous system are presumably accompanied by differences in function, or psychologically speaking, that the mental traits which characterize

1

different individuals are distributed in varying manner
among different races. . . . The evidence that has been
brought forward does not justify us, however, in claiming
that the characteristics of one race would be an advance
over those of another, although they would be different.
[1910:371]

Boas advocated a theoretical approach to the study of human behavior that represented a balanced view of the influence of biology
and culture in shaping behavior. Melville J. Herskovits has described
this approach:

Because of his rounded view of the problem, Boas could
perceive so clearly the fallacy of the eugenist theory, which
held the destiny of man to be determined by biological
endowment, with little regard for the learned, cultural
determinants of behavior. By the same token, however, he
refused to accept the counter-dogma that man is born with
a completely blank slate, on which can be written whatever
is willed. [1953:25]

As Boas saw it, the scientific problem was to determine the relation
between environmental and hereditary factors. While Boas believed
that the human species was first and foremost a *cultural* animal, it is
noteworthy that Marvin Harris, in his book *The Rise of Anthropological
Theory* writes that "Boas systematically rejected almost every conceiv-
able form of cultural determinism" (1968:283). Derek Freeman, on the
other hand, maintains that Boas espoused a position of cultural determinism (often referring to him or his students—Kroeber, Lowie,
Benedict, and Mead—as "absolute cultural determinists") and charges
that Boas was a man who promoted a concept of human nature as a
"*tabula rasa.*"[1]

How it can be claimed that Franz Boas did not take the biological
component into consideration in the study of human behavior is
beyond comprehension, considering the fact that Boas spent his first
two years at Columbia University as a lecturer in physical anthropology. Boas was also a major promoter of the American Association of Physical Anthropologists and its journal.

The anthropological perspective promoted by Boas was a holistic,
four-discipline approach involving cultural anthropology, physical
anthropology, archaeology, and linguistics. All graduate students in
American universities are required to take courses in both cultural
and physical anthropology and answer questions in both of these
areas in comprehensive examinations. On this point Marvin Harris
has commented:

Unlike its European counterpart, American anthropology
has always been concerned with the relationships between

nature (in the guise of habitat and genic programming) and culture (in the guise of traditions encoded in the brain, not in the genes).

Neither Boas nor his students ever denied that *Homo sapiens* has a species-specific nature. What they denied in the first instance was that variations in human nature—especially those associated with racial groupings—could account for a substantial portion of the enormous variations in cultural coding found all over the world in the past 10,000 to 20,000 years. [1983:26]

Following World War I there was considerable speculation concerning the meaning of the results of Stanford–Binet tests, which had been given to large numbers of American servicemen. The fact that Blacks scored lower than whites was interpreted by many as evidence that the achievements of particular races were an expression of their genetic statuses and that biology alone established the ceiling for performance. But it was also discovered that northern Blacks had a tendency to score higher than southern blacks, and it was Boas' opinion that environmental factors could not be dismissed. For Boas, cultural environment exerted a profound influence on behavior and mental functions, and cultural differences could account for differences in achievement without postulating an innate component.

The Stanford–Binet issue was but one skirmish in a nature/nurture controversy that was hotly debated during the first four decades of this century. An analysis of nature vs. nurture advocates during this period reveals that those who emphasized environmental factors—William Bagley, James Cattell, Charles H. Cooley, J.B.S. Haldane, Hermann Muller, Lester Ward, John Watson, and Franz Boas—tended toward political liberalism, while those emphasizing hereditary factors—Charles Davenport, Francis Galton, G. Stanley Hall, Karl Pearson, and Edward Thorndike—leaned toward political conservatism. The controversy was clearly both sociopolitical and scientific.

FRANZ BOAS AND G. STANLEY HALL

Boas was an ardent environmentalist who believed that the mission of anthropology, and his mission as an anthropologist, was the destruction of certain dangerous American prejudices. Examples of these "prejudices" for Boas, according to Nicholas Pastore, involved such notions as "the identity of the race and nation, the superiority of the White Race, the identification of absolute ethics with our modern code of behavior, the resistance to fundamental criticism of our civilization" (1949:140).

Boas was also a vigorous advocate of academic freedom and it was a violation of this cherished trust that initially caused him to quarrel with his first employer, G. Stanley Hall (President of Clark University), and later to submit his resignation. Concerning this incident, Herskovits writes: "The intensity of Boas' reaction to what he conceived to be Hall's irresponsibility never diminished, a feeling not lessened by his view as to the inadequacies of Hall's psychological position" (1953:15). It is not surprising, therefore, given Boas environmentalist position and the nature of his relationship with Hall, that he was particularly interested in a book written by Hall in 1904. This two-volume work, titled *Adolescence*, might be called a treatise on recapitulation in development. Maintaining that the psychological growth of an individual can be seen as the repeating of the life history of the race, Hall postulated that the individual behavior was determined not by cultural or social environmental influences but by the nature of the person's racial past and level of maturation.

Describing adolescent years, Hall wrote:

> Important growth-changes characterize this period . . . making possible still more striking and important psychic and social transformations. . . . Variations often thought pathological are normal at this age. [1904:827].

Hall maintained that the child would pass through a series of stages, each providing the necessary stimulus for the next. Believing that emotional disturbance marked adolescence in all human societies, Hall alleged that "first there is a marked increase of crime at the age of twelve to fourteen, not in crimes of one, but of all kinds, and that this increase continues for a number of years" (ibid.:325). "Fourteen is the maximal age for incorrigibility and malicious mischief and trespass; fifteen for petty larceny, vagrancy, disorderly conduct and assaults; sixteen for larceny, burglary and public intoxication; and seventeen for fornication" (ibid.:333). According to Hall, adolescence was inevitably a time of storm and stress, or what German theorists at that time had been calling "*Sturm, Drang und Weltschmerz.*"

ENTER MARGARET MEAD

In the fall of 1920, a young woman named Margaret Mead entered Barnard College in New York City as a transfer student from Depauw University. Barnard and Columbia University shared a number of faculty members, and in her senior year Margaret Mead was faced with a choice of taking either a philosophy course taught by Columbia Professor William Pepperell Montague or a course in Columbia's anthropology department taught by Franz Boas. She selected the latter. She found Boas a "surprising and somewhat frightening" (1972:112–114) teacher but she was drawn to the subject matter and greatly impressed by the dedication of Boas' teaching assistant, Ruth Benedict, who lured Margaret Mead into the profession by promising that "Professor Boas and I have nothing to offer but an opportunity to do work that matters." And Benedict stressed the urgency of that work: anthropology had to be done *now*.

After completing a doctoral dissertation on stability and change in Polynesia that was based solely on the existing literature, Mead was anxious to try her wings as a field researcher in an exotic culture, particularly Polynesia. Boas, however, thought the Pacific area too dangerous for a 23-year-old girl who weighed only 98 pounds and stood 5 ft. 2 in. tall.

She recalls the circumstances surrounding preparations for the field:

> The choice of where I went to the field and what problem I would work on was not mine alone to make. The final decision rested with Boas, and he wanted me to study adolescence. He decided that the time had come to tackle a set of problems that linked the development of individuals to what was distinctive in the culture in which they were reared. In the summer of 1924, when Ruth Bunzel said she wanted to go to Zuni, he suggested that she work on the role of the individual artist. Now he wanted me to work on adolescence, on the adolescent girl, to test out, on the one hand, the extent to which the troubles of adolescence . . . depended upon the attitudes of a particular culture and, on the other hand, the extent to which they were inherent in the adolescent stage of psychobiological development with all its discrepancies, uneven growth, and new impulses. [1972:126–127]

Boas had advised Mead specifically not to collect a general ethnography of Samoa but to focus on a particular problem. Although Boas had conveyed nothing of what her methodology should be, Mead approached the problem as one of cross-cultural analysis. Such analysis has long been used in cultural anthropology to determine, among other things, whether a given behavioral phenomenon is cultural (primarily learned) or inherited through the genes. Mead, who suspected that American adolescent stress resulted from the American cultural environment, chose to go to a different civilization and make a study of human beings under different cultural conditions in some other part of the world. For such studies the anthropologist chooses quite simple peoples, whose society has never attained the complexity of our own. In this choice of primitive people . . . the anthropologist is guided by the knowledge that the analysis of a simpler civilization is more possible of attainment. [1928a:7–8]

From such societies, those that are different from one's own in historical development, language, and religious ideas, Mead believed "it is possible to learn many things about the effect of a civilization upon the individuals within it" (ibid.:8).

MEAD'S FIELD PROBLEM

By investigating the lives of adolescent girls in Samoa Mead hoped to test whether the teenage years were everywhere a time of rebellion and psychological upheaval, as Hall had predicted. If she found that such behavior did not occur in Samoan culture then she could use this "negative instance" to challenge claims of a physiological determinant for adolescent behavior.

While Derek Freeman insists that Boas assigned the problem of testing the G. Stanley Hall hypothesis about adolescence to his young student Margaret Mead, Victor Barnouw, also a Boas protégé, writes:

Boas' influence on Mead's research may not have been as far-reaching as Freeman maintains. We are told that she received only half an hour's worth of advice from him, and the letter that Boas wrote to Mead about her forthcoming research does not seem heavy-handed. Boas appears to have been making suggestions which Mead might follow up if she wished. . . . Mead herself said of Boas that "he did not teach us by laying out a systematic plan for future research, such as is possible in an experimental science." [Barnouw 1983:431].

Nor do we see the heavy hand of an inflexible pedant in Mead's presentation of her findings to Boas after her return from the field. Mead states that she was very apprehensive about how Boas would receive her manuscript. She feared that she had "betrayed him like all the rest" and that she had wasted her opportunity to properly record the nature of a disappearing culture (Cassidy 1982:31). Apparently, however, Boas suggested only a few minor changes.

From the following sections of the letter Boas wrote Mead on the eve of her departure for the Pacific it can be seen that Boas sent her out to *investigate* something and not to *prove* something, as Derek Freeman would have it (1983:59–60).

> One question that interests me very much is how the young girls react to the restraints of custom. We find very often among ourselves during the period of adolescence a strong rebellious spirit that may be expressed in sullenness or in sudden outbursts. . . . I am not at all clear in my mind in how far similar conditions may occur in primitive society and in how far the desire for independence may be simply due to our modern conditions and to a more strongly developed individualism. [Mead 1972:138]

Armed with these somewhat casual comments from her mentor, a twenty-year old theory to test, six cotton dresses, a strongbox for money and important papers, a small Kodak camera, a portable typewriter, and a few notebooks, Margaret Mead boarded a train for California, the first leg of her trip to the South Seas, a journey she would make many times in her life.

IN THE SOUTH SEAS

Mead arrived in Pago Pago, American Samoa, on August 31, 1925. Although the U.S. Navy (which governed the islands at that time) knew of her impending visit, no one was at the dock to meet her. Nonetheless, she did manage to find the one hotel in town (the one that had inspired Somerset Maugham to write the short story "Rain") and she settled in for a six-week stay that would consist mostly of an intensive study of the Samoan language. She was assisted in her efforts by a bright young Samoan nurse, Pepe, who had visited the United States and spoke excellent English. Pepe worked with Mead one hour a day, and then left her to put in an additional seven hours on her own, memorizing vocabulary, courtesy phrases, and simple sentences.

Mead believed that she would have greater success with the language if she could live for a time in a Samoan household. She arranged for a short stay in Vaitogi village in October 1925. There she was able to practice her language skills, learn about Samoan etiquette, acquire a taste for Samoan food, and receive her first instruction in the art of Samoan dancing, called *siva*.

In November 1925, still far from fluent in the language, Mead decided to begin her field study of adolescent girls. For this she had chosen the island of Ta'ū in the Manu'a island group (60 miles east of

Tutuila). According to her letter to Franz Boas, Ta'ū was "the only island with villages where there are enough adolescents, which are at the same time primitive enough and where I can live with Americans. I can eat native food, but I can't live on it for six months, it is too starchy" (Mead 1977:28)

She went on to describe the remote area where she would reside as follows:

> There are no white people on the island except the Navy man in charge of the dispensary, his family, and two corpsmen. There is . . . a cluster of four villages there within a few minutes' walk of each other. The chief, Tufele, who is also district governor of Manu'a, was educated in Honolulu and speaks excellent English and is probably the most cooperative chief in American Samoa. [Ibid.: 29]

From November 1925 to June 1926 Mead lived in Ta'ū village on the screened back porch of the dispensary which was presided over by Chief Pharmacist Mate Edward R. Holt. Here she had easy access to a group of about 50 girls ranging in age from eight to twenty years. She developed close friendships with many of them and they dropped by to see her at all hours. She also "borrowed" a schoolhouse to give "examinations" and under that heading she stated:

> I was able to give a few simple tests [color naming, rote memory for digits, digit symbol substitution, opposites (23 words), picture interpretation (of *Moana* stills) and ball and field] and interview each girl alone. Away from the dispensary I could wander freely about the village or go on fishing trips or stop at a house where a woman was weaving. Gradually I built up a census of the whole village and worked out the background of each of the girls I was studying. Incidentally, of course, I learned a great deal of ethnology, but I never had any political participation in village life. [1972:151]

Mead conducted much of her investigative work in the Samoan language, in which she had developed rather surprising skills considering her two month acquisition period. However, many areas of information were closed to her because she was a woman, and a young one at that. She was not permitted to attend village council meetings (except for an occasional courtesy when she served as honorary *taupou*). Most details of village ceremonial life and social structure were provided to her by certain sympathetic and cooperative chiefly informants such as High Chief Tufele who had to a large extent taken Margaret under this wing. A number of informants and anthropologists (particularly, Derek Freeman[2]) have accused Mead of "going native" in an attempt to experience the sexual joys of "under the palms" relationships for herself. However, no informant that I utilized, who knew Margaret Mead when she was in Ta'ū village (including Mrs. Sotoa who ran the village store by the church and with whom Margaret often stayed for several days at a time), were aware of any untoward behavior on her part. Jane Howard records in her biography of Mead:

> One Samoan man, Mead later told Luther Cressman, had in fact made quite clear his willingness to demonstrate his sexual prowess in order to provide her with firsthand knowledge. And though it was rumored she had taken him up on the offer, she abstained, and learned all she could in conversations which persuaded her that Samoans were so familiar with sex, and so given to dealing with sex as an art, that they had produced "a scheme of personal relations in which there are no neurotic pictures, no frigidity, no impotence, except as the temporary result of severe illness, and the capacity for intercourse only once a night is counted as senility." [1984:85–86]

WRITING UP THE DATA

In June 1926 Mead returned to Pago Pago and two weeks later left for home by way of Australia and England. Upon her return to New York Mead began her first job in anthropology—Assistant Curator of Ethnology at the American Museum of Natural History. Her new job gave her time to write, and within a few months she had completed all but the last two chapters of *Coming of Age in Samoa,* the chapters in which she would compare adolescence in Samoa and in the United States.

Mead had targeted the book more for schoolteachers, psychologists, and parents than for anthropologists. The subject matter was vital information for the rearing of future generations, she reasoned, and therefore she purposely had used layman's language and had not engaged in the usual anthropological practice of inserting an abundance of native words. But despite her efforts to make the book relevant to non-anthropologists, the first publisher she approached, Harper & Brothers, rejected the manuscript. However, the book was brought to the attention of William Morrow, president of a newly established publishing firm. Mead recalls that Morrow had a good deal of influence in the shaping of the final draft of *Coming of Age in Samoa.*

> Mr. Morrow had dealt with educational books all his publishing life, and when he had read the manuscript (which

then ended with the final chapter on Samoa), he asked me: "What would you have to say if you wrote some more about what all this means to Americans?"

Fortunately, I knew. When I came back from Samoa I was asked to give lectures before an assortment of audiences— in schools, in the Long Island town where a cousin lived, in a new housing project for intellectuals—and, when I was asked about the meaning of what I had found in Samoa, I was compelled to think through the answers. It seemed clear, to start with, that if girls in Samoa did not have to live through the difficulties that face American girls in adolescence, then the problem is not the inevitable, universal one that it was assumed to be. If one society could bring its children through adolescence painlessly, then there was a chance that other societies could do so also. What then, audiences wanted to know, did this mean to us, as Americans? During the same winter, I was also teaching an evening class of working girls, and their questions, which I had to answer, were quite different from those I had thought of.

Fresh from these experiences, I was ready to write the last two chapters—one comparing the lives of Samoan and American girls and one called "Education for Choice." This chapter, written in 1928, is still relevant. The problem of bringing up children who are free to choose among many alternatives is one we shall be trying to solve, in new and better ways, as long as we are a democracy.

The manuscript was at last complete. [1965:124–125]

TWO

Restudies: Use and Misuse

In 1966 and 1967 I received a series of letters from an anthropologist named Derek Freeman, posted in Sa'anapu village, Western Samoa, stating that he had returned to resume his studies of the society after more than 20 years. He requested that I send him reprints of some of my publications on Samoa and asked if I could provide him with xerox copies of particular sections of my 1957 doctoral dissertation, "A Restudy of Manu'an Culture: A Problem in Methodology," which had been a systematic analysis of the quality of Margaret Mead's research in American Samoa in 1925–26.

The tone of his inquiries was such that I surmised that this was something other than a scholarly endeavor, and after a couple of letters it became obvious that Freeman was primarily interested in obtaining evidence damaging to Mead and that he was not doing a general study of Samoan culture at all.[1] Therefore, it was no surprise when on January 31, 1983, I saw the article on the front page of the *New York Times* with the headline reading "New Samoa Book Challenges Margaret Mead's Conclusions." "Two months before its official publication date," the article reported, "a book maintaining that the late Margaret Mead seriously misrepresented the culture and character of Samoa has ignited heated discussion within the behavioral sciences."

The book that stirred this advance notice and notoriety was *Margaret Mead and Samoa: The Making and Unmaking of an Anthropological Myth*, by Derek Freeman, an emeritus professor of anthropology at the Australian National University in Canberra. The book attacks the

11

conclusions of Mead's first research project, which she began when she was only twenty-three, and which was documented in her book *Coming of Age in Samoa*. "The entire academic establishment and all the encyclopedias and all the textbooks accepted the conclusions in her book, and these conclusions are fundamentally in error," Freeman told the *Times* reporter. "There isn't another example of such wholesale deception in the history of the behavioral sciences."

The Freeman/Mead controversy had become a full-blown conflict before I was able to obtain a copy of bound page proof from Harvard University Press. Once in hand, I eagerly set to work analyzing Freeman's case against Margaret Mead.

The first comments on *Margaret Mead and Samoa* were those volunteered by a select few who had received advance copies of the book, presumably at the author's suggestion. Their evaluations were ultimately printed on the dust jacket, used in promotional ads, or were quoted by journalists in early articles in *The New York Times, Time,* and *Newsweek*. For example, Niko Tinbergen, a Dutch zoologist, ethologist, and sociobiologist (with no research experience in Samoa) is quoted on the dust jacket to the effect that he found the book "a masterly treatise" and commented on its honesty. Bruce Mazlish, an MIT historian and an authority on Richard Nixon, Henry Kissinger and Jimmy Carter, but with no Samoan research experience, found it "an extraordinary book," reading "like a detective story, as Freeman quietly but devastatingly shows us how and why the great Margaret Mead perpetrated a myth about Samoa's untroubled and free-loving adolescents." Ernst Mayr, a Harvard ornithologist and expert on Darwin and birds of the South Pacific, maintained that the Freeman work "Is not only a contribution to cultural anthropology, but it will also have a major impact on psychology and other aspects of human biology. It necessitates a careful rethinking of some of the most basic problems in all these fields." The Harvard University Press promotional ad for the volume, which appeared in the *New York Times* (13 Mar. 1983), quoted I. Eibl-Eibesfeldt, a Viennese zoologist and human ethnologist with no Samoan research experience, as follows: "Derek Freeman's book is a most remarkable contribution to anthropology and it will mark the end of radical cultural anthropology. Derek Freeman's contribution sets the record straight. We can consider this scholarly contribution as one of the milestones in cultural anthropology."

The book in question is, according to its author, a refutation of the anthropological classic *Coming of Age in Samoa*, written in 1928 by Margaret Mead as a result of some six months research in Ta'ū village, American Samoa, in 1925–26. Freeman claims that Mead's findings were totally wrong because she was inexperienced in fieldwork, she did not stay long enough, she could not speak the language adequately, she was duped by her adolescent informants (who enjoy putting people on), and she was completely biased, since she knew what she wanted to find in Samoa before she ever left New York. She wanted to find a society where adolescence was not marked by storm and stress to the extent it was in the United States and therefore be able to confirm her mentor's theory that human behavior is totally determined by culture and that nature (biology) can be completely ignored.

Motivated by Karl Popper's declaration that true scientific generalization is deductive and not inductive,[2] and that the progress of scientific research should consist essentially of attempts to refute established theories, Freeman attempts to discredit the Mead premise that Samoa represents a "negative instance" and therefore destroys the G. Stanley Hall theory that adolescent psychological stress is a universal phenomenon and can be explained as resulting from physiological developments associated with maturation. Although Freeman rejects the label sociobiologist, his main orientation appears to be ethological and his tendency is to rule out the forces of culture as an explanation of behavioral differences between young people in the United States and Samoa. Referring to Franz Boas, Margaret Mead, and the majority of American anthropologists (particularly those Samoan specialists who oppose his views) as "inductivists" and "absolute cultural determinists," Derek Freeman presents his refutation of the Mead study as an example of the proper manner in which to advance the science of anthropology as a discipline that will present a more balanced perspective of the forces of nature and nurture.

While Margaret Mead described Samoa as a paradise relatively untouched by competition, sexual inhibition, or guilt, Freeman maintains that Samoans are by nature sexually inhibited (even puritanical), aggressive, and highly competitive, prone to jealousy and subject to a whole range of pathological types of behavior including assault, rape, "surreptitious rape," suicide and murder.[3]

The early journalist-produced reviews of, or feature articles about, *Margaret Mead and Samoa* tended to be highly supportive of Freeman (for perhaps no other reason than that an attack on a person of legendary reputation makes good copy). For example, in Natalie Angier's article in *Discover* (April 1983) she suggested: "Her [Mead's] novelistic depiction of primitive bliss does seem in need of skeptical scrutiny," and "He [Freeman] seems far more of a 'scientist' than Mead; he did everything she did not." And Jane Howard, a biographer of Mead who also did a special report on the controversy for the *Smithsonian,* commented: "He's done his homework. I don't think he can be ignored."

Freeman's book had special meaning for me, because, in 1954, I lived in Ta'ū, where Mead had worked twenty-nine years earlier. I talked to many of her informants and analyzed every word she had written about life in that village. In that year I was conducting what is known as a methodological restudy. I retraced Mead's steps with the express purpose of testing the reliability and validity of her investigation and establishing the kinds of errors of interpretation that she might have made. Margaret Mead was a woman in a male-dominated society; she was young in a culture that venerates age; she was on her first field trip at a time when research methods were crude; and she was a student of the influential anthropologist Franz Boas, and so went armed with a particular theoretical frame of reference. Not only did I intend to analyze how my findings differed from hers (if they did), I was also interested in how our differences in age, status, personality, gender, and outlook might have accounted for differences in our collecting and interpreting of data.

A major consideration throughout the study was whether differences between my findings and Mead's were due to cultural change or other personal or methodological factors. Because of this problem, I had to document the culture for the periods of (1) the mid-nineteenth century, a period of prolific ethnographic writing by missionaries; (2) the 1920–30 period, when Samoa was studied by Mead, Peter Buck, N. A. Rowe, and Felix Keesing; and (3) the contemporary scene as I observed it in 1954. Through a constant comparison of these periods I was able to establish when major cultural changes had taken place in Samoa that might explain differences in the observations of Mead and myself. And, in order to evaluate her statement that it was easier to come of age in Samoa than in the United States, I also found it necessary to investigate what it was like to be a teenager in America in 1925.

As far as I know, my research effort was the first methodological restudy ever conducted with the specific purpose of evaluating the validity and reliability of an earlier observer's work. Other researchers had commented in their field reports on the quality of a predecessor's data, (e.g., A. L. Kroeber's evaluation of W. S. McGee's Seri material; Li An-Che's critique of Benedict and Bunzel's interpretations of Zuni; M. B. Emeneau's evaluation of Rivers' Toda study; and Oscar Lewis' criticism of Redfield's Tepoztlan investigation), but none had set out with the express goal of systematically evaluating earlier work. My general motive was not necessarily to prove that I was right and that Mead was wrong (if great discrepancies might be discovered), but to investigate the personal equation in ethnographic field work (i.e., what kind of errors might be made by what kind of people under what kind of conditions). In other words, would a married man of 29 with a wife and child accompanying him arrive at the same conclusions about Samoan culture as a young woman of 23 living as a single individual. Since I was a student of a student of Franz Boas, Melville Herskovits, both Mead and I had a similar theoretical orientation, although the methods of field ethnography had been greatly refined between 1925 and 1954.

It is surprising that no one prior to 1954 had conducted a methodological restudy. As early as 1933 Paul Radin was lamenting the fact that ethnographers saw the specific society of their inquiry as a private preserve. Radin stressed that this caused "inestimable harm and frequently meant that a tribe had been described by only one person" (1933:106). He deplored further the fact that this sole investigator was very likely bereft of an adequate knowledge of the society's language. This lack of control, states Radin, "must strike an outsider as unbelievable, indeed almost as amazing as the fact that ethnologists have tolerated it for so long a time" (1933:106).

In 1949 Margaret Mead commented that "there is no such thing as an unbiased report on any social situation. . . . All of our recent endeavors in the social sciences have been to remove bias" (1949:299–300). On another occasion she went so far as to suggest that a field worker be psychoanalyzed before going into the field in order to assess bias (1952:345). Although Mead never maintained that her field methods were infallible, she is on record (1949:296) expressing doubt concerning the value of restudies. She held that the drawback of the restudy is that the second observer must work within the frame of reference of the first, either trying to prove or disprove the former's material. This, interestingly enough, seems to be a rather accurate description of what Derek Freeman has attempted to do in his book *Margaret Mead and Samoa*, although it is my impression that Freeman has worked much harder at trying to refute the Mead data than trying to confirm them.

My own view is that a restudy should be a holistic analysis of the total cultural configuration, always taking into account, of course, the events that have taken place since the earlier research. A restudy should not be confined to the limits of the scope of the earlier study; in fact, it is desirable if the second investigator can apply new methods and perhaps a frame of reference somewhat different from that which oriented the first. Each anthropologist will view the culture in terms of his/her own personality, interests, and methodological training. It is inevitable that the results of the two studies will be somewhat different, but there is nothing wrong with this. It does not necessarily mean that one ethnographer is "right" and the other is "wrong." It means that the two have come to the culture from different perspectives, at different times, and with biases that grow out of their unique backgrounds and life experiences. As the Japanese film classic *Rashomon* illustrates, several people viewing the same situation will invariably interpret it differently.

One thing that I did share with Margaret Mead was a belief in the force of culture to fashion human personality and to affect the nature of value orientations and social institutions. I do not believe, nor did Margaret Mead or Franz Boas believe, that heredity is an unimportant factor in understanding human nature. My basic approach to the nature/nurture question might best be characterized by the following example I developed for a discussion of human nature in a general textbook I first published in 1965. I described human nature as

> the nature of the human animal arising out of the fact that Man is one species and shares the same kind of basic physiology. It is the nature of human beings to experience live birth, feel pain, meet with hunger, respond to feelings of sexual excitement, weaken with age, and finally die. The human animal walks upright on the earth; it does not burrow in the ground, live in the trees or under the sea, or fly through the air under its own power like the birds. People have a certain set of needs that must be met, certain physical and mental limitations, and certain abilities. At the moment of birth, every child of every race and culture inherits these needs, abilities and limitations; they are its heritage as a human, its human nature. From that moment on, however, this bundle of raw material will be shaped by its group and its culture. The processes of developing a human being might be compared to the process of a sculptor carving a statue out of wood. The sculptor knows the limitations and strengths of his material, and must work in terms of its physical nature. By observing certain precautions, the sculptor can develop a finished product. Two sculptors, however, both working in terms of the nature of the same raw material, might fashion quite different products, one producing a heavy and strong figure, the other a delicate, fragile, and beautiful one. The two figures will be alike in some respects—in their material, with its color and grain, but they will also differ greatly in their appearance due to the different approaches of the two artists. For human beings, this development of a finished product from a raw material amounts to growing up in a culture with its own unique material artifacts, ideologies, system of family, and configuration of values. [1981:303–304]

In addition to the notions above, I also went to the field armed with yet another theoretical orientation—the concept of cultural relativism. This concept characterized the Boasian approach to anthropological phenomena, and represented a major theoretical aspect in the work of Mead, Benedict, Herskovits, and the majority of American anthropologists during this century.

Cultural relativism is both a methodological tool (demanding objective, unbiased data collection) and a philosophical and theoretical principle, calling for open-mindedness with respect to cultural diversity. It requires that no single culture be held up as offering the "right" or "natural" way of doing things or valuing things. It reminds people of all nations that each society should be free to solve cultural problems according to their own time-tested methods without condemnation from those who would choose different solutions. Having been trained in such a philosophical tradition, Mead, myself, and the bulk of American anthropologists would believe that behavior associated with adolescence or other aspects of the life cycle must be evaluated *only in terms of the cultural context in which they occur.*

Derek Freeman's theoretical stance is somewhat at variance with this position. In a 1965 article, in which Freeman distorts the relativist's conceptualization of culture (among other things), he wrote:

> The cultural relativist, we have seen, looks on culture as a thing in itself, conceptualizes it as a closed, self-explanatory system. He accepts culture as something given, and does not enquire into its origins. This, it may be noted, is close to the view of the uneducated who accept the culture into which they happen to have been born, rather as a teapot accepts hot water.
>
> The evidence of research in palaeo-anthropology, a branch of anthropology which in recent years has made great progress, enables us to view human cultures in what is, I believe, a more scientitic way.
>
> There is now decisive scientific evidence that man is an animal, and has evolved from a primate stock. This means that an early stage in this evolution there were proto-hominoids without any form of culture. It follows that man's nature, as a phylogenetic entity, was evolved prior to the emergence of culture. Thus, the scientific way to look at culture is as biological adaptation by way of which evolving human animals have come to terms with their natural impulses and their environment (including their social environment). [1965:65–66]

The statement not only distorts the relativist's conceptualization of culture but indicates that Freeman does not understand the concept of culture himself or the research capabilities of the area which he refers to as "palaeo-anthropology." Culture cannot be studied phylogenetically, i.e., traced through the fossil record, as morphological changes in teeth or skeletal material can, although it would be an ideal situation if we had the ability to study changes in culture or any other form of behavior in that way. Kinship systems, aesthetic judgments, moral precepts, and supernatural belief systems just do not fossilize. A problem also arises from the fact that all cultural organisms are social, but not all social organisms have culture. Ants, wasps, fishes that school, some birds, ungulates, elephants, various carnivores and primates are all social, but they do not have social organizations that reflect cultural organization.

FIELD PREPARATION

It was only because of a series of unusual circumstances that I went to Samoa at all. Originally I had planned to go to Africa to do research (among the Kru of West Africa), but due to some mix-up at the Social Science Research Council, the year I applied for funds was one in which not a single grant was awarded to Northwestern University graduate students for field research. While my classmates settled for doing library dissertations, I ran across an announcement of money being available for field research in the Pacific through the Tri-Institutional Pacific Program. Having long been interested in Polynesia as a cultural area and having been particularly interested in the phenomenon of cultural change, especially acculturation, I submitted a proposal to study change in Rarotonga, Cook Islands, and was awarded $4,500. About a week before I was to present the plan of my proposed research to my dissertation committee, I received a phone call from the head of the Pacific Science Board requesting that I change the site of my forthcoming research. Because of political problems arising from the activities of an American anthropologist who had become too involved in island election campaigns and had been asked to leave the island, the Pacific Science Board thought that perhaps Rarotonga ought to have a brief respite from Yankee anthropologists.

I took my problem to Dr. Melville Herskovits and he suggested I go to Samoa. He maintained that for some time scholars (including himself) had been skeptical about Mead's findings in American Samoa and that it might be a good idea, and an excellent dissertation project, to undertake anthropology's first methodological restudy, which in this case would be a systematic reappraisal of the reliability and validity of Mead's *Coming of Age in Samoa*.[4]

My restudy of Margaret Mead's Samoan material is based on nine months of field work in American Samoa, beginning in February 1954. My wife, infant daughter,and I spent five months in the Manu'a group of islands working in the villages of Lumā and Si'ufaga, collectively known as Ta'ū village. This community on the island of Ta'ū was the site of Margaret Mead's research twenty-nine years earlier. We spent another four months in Pago Pago, where it was possible to work with Manu'an chiefs temporarily in residence, and to consult government records. We had originally planned to spend six or seven months in Ta'ū village, but the serious illness of our daughter forced a withdrawal to the administrative center where better medical facilities were available. During the last three months of our stay in American Samoa my wife worked as a head nurse in the Pago Pago hospital. In this position she supervised the work of Pepe Halek, the same Samoan nurse who had been Margaret Mead's language teacher in 1925.

Residence in Ta'ū village was in the Samoan house *(fale)* of High Chief Tufele. Since the traditional Samoan house is completely open on all sides it afforded excellent opportunities for the observation of life as it went on in the several houses grouped around it. The house also permitted careful observation of child behavior, as the grounds boasted the only stretch of grass in the village and therefore was preferred by the children in their play activities.

Entrance into the society of Manu'a was made through the Tufele family. A successful ethnographic study is possible in Samoa only through the good will of the high titled chiefs. It is not possible to first take up residence with an untitled man, and expect to subsequently gain the confidence and good will of the titled members. One must start at the top and work down.

Because my study dealt primarily with methodology in field work, the following discussion of rapport is pertinent. Chance played an important part in this. My first trip to Manu'a was made in the company of the Crown Prince of Tonga (now the King), and it was consequently possible to participate in some of the most elaborate welcome ceremonies ever accorded visitors in Manu'a, in honor of the King of Tonga. Legends that tell of the relationships between the kingdoms of Tonga and Manu'a are an important aspect of Manu'an folklore, and the King of Tonga (Tuitonga) is considered equal in rank to the King of Manu'a (Tuimanu'a). Association with a person of this stature eliminated suspicions that other investigators in Manu'a might encounter, and was probably the single most important factor in making it possible to obtain esoteric information. In the months that followed I was often referred to as "the man who first came here with the Tuitonga."

The sex and age of the observer are important in establishing the contacts necessary to an accurate description of Manu'an culture. Manu'a is generally a male-dominated society. Only males may hold titles[5] and participate in the political affairs of the villages, and in the Ta'ū village council (*fono*) only men may wring the kava. Only during the special ceremonies of greeting of visiting parties (*malaga*) does a female, the ceremonial maiden (*taupou*), fulfill any ceremonial function whatsoever. While the wives of the Chiefs and Talking Chiefs have a council organization analogous to that of their husbands, it functions only on social occasions. Although the women serve as orators, the elaborate oratory which draws on Samoan mythology and tradition is not approached.

Genealogies, family tradition, and other lore are transmitted by the men of the group. Adult women of families of rank who were interviewed on several occasions were found lacking even in knowledge of their own family, let alone the intricacies of political organization or ceremonial detail. Women never attend the village council and are not included in family discussions of tradition. At formal village functions, women are not even permitted to serve food or kava. In view of the position of women in ceremonial and political life, there is real reason to doubt whether an investigator who was not a man could ever establish adequate rapport for the study of problems involving these matters.

My presence in the village was explained by stating that I was a teacher sponsored by the University of Hawaii to study Samoan culture. This was understandable to the Samoans, for all the villages have resident native government school teachers. Moreover, school teachers are respected and enjoy a great measure of prestige. Recent developments in education also facilitated the accurate recording of Samoan tradition. The people of Manu'a recognized that the recording of their traditions for posterity is important; they even have a term for anthropologists, a'o a'o aganu'u—which translates as "one who studies the customs of the country."

The factor of age, however, was a considerable handicap in establishing complete rapport with the older men (I was 29 at the time). There were repeated comments such as, "You are very young to be a teacher in a University." The fact that my wife and infant daughter accompanied me to Manu'a helped somewhat to alleviate this, since in Manu'a one is really considered an adult only when he is married and has a family. Living as a family was beneficial in still another way, since some suspicion surrounds any single person taking up residence in Manu'a. One tourist who stayed for a time at our home during this study was believed to be a "spy" by some of the Manu'a chiefs who could not fit him into any familiar category which would explain his presence.

Since the problem of my restudy was methodological, involving Samoan culture in its entirety and not just adolescence, an attempt was made to document all facets of Samoan life, material as well as nonmaterial. Village mapping and a complete census were undertaken. The results closely paralleled Mead's. The exact age of each individual was established, which Mead states was impossible in 1925 (1928:21, 282). The relationship of each household member to the family head was also recorded. Statistical records were used whenever possible. Quantitative measures were obtained for such factors as mobility, mortality and birth rate, size of family, composition of family, age composition of the village, family income, age at marriage, frequency of divorce, and incidence of illegitimacy.

In considering adolescent behavior, a significant area of investigation was that of sexual behavior. This topic is by far the most difficult of all areas of Manu'an culture to discuss. Even esoteric spirit lore and data on bush medicine and magic were simpler to obtain. Informants who were consulted daily for a period of several months still showed great embrassment and reticence to speak of sexual matters. Even close Manu'an friends couched their replies to sexual questions in very general terms. No better success was had by my wife when she tried, showing that rapport in this matter is not simply a question of the sex of the investigator.

During the entire residence in Samoa it was impossible to obtain details of sexual experience from unmarried informants, though several of these people were constant companions and part of our household. The housegirl, who resided within the household more as a friend than a servant, never once confided that she was the mother of three illegitimate children and the partner in a common-law marital relationship. This information came from another source. One cannot explain this reticence by suggesting that religious sanctions have become stronger since Mead's study. To the contrary, earlier doctrines of the church appear to have been stricter than those in force in 1954.

The major informant in this study, Lauifi Ili, said on this point that "while boys are prone to brag about their sex activities, the girls are very close-mouthed and 'ashamed.'" Other informants stated that girls do not discuss their love affairs with other girls, and the only one who would know of their activities would be their intermediaries (*Soa*). Mead recognized this: "The girls learn from the boys and do very little confiding in each other. All of a man's associates will know every detail of some unusual sex experience while the girl involved will hardly have confided the bare outlines to anyone" (1928:150).

The high degree of rapport attained by Mead in this area of culture might have been due to the fact that she appeared to be single when she carried on her study. At the close of this period of research, I lived alone in Si'ufaga for two months, and found that, being accepted more as a single man, I was in a better position to observe courtship activities than was possible while my wife and child were living with me.

This study was carried on almost entirely with English-speaking informants, the direct use of Samoan being restricted to matters of material culture, later checked with interpreters. Often the halting interviews with older non-English speaking men served only to give ideas for later discussion with other informants where communication was more dependable. Even after nine months of work in Samoa it was not felt that information obtained only in the Samoan language could be relied upon.

Three main informant-interpreters were utilized, all of them proficient in the use of English. All three were schoolteachers although one was retired. As teachers, all five were respected members of the village. One received the title of Ili, one of the five highest titles of Fifiuta village, during the period of fieldwork. The second was an untitled man of the family of High Chief Moliga of Si'ufaga village. The retired teacher held a Talking Chief title in Si'ufaga and was very active in village politics. Certain other men who had excellent command of English were used as informants only to a limited extent because they were recognized as deviants, and their information was carefully checked. All information on matters of Samoan life felt to be noncontroversial was checked with at least one other informant familiar with this aspect of life. In controversial matters or matters dealing with custom no longer practiced, many informants were used, and cross-checking was intensive.

With regard to the original choice of informants, the following data are pertinent. The wife of Tufele, who helped establish us in our Ta'ū village home, suggested several men of the village who she thought were respected, well-versed in Samoan custom, and acquainted with the English language. These men were used as principal informants and interpreters. It might be added that her suggestions did not prove advantageous to her, for in discussing matters of rank these informants mentioned other chiefs as having equal or higher rank than the Tufele title. It is not believed, therefore, that they were chosen because they would tell what the Tufele family wanted to be known.

Esoteric lore was not barred by the use of English-speaking informants, one of whom was recognized in the village as a specialist in matters of supernatural lore and "bush medicine." All three of the informant-interpreters became my personal friends, and none hesitated to correct my errors, although this is often a major problem in Samoan field study.[6]

The culture of the Samoans who resided in Ta'ū village, American Samoa, in 1954 is described in the following four chapters. I have attempted to record the full range of social and cultural patterns as I observed them or had them described to me by informants. My data constantly take into consideration the historical stream of culture which was often of great importance in interpretating events and understanding values. While much of the indigenous religion was no longer viable, for example, knowledge of that belief system provided a means for understanding the manner in which Christianity had been accepted, reinterpreted, and, just how it was being observed in 1954. The traditional ways that family, village politics, and the economic system functioned told me much about the nature of my human subjects and how to interpret and anticipate their patterns of behavior.

Restudy headquarters Ta'u village (1954)

THREE

The Culture of the Village of Ta'ū—1954

ISLANDS AND PEOPLE

The Samoan archipelago, consisting of nine inhabited islands, lies in a general east to west line at 14° south latitude and between 168° and 173° west longitude. The group is divided politically into American Samoa and Western Samoa. The American portion is a territory of the United States administered by the United States Department of Interior and consists of the islands of Tutuila (with the port of Pago Pago), Aunu'u, Ofu, Olosega, and Ta'ū, the latter three islands being collectively known as the Manu'a group. Western Samoa is a sovereign nation, having gained its independence from New Zealand in 1962. This nation is made up of the islands of Upolu, Savai'i, Apolima, and Manono. The inhabitants of the entire archipelago are remarkably homogeneous culturally, linguistically, and racially. Ninety percent of the 135,000 inhabitants of this island chain are classified as full-blooded Polynesians and the majority of them practice the traditional economic pursuits of subsistence agriculture and occasional reef and deep-water fishing.

Ta'ū village, the focus of this study as well as Margaret Mead's in 1925–26, lies 60 miles east of the American Samoan island of Tutuila. The village, with a population of over 700, is actually two villages. That is to say, it recognizes civic subdivisions known as Si'ufaga and Lumā (see Figure 3.1). There are two other villages on the island, Faleasao, situated on the next bay to the north, and Fitiuta, some five

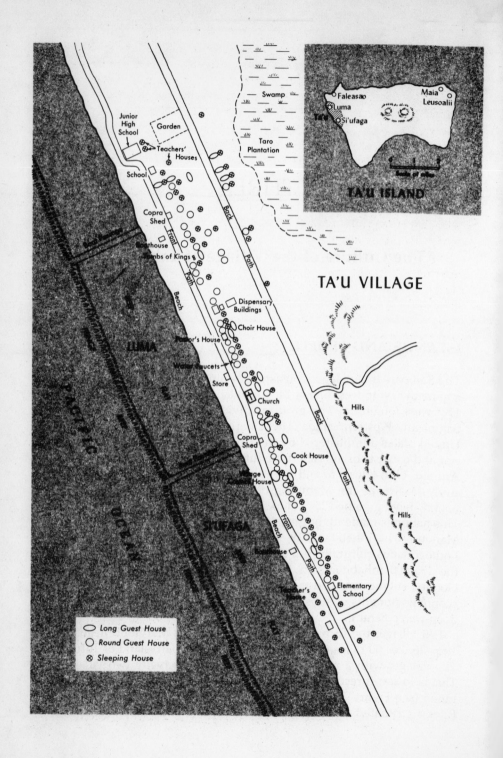

Junior
High
School

Garden

Teachers'
Houses

School

Copra
Shed

Boathouse

Tombs of Kings

LUMA

Dispensary
Buildings

Choir House

Pastor's House

Water Faucets

Store

Church

Copra
Shed

Cook House

Village
House

SIUFAGA

Boathouse

Teacher's
House

Elementary
School

Swamp

Taro
Plantation

TA'U VILLAGE

Hills

Hills

Back
Path

Front
Path

Beach

Back
Path

Front
Path

Beach

PACIFIC

OCEAN

○ Long Guest House
○ Round Guest House
⊗ Sleeping House

Faleasao

Luma

Ta'u

Si'ufaga

Maia

Leusoalii

TA'U ISLAND

to six miles over mountain trails to the east. Ta'ū, like all the islands in the Samoan chain, has low coastal areas with sand beaches (where the villages are located) from which the land rises sharply to highland ridges. Mount Lata on Ta'ū has a summit 3056 ft. above sea level while the island of Savai'i boasts a 6000-ft. peak; Matafao, on Tutuila, has an altitude of 2141 ft. Nearly all of the coastlines are fringed with coral reefs with breaks only where freshwater streams enter the sea.

Since this region is tropical, with warm temperatures and abundant rainfall (averaging 150 in. per year), vegetation is dense and green. Bushes, ferns, grasses, and vines carpet the mountain slopes beneath stands of high-quality timber such as *ifi lele (Intsis bijuga), tavai (Rhustaitenis),* and *asi (Syzygium inophylloides).* Mountain tops are covered with mosses, lichens, and ferns, and are fairly barren of trees.

The animal population of the archipelago, aside from domesticated varieties—chickens, pigs, dogs, and a handful of horses and cattle—is meager. There are a few wild bush pigs, two species of nonpoisonous snakes, a dozen varieties of lizards (including the gecko), and land crabs. *Fruit bats (Pteropus ruficollis),* sometimes referred to as "flying foxes," are common, as is the small Poynesian rat *(Rattus exulans Peale).* While this rodent probably arrived in Samoa with the original settlers, the large wharf rat, *(Rattus norvegicus)* found around port towns, is of recent introduction, having arrived on European vessels. There are thirty-four species of land birds including such game fowl as the golden plover, wild duck, and three varieties of pigeon. The most important bird culturally, is a small green parakeet with red markings, the *sega,* referred to as "the chief's bird." Its colorful feathers are used to decorate the Samoan's most prized possession, the finemat.

Insects are numerous in this tropical climate, but only a few cause serious problems. The mosquito *(Stegomzia pseudoscatellaris)* is a carrier of filariasis, the disease which in its advanced stages develops into elephantiasis. There is no malaria in Samoa. The rhinoceros beetle *(Oryctes rhinoceros)* is a costly pest; it destroys coconut palm. Two varieties of centipede and one type of scorpion are present. Their bites, while painful, are seldom fatal. Cockroaches, which often attain a length of two inches, are annoying creatures that persist in destroying clothing and finemats. Flies are present in abundance and are a serious health hazard, for they breed in human waste, disposal of which is a problem.

Culturally (and geographically) the Samoan people are identified as Western Polynesians, a category they share with the inhabitants of Tonga, Niue, the Tokelaus, and to a certain extent, with the people of the Fiji Islands.[1] Although there are cultural similarities and numerous historical traditions concerning political interaction between Samoans and Fiji Islanders, the two are markedly different in physical type. While Fijians are usually classified as Oceanic Negroes and related to Melanesians to the west of them, Samoans are Polynesian in physical type and thus constitute a racially hybrid group exhibiting a blend of physical characteristics.

Some claim that Samoans resemble Europeans more closely than do any other groups of Polynesians. The color of their skin is a medium yellowish brown and their hair is black or dark brown and wavy or straight in form. Samoans are relatively tall, with men averaging five feet seven and one-half inches and women five feet three inches. Faces are broad with straight noses of medium breadth, dark brown eyes, and full but not protruding lips.

The language of Samoa is a dialect of the linguistic family known as Austronesian (formerly called Malayo-Polynesian). It has been placed in the subgroup Samoic, a category that also includes the languages spoken by the inhabitants of the Tokelau and Ellice Islands, Eastern Futuna, and Tikopia. It is a pleasant sounding language because of its liberal use of vowels and has often been referred to as the "Italian of the Pacific." Roger Green (1966:34) maintains that Samoan was one of the earlier established languages of Polynesia although of more recent development than Fijian or Tongan.

Samoan has only nine consonants: p, t, f, v, s, m, n, g (pronounced ng), and l. The five basic vowels used by English-speakers—a, e, i, o, u—are augmented in Samoan speech by the use of long vowel sounds. For example, *tama* (boy) ends in a short *a* and is pronounced *tahm-uh*, but the word for "father" is *tamā* (long vowel indicated by the accent mark above the letter *a*) and is pronounced *tahm-ah*. As is true of most Polynesian languages, every consonant in Samoan is separated by one or more vowels as may be seen in the following sentence: *O le a o fafine a tata lavalava i le vaitafo* ('The women will go to wash clothes in the river.') Furthermore, there is the feature of the glottal stop indicated by ') which is a choking off of sound as in words like Savai'i, Ta'ū, Manu'a, or *va'a* ('boat'). This interruption of sound is phonemically very important, as a similarly spelled word without the glottal stop has a very different meaning. For example, *fai* means do, and *fa'i* means banana; *sao* means to escape, and *sa'o* means straight.

Relative to English, Samoan has a small vocabulary. Its basic stock of morphemes is often called up to do yeoman service in satisfying the society's communication needs. The word *lau*, for example, has nine meanings: leaf, lip, brim of a cup, thatch, breadth, hundred, your, fish drive, and to sing a song verse by verse.

The most unique feature of the Samoan language is the special set of honorific terms known as the "chief's language." This is a class of polite or respectful words which are substituted for ordinary words when one is speaking to someone of chiefly rank. For example, a untitled man has an *'aiga* ('meal'), but a chief has a *taumafataga;* an untitled person puts his hat on his *ulu* ('head'), but a chief places it on his *ao;* an untitled person may become *ma'i* ('ill'), but a chief becomes *gasegase;* and a chief may *maliu* ('die'), but a commoner will merely *oti.*

With the exception of those who reside around the Pago Pago Bay area on the island of Tutuila, most of the inhabitants of American Samoa live in traditional villages located near the sea. These consist of a long string of thatch roofed houses *(fale)* which front on beaches of white coral sand. *Fale* have great beehive-shaped roofs suspended by posts set three feet apart in a round or elliptical floor plan. The open spaces between the posts can be closed against inclement weather by lowering plaited coconut leaf blinds. The roof is a complicated frame-work of beams, purlins, rafters, and ribs, securely lashed together with sennit and erected in three sections, a center portion *(itū),* and two round ends or gables *(tala).* Center posts *(poutū)* and ridge poles *(aū aū)* support the weight of the roof and add strength to the super-structure. Thatch, consisting of units of sugar cane leaves, or in rare cases, coconut leaves, is secured to the framework of the roof with sennit. Informants state that the Samoan house was traditionally constructed entirely of breadfruit wood, but newly constructed houses contain inferior woods that do not have its lasting quality.

In some villages of Manu'a the houses rest on elevated platforms *(paepae),* whose heights correspond to the rank of their occupants, but in Ta'ū village this feature is not found, since the rank of all chiefs was considered unimportant compared to that of the King who resided in this village. Flooring consists of a three or four inch layer of coral fragments over a level earth base.

Construction of round and elliptical houses is similar, in that the center portion is merely elongated in the elliptical house while retain-ing a common form of gable. Guest houses may be round *(fale tele)* or elliptical *(fale afolau).* Sleeping houses *(fale o'o),* also round or elliptical, vary from guest houses only in their smaller size and more simple construction.

In addition to the guest and sleeping houses, every household unit also includes a separate cook house *(faleumu),* a simply constructed building about twelve feet long, six feet wide, and ten feet high, with a peaked thatched roof supported by four to eight posts. This struc-ture, containing the oven *(umu),* lies to the rear of the living quarters.

In recent years European building materials have been employed— galvanized iron for roofing and scrap lumber for structures with permanent walls. European materials are usually used for storage sheds or cook houses, only rarely in sleeping houses, and never in the construction of guest houses. A survey of Ta'ū village in 1954 revealed the following types of dwellings:

Traditional guest houses (round)	49
Traditional guest houses (elliptical)	23
Traditional sleeping houses	61
Sleeping houses and sheds containing European materials	21 (14%)
	Total 154

The Manu'an house has little in the way of furniture; the coral flooring is covered with a minimum of pandanus mats on which the members of the household sit cross-legged. A few of the homes of the High Chiefs boast wooden chairs, but these are used only when Europeans are entertained. Bedding consists of piles of sleeping mats, a bamboo headrest, and cotton sheets. Four or five large wooden beds are found in the village, but these are confined to the homes of chiefs of high rank. The bamboo headrest, which measures four inches in diameter and one and one half to five feet in length, is used mostly by older people, as the younger generation finds European pillows more to their liking. During the daytime bedding is rolled within the sleeping mats and placed on a special shelf (*fata*) which is built into every Samoan house.

Food is served on plaited coconut leaf mats (*laulau*) covered with breadfruit leaves and eaten with the fingers; coconut cups are used for drinking. There are few families, however, who do not own china plates and cups and silverware for entertaining European visitors. These are stored in glass-doored china cabinets. Personal belongings are kept in trunks, suitcases, or wooden boxes.

THE ECONOMY

Agriculture is by far the most important economic activity of the Manu'an people. Although some men are titled and some are not, and some are carpenters and some "bush medicine" specialists, all are farmers. Every man and woman in the Samoan family is responsible for a share of agricultural work on family lands.

In the preparation of plantations, the land is cleared by the family head (*matai*) and the untitled men of the family. Large trees are felled with axes, and small trees, bushes, and high grass are cleared away with a machete. After a week the trees and underbrush are burned, but the land itself is never burned over. Beside the axe and the machete, the pointed digging stick (*oso*), measuring three to four feet in length and two to five inches in diameter, is the only tool used in plantation agriculture. Digging sticks are made of local hardwoods; they are used in turning soil and prying out rocks. Samoan agriculture does not include the techniques of irrigation or terracing. There is no system of draining ditches used to carry off surplus rain water, although these are often found in the villages.

Keesing (1934) recognized the following traditional categories of land in Samoa and his classification was general valid for Ta'ū in 1954.

(1) *Village house lots:* Each Samoan village is divided into family household lots. The portion on which the family dwellings stand is called *tulaga fale* while the surrounding yard is known merely as *fanua* (land). The boundaries of village lots are indicated by trees, rocks or other natural features and are well known to the whole village. Each lot has a name. Beneath the pebbled, sandy, or grassy surface of the yard are the remains of ancestors whose graves are often marked by cairns or concrete markers.

Breadfruit, coconut and papaya trees or a small patch of taro may be found on house lots. These foods are useful when it is inconvenient to go to the plantations, but house lots are not considered the proper place for agriculture.

(2) *Plantation lots:* These lie around and behind the village (which usually faces the sea), their extent depending on such factors as the size of the community and the suitability of land and water resources. Farrell's data indicate that Samoan-owned lands (excluding forests and lava fields) averaged 535 acres per village (Cumberland and Fox 1962:115, 185–186). The major stands of coconut trees are found here on coastal lots and the larger quantities of breadfruit trees and banana plants on the inland slopes. Some taro is found in this area but the main plantings are usually higher on the slope. The plantations contain a great deal of underbrush, and plantings are not in orderly rows. A person unfamiliar with island flora could walk through a plantation without realizing it was a valuable agricultural area.

(3) *Family reserve sections:* Beyond the plantation lots and often higher on the mountain slope are additional lands traditionally associated with the several families of the village. Title to and boundaries of these lands are known to most villagers. Only portions of them are cultivated at any one time in order not to exhaust soil fertility. This land generally accommodates the main taro beds, *ma'umaga*, since taro requires soil which has been fallowed. Family reserve sections consist mainly of dense secondary forest which must be cleared before planting.

(4) *Village lands:* Beyond the family or title sections are lands that lie within the village boundaries but are not the property of specific families. These include not only potential agricultural lands on the upper slopes of mountains or adjacent to the ocean but also reef and sea frontages which have value to the entire community. On bush land in this category individuals may acquire additional landholdings merely by clearing and planting, though this may require the permission of the village council. If, however, the land is unattended and there is no evidence of cultivation, others are free to use and claim it. Families who are interested in permanently increasing their landholdings plant coconuts there to provide continuing evidence of long-term rights. It thereupon falls into the category of plantation lots.

Another enterprise associated with village lands is the *taloloa,* a group taro planting operation undertaken by the village organization of untitled men, the *'aumaga,* either on their own initiative or as the result of an order from the village council.

The principal Manu'an crops include coconuts, taro (three varieties), breadfruit, bananas (nine varieties), manioc, yams, sweet potatoes, Tahitian chestnuts, cocoa, oranges, grapefruit, limes, mangoes, arrowroot, papaya, guava, avocados, tobacco, and sugar cane. Tomatoes, cabbage, corn, beans, and carrots have recently been introduced by the government but have not found favor among the Manu'ans. Kava, used for ceremonial and leisure drinking, is cultivated on the plantations and on village household plots. Kava matures after one year, and at this time it is dug up and the roots and tubers are allowed to dry for three days. The outer coverings of these are then removed and the whole crushed and mixed with water for drinking. Copra is the only agricultural product that is exported, although cocoa is now being grown and should serve as a valuable cash crop in the future.

There is a commonly held fallacy that Polynesians spend a great deal of their time fishing and gathering shellfish. This is not true. While Samoans are extremely fond of fish and really prefer it to other forms of protein, they spend very little time angling, spear- or net-fishing, or scavenging on the reef. Undoubtedly more time was spent in these activities in the past, but today it is often easier to send someone to the bush store for a tin of sardines, tuna, or salmon than to spend hours trying to catch fresh fish.

While fishing activities consume perhaps a tenth of the time and energy devoted to agriculture, Samoans have devised an impressive array of methods for exploiting their sea resources. Ta'ūans fish singly or in groups for a variety of creatures ranging from reef worms to giant turtles and sharks. Individual methods include the use of three kinds of throwing nets for capturing a host of brilliantly colored reef fish; wooden traps for taking eels, lobsters, crayfish, and crabs; bamboo rods and lines outfitted with metal hooks and lures of stone or shell or live bait for catching sea bass or red snapper; nooses for snaring small eels when they have been partially lured out of their lairs in the coral by sticks with small fish secured to the end; three-pronged spears for impaling, or bush knives for slashing a variety of fish and sea creatures; poisons and dynamite for killing whole schools of fish within the fringe reef; and spear guns, resembling sling shots, made of wood and strips of innertube which launch long missiles made of heavy fencing wire. The latter device is used on the reef flat or by swimmers operating well offshore who tread water for hours collecting whole strings of fish which they wear like a belt.

Three-man crews in 27-foot outrigger canoes fish for bonito often well out of sight of land, and danger-loving shark fishermen in rowing boats stalk their prey with heavy rope nooses which they slip over the heads of the sharks, lured to the side of the boat with chunks of meat. Turtles are captured by men in boats who place large banana leaves on the water as shade for the animals. The men return later and pick up the leaves. If they are lucky they will find at least one turtle under the leaves and be able to wrestle it into the boat. Community fish drives (*lau*) are carried out on the reef flat by large numbers of men and women who drag long streamers (made of coconut fronds twisted about vines) through the water and drive schools of fish toward men who wait with gill nets and spears. In some cases a rock cairn is prepared beforehand so that the frightened fish, in seeking its shelter, are concentrated in one small area. Gill nets are placed around the cairn and, as one man unpiles the rocks, others spear or shoot the fish with missiles launched from spear guns.

Reef scavenging is carried out almost entirely by the women. They probe the holes in the coral reef with sticks and occasionally are successful in locating small octopuses which they drag from their shelters and kill by biting or by beating the creature on a rock. Crabs, lobsters, crayfish, and squids are also objects of their search.

Samoa is a society with little labor specialization other than that based on sex, and there are few tasks aside from ceremonial cooking that cannot be undertaken by members of either sex if they wish. There is a great deal of cooperative labor within the *'aiga* and within the village.

There are no definite categories of "children's activities," "adult activities," and "old people's activities." There is a smoothly flowing continuity in the life cycle and the tendency to allow people to perform day-to-day tasks according to their ability.

Samoa, with its lack of emphasis on individual as opposed to situational status and with its comfortable ideological environment, allowing a smooth and unrestricted maturation process, seems to have been able to promote a positive attitude toward its elders and an atmosphere of freedom in which they can participate fully in their society.

As has been noted above, old age in Samoa is not viewed as a period of retirement from work (although that is not looked down upon) but merely a time when work activities are different, i.e., altered to match the strength and interests of the aged. It is not a time, however, when Samoans are relegated to doing jobs of little importance.

Since Samoans believe that patience is supposed to increase with age, the elderly are often asked to do jobs that involve a certain amount of tedium but which are important jobs nonetheless, vital to the economy and, most important of all, jobs which can be done sitting down or at least with a minimal outlay of physical exertion.

There is some craft specialization. Members of the guilds of house and boat builders are designated by a special name and participate in special ceremonials. Specialists in fishing, dancing, medicine-making, and spirit control are also acknowledged but are not organized into guilds. The knowledge and ability of massage (*fofō* or *lomilomi*) is handed down within certain families. In some cases this is also true of medicine making and the control of the spirits. Knowledge in these spheres is held by both men and women in the society, and certain individuals are specialists in certain types of illness, but ability is not necessarily handed down, as is massaging.

While there is a great deal of specialization in housebuilding, boat building, fishing and medicine, most Samoans have some ability in each of these activities. If need be, they can handle the simpler tasks for the family, therefore making the household largely a self-sufficient unit.

The economy of Manu'a is one of plenty. Within the memory of the Manu'an people there is only one occasion, a hurricane, when there was a shortage of food. The average family in Ta'ū can provide itself with ample food by working its plantations only about three days a week. In Samoa no one goes hungry. The extended family provides for all its members, whether they be old, infirm, or lazy. All have claim to the benefits—widows, relatives by marriage, and even the illegitimate or adopted children of the family members. As long as they nominally place themselves under the control of the family head (*matai*) each has a share in the products of the family. They also share in remittances that come from family members outside of Manu'a (Mead 1930:65; Keesing 1956:220; Shankman 1973).

Salaries from government positions, Fita Fita Guard (Samoan reserve unit under naval administration) pensions, or dependency allotments from family members in military service supplement the usual income from copra and allow families to provide food for the village council, give large church donations, and gain added prestige by public expenditure of wealth.

Property in this society consists mostly of land and is collectively owned by the descent group. While the land technically belongs to the entire family, it is administered by the family head (*matai*). No land may be given away by the family head or alienated in any way without the consent of the family as a whole. Disposal of land by the *matai* without the consent of the family is considered grounds for removal of the *matai*'s title by the family. However, methods are sometimes used by family heads to circumvent these principles. By playing one branch of the family against another the family head may be able to deal with the land in a manner suitable to his purposes.

The buildings erected on household land are also jointly owned by the family and administered by the *matai*. All items used by the family as a whole, such as floor mats, boats, cooking utensils, agricultural and carpenter tools, and fine mats are, in like manner, administered by the *matai* but collectively owned.

Personally owned property includes such things as clothing, mats (beyond the family's requirements), musical instruments, jewelry, special tools, and land carved out of the unclaimed bush land.

At his death, property owned by the *matai* in the name of the family is passed on to the next titleholder, but personal property is inherited by the wife. Debts are not inherited but merely canceled at the death of the debtor. The only type of will known in Samoa is the last wish (*mavaega*), which is carried out because of the family members' fear of angering the dead person's spirit.

Prior to about 1940, any income from the land earned by individual family members (mainly cash from copra) was turned over to the family head who provided for the needs of the family. Copra receipts, which name the individual who received payment for the copra sale, were examined for the eight-year period from 1946 to 1954. They showed an increasing trend away from giving the total income to heads of families, with a concomitant tendency to divide the money between the various immediate families that comprise the household. This tendency is somewhat more pronounced in households where the family head receives Fita Fita Guard pensions or allotment checks from family members in the armed forces.

The increasing financial independence of members of the household does not appear to affect their loyalty to the family head. Both their respect for him and their cooperation in working the family land are as evident today as was recorded in former years. Despite these economic changes, the structure and unity of the Samoan family have remained unchanged.

Reciprocal exchanges of property are an important part of the Manu'an economy and mark all important events in the lifetime of the Manu'an people. At marriage, dowry (*toga*) and bridewealth (*oloa*) are exchanged by the families of the couple involved. *Oloa*, consisting of food, bark cloths, and money, is given by the groom's family in return for *toga*, consisting of fine mats, which is supplied by the bride's family. *Toga* and *oloa* should be of equal value reckoned on the basis of $20 for a fine mat (1954 value) and $1.50 for a *tapa* cloth. Currency has not replaced the fine mats as a standard of value in the exchange system, but it is substituted for many of the bulkier goods that serve as reciprocal payment for fine mats. The Samoans have found it much easier to carry currency to another village than their equivalent in pigs, chickens, other foodstuffs, and *tapas*.

On occasions of the exchange of property at marriage and the outlays of property connected with the making of a *taupou*, the taking of a title, the birth of a child, and the burial of a high chief, one of the cardinal principles of Manu'an economy is displayed. This is that wealth is dynamic, and prestige comes through its use, rather than simply its ownership. Prestige within the village often is as dependent upon the display of wealth as is the holding of a traditionally high title. A High Chief who does not maintain his position by the distribution of property is often in danger of being overshadowed by another of lesser traditional rank.

Capital investment is found only in the ownership of bonito boats. Most owners of these boats in Manu'a do not fish in them but arrange for specialized fishermen to captain their craft. Consequently, a share of the catch is the property of the owner. A few of the wealthier individuals of the village own as many as three of these fishing craft and receive a sizeable return on their investment during bonito season.

FOUR

Social Organization: Family and Fono

Social organization in Samoa is a principal preoccupation. It has been so important in everyday life that one observer maintained that while other Polynesians worshipped deities, the Samoans worshipped their own social and political system. Regardless of whether we are observing household interaction or the deliberations of the village council *(fono)*, it can be seen that individualism has little significance in this culture. An individual is regarded as a necessary, but minor, component of the family. Although Samoan society is democratic in many ways, the basic principles of Samoan social structure hinge on hereditary rank (but not primogeniture), the functions and privileges of relationship groups, and the recognition of the rights of the village. Mead cites that this continuous use of cooperation units and the continuous recombinations thereof is an important feature of Samoan economic and social life (1937:289–291).

Reciprocity works to reinforce the attitude of cooperation. At any given ceremonial function—such as a wedding, an installation of a family head *(matai)*, or a funeral—there is always an exchange of property. Custom dictates the kind of property to be given and demands that the property exchanged be of equivalent value. Each of the family members is called upon to donate a share, and therefore every one in the family, and in some cases, in the village, is tied to everyone else through the exchange of gifts.

The Samoan cultural environment is described by Rose as follows:

> First of all, and of paramount importance, Samoans are
> born into a culture of almost complete individual security.

37

emotions are early diffused over a wide group of ople (as compared with our far more compact family group) and they are never without relatives who are always ready, and obliged by custom, to aid them. This mutually-assisting social unit is fostered and promoted. There is little individual striving; there is little need for striving. Food, if not always plentiful, is usually in adequate supply; if it is not, other people, or villages, or even districts, will help out.

The Samoan can (or could in former times and can still up to a point) travel the whole of Samoa without coin or kind, obtaining, wherever he chooses to stop, food, shelter, and the means of travelling further. It is necessarily a reciprocal system. When his turn comes, he must aid the traveller, too. [1959:83]

FAMILY

The Samoan individual is identified with three familial groups: the immediate family, the household (*fua'ifale*), and the *'āiga* (or extended family). There is no clan or tribal organization. In ancient Samoa, warfare was carried on in terms of territorial units rather than any form of kin affiliation. Relatives often fought each other. The immediate family, of course, is the most basic unit in the social system, and the household, made up of one or more immediate families, is presided over by a *matai*. The extended family (*'āiga*) includes all the members of the *matai's* household plus individuals in other households who are related to him through blood, marriage, or adoption.

Each village has from ten to fifty *matai* titles which have been created at various times by important persons or by the village council (*fono*). Many families can name the original titleholder and the circumstances (usually meritorious service in peace or war) under which the title was conferred. Certain sections of village and plantation land are associated with each title.

Within each large extended family there are subgroupings known as *faletama* (houses of the children) which are said to have been established by the offspring of the original titleholders. Thus, if the first man to hold a title had three sons and a daughter there would be four branches within that family—three male lines and one female. Often there are separate subtitles held by *faletama* heads who are elected in much the same way as the paramount titleholder. The lands are also subdivided accordingly. Members of the larger titular family therefore owe allegiance to the man who holds the paramount title of their family and also to the holder of the title of their *faletama*, but the latter is the more important for matters of land allocation and use within subgroups.

Because descent is traced through both parents, a Samoan can trace a kinship relationship to a dozen or more *matai* in his own or other villages. As a result he may, in theory, express an opinion on the disposition of lands with any of those titles. He is also theoretically eligible to be elected to any of those titles which fall vacant. In practice, however, his influence in each case depends on his participation in the affairs of that family as well as on his personal prestige. One's influence is normally greatest in the family in which one resides, that is, in the same locality as the *matai* of that family. In any family one's influence is enhanced by skillful oratory, effective organization at times of family crises or celebrations, and generous giving to enhance the interests of that family.

In addition to directing the day-to-day affairs of his household, the *matai* represents them in the village *fono* where he acts in accord with his relative rank in the village hierarchy of titles and according to his role as *ali'i* (chief) or *tulafale* (orator) which are the two categories of *matai*. To maintain family prestige the *matai* must have resources to give lavish feasts or to manage impressive property exchanges at funerals or marriages, and to contribute to the church—a major prestige source for the last 150 years.

In some families the household group works the land in common, moving as a single work force from section to section to plant, weed, and harvest. The fruits of the family's labor are nominally the property of the family head, but since he is responsible for the welfare of all living with him and is concerned with keeping his household satisfied so they will continue to help him work the land, an equitable distribution is made. In other families the untitled men *(taulele'a)* who head the nuclear families comprising the *'āiga* manage specific sections of the land, using the produce to feed their own immediate families or to provide them with income if cash crops are involved.

The *matai* occupies the traditional dwellings and land associated with his title. With him live the *fua'ifale* (household group) who constitute the residential core of the *'āiga*, and may contain several nuclear families as well as widows and others. This household group is often very fluid in composition owing to relatively frequent shifts of residence of single as well as married people. Thus in Ta'ū, half the residents of many households in 1950 had changed to other households by 1954. Post-marital residence may be either in the husband's or the wife's village and household of birth, or with other relatives of either. When a *matai* dies or relinquishes his title because of age, the family will hold a *filifiliga*, or special meeting to elect a successor. All men who believe that they are related to the title and who are interested in playing a part in selecting the new *matai* will attend. Some writers claim that there is a tendency toward primogeniture and others refer to a 'right of the brother' in the selection of *matai*. Though the author found that it was quite common for a son to succeed to a father's title, he found no evidence of a 'right of the brother' either in the contemporary scene or in an analysis of genealogies.

The *matai* has *pule* over the family lands; that is, he has power to determine the uses to which they will be put by household members. He also has power to lend land to distant relatives on a short-term basis, but any transaction which will alienate land from the family must be entered into by all members of the family who have an interest in the title and its lands. Mead (1930) and others have stressed the balance in the bilateral Samoan family between the influence of the male and female sides, and noted the latter's power to control land transactions through the veto. This concept defines a pattern of respect which men must pay to their sisters, father's sisters, father's father's sisters, and to the children of these female relatives. The term *tamasā* (father's sister), designates this respect relationship. It is also referred to as *tamafafine* (sister's children), *ilamutu* (father's sister), *feagaiga* (relationship between male and female relatives) and *se'e talaluma* (female relatives). In modern Samoa, at least, the influence of the female side is exerted positively by participation and persuasion rather than negatively by the veto, which is used very rarely.

The *tamasā* relationship also applies to female siblings and underlies the avoidance and respect patterns observed between brothers and sisters. These patterns extend to adopted brothers and sisters and to cousins, who are referred to as "brothers" and "sisters." Kinship reckoning is classificatory and appropriate behavior extends to all relatives who are referred to by a common term.

When brothers and sisters have reached the age of fifteen or sixteen, they must use extreme discretion in their behaviour toward one another. They may not intentionally touch one another nor wear one another's clothes, and brothers are not even permitted to go near where their sister's clothing is kept. A brother and sister may not dance at the same time unless the entire village is present at the festival. While brothers often refer to one another with derogatory nicknames, this is not permitted between brothers and sisters, and it is prohibited for a brother to mention his sweethearts to his sister, no matter how innocent the relationship.

Margaret Mead has noted (1928a:210–212) that in Samoan families there is a relative lack of strong emotional attachment between children and their biological parents. This is in part due no doubt to the classificatory system of kinship, in which all women of the family of the mother's generation are called *tinā* (mother) and all men of the mother's generation are *tamā* (father). And since appropriate behavior in large measure matches kin terminology, every Samoan child has several "parents" who provide, educate, and discipline. The weaning of a child begins a longer and more gradual process of lessening dependence on the mother. An older sibling takes over much of the baby tending and a grandmother feeds a child while the mother is working in the fields. A paternal or maternal aunt or grandmother often instructs a young girl in handicraft and other work. An uncle or an older brother takes a young boy on his first fishing expedition, or teaches him the methods of agriculture. In identifying with a number of real or surrogate parents the child's personal attachments do not become so intense that the loss of one of them is as traumatic an experience as in America. In the same way, the child's hostility or resentment is diffused because more than one individual can punish him. The flexibility of this parent–child relationship can be seen in the relative ease with which an adopted child adjusts to a new household. Adoption is common in Samoa, and the adopted child has basically the same rights within the family as do the *tama moni* (true offspring).

In many cases too harsh discipline prompts a child to leave the household for the home of another relative and remain there for a month or more. One person told how when he was a child, he circulated between several households of relatives escaping from each when disagreeable work was forced upon him.

The *matai* is a "father" to all who live beneath his roof. He is responsible for the welfare of the group through efficient administration of family lands and resources. The chiefs of Samoa may be considered a privileged class but not without special obligations and demands. This is best expressed in the following statement of the young chief, recorded by Mead.

> I have been a chief only four years and look, my hair is grey, although in Samoa grey hair comes very slowly. . . . But always, I must act as if I were old. I must walk gravely and with measured step. I may not dance except upon most solemn occasions, neither may I play games with the young men. Old men of sixty are my companions and watch my every word, lest I make a mistake. Thirty-one people live in my household. For them I must plan, I must find them food and clothing, settle their disputes, arrange their marriages. There is no one in my whole family who

dares to scold me or even to address me familiarly by my
first name. It is hard to be so young and yet be a chief.
(1928a:36–37)

The main labor force within the household consists of the untitled
men *(taulele'a)* who work the family land. The untitled men in each
household are headed by the *matai taule'ale'a*, an untitled man who is
chosen by the *matai* to direct the family in his absence. This individual
may not represent the household head in the village council, because
he is untitled, but within the household he is looked to as the director
of family activities. When both the *matai* and the *matai taule'ale'a* are
present, the latter serves as an assistant, directing the family labor
force without shirking any of the labor himself. Each morning he goes
to the family head to receive the work orders of the day.

THE AUMAGA AND AUALUMA

The untitled men of the village are organized into a cooperative work
group *(aumaga)* which constitutes an important ceremonial and labor
unit serving the village council and the village as a whole. The *aumaga*
has been referred to as the "strength of the village." Nearly all of the
village's cooperative labor projects are in its hands, and while chiefs
may join in, the majority of the work is planned and carried out by the
untitled men. Cutting copra for church projects, repairing village
paths, house building, operating the longboats, planting and harvest-
ing of the village taro patch, and organizing community fishing parties *(lau)* are but a few of its activities. All passengers and cargo from
interisland vessels are unloaded and ferried ashore through the chan-
nels in the reef by this group. They are servants of the chiefs, cooking
and serving food at all meetings of the village council, and preparing,
wringing, and serving ceremonial kava. They are also the enforcers of
village council law.

Aside from their part in labor activities, this group of untitled men
take an important part in the social activities of the village. The arrival
of a visiting party *(malaga)* is a signal for them to make a ceremonial
call *(aiavā)* on the visiting ceremonial maiden *(taupou)* for purposes of
feasting, dancing and singing. Less formal calls are paid to individual
girls visiting the village when feasting and dancing are again in order,
to entertain and get acquainted with them.

The female counterpart of the *aumaga*, the *aualuma*, is composed of
the unmarried women of each family and it also performs ceremonial
and labor functions for the village. During the last generation, when
these groups were still important in every village, they were often

visited by other *aumaga* whom they received as their guests. After feasting and dancing, the two groups slept together in the house set aside as the residence of this female group *(faleaualuma)*. These visits were of extreme importance if the occasion was the marriage of a village prince *(manaia)* or a ceremonial maiden *(taupou)*.

In recent times the *aualuma* serves a somewhat different function. It is now but a part of a greater village organization known as the Women's Committee. This group is made up of the wives of untitled men and the wives of Chiefs and Talking Chiefs. Although still a recognizable entity, the *aualuma* cooperates with the larger group in public health and infant welfare activities, in money-raising for the church, and in the entertainment of visiting parties *(malaga)*. The principal leadership of the Women's Committee comes from the wives of titled men; they rule the organization by virtue of their husband's positions in the village hierarchy.

VILLAGE ORGANIZATION

Although each household in the village of Ta'ū is headed by a *matai*, there are actually fewer extended families in the village than the number of *matai* titles. This is because in some cases there is more than one *matai* in an extended family. This is the case in approximately four of the larger, higher ranking extended families, such as those of Lefiti and Tufele. The family heads, or more correctly, household heads, are all titled chiefs of various ranks. In Manu'an society three ranks of Chiefs and three of Talking Chiefs are recognized:

CHIEFS

1. *Ali'i Sili*—'high chief'
2. *Ali'i*—'chief'
3. *Ali'i Fa'avaipou*—'between the posts chief'

TALKING CHIEFS

1. *To'oto'o*—'high talking chief'
2. *Vae o to'oto'o*—'foot of the talking chief'
3. *Lauti Laulelei* or *Tulafale Fa'avaipou*—'common talking chief' or 'between the posts talking chief'

Titles are as much family property as land. In Manu'a, Chiefs and Talking Chiefs of the third, or lowest rank, are appointed by the village council. After the council has conferred with members of the family or with chiefs related to the family in which a title is vacant, a "calling meeting" is held, at which the candidate is called in from the group of untitled men *(aumaga)* assembled outside to take the seat to which he is entitled as the new family head.

Titles of first and second rank are conferred by the family after a lengthy deliberation. Important qualifications for the position include knowledge of Samoan tradition, intelligence, ambition, claim to the title through either direct patrilineal descent or adoption into the family, and nomination by the former family head in his "last wish" *(māvaega)*. If no wish has been expressed by the former family head, the usual processes of family selection ensue. The role at *māvaega* in title succession is not mentioned in other literature and may be an innovation. Certainly it is unique to Manu'a.

Most family heads hold their titles for life. In Manu'a a title is never taken from an individual merely because of old age, though there have been rare cases where titles were taken away because of misuse of the office. The official grounds for removal from title are: (1) absence from the village of six months or more, and (2) failure to perform traditional duties. Impeachment requires the unanimous vote of the titular extended family.

The holders of the various ranks of Talking Chief and Chief have a number of duties and privileges within the family and village. The High Chief *(ali'i sili)* settles arguments in the council *(fono)* and advises the Talking Chiefs. He is a leader of the village and maintains a great guest house for the entertainment of visitors. In most cases the High Chief has the right to maintain a village ceremonial maiden *(taupou)*, and his son is usually the leader *(manaia)* of the untitled men. On ceremonial occasions a High Chief, his *taupou* and *manaia* may wear the headdress known as the *tuiga*. The High Chief receives first kava, and the first portion *(sua)* of food served at a meeting of chiefs. At any distribution of food, choice portions of pigs, fish, or fowl are the share of the High Chief. Some Chiefs, depending upon traditions surrounding their titles, have the right to impose taboos, but most taboos are edicts of the village council. In Manu'a the general name for High Chiefs is *fa'atui*, which means "second to the King."

The High Talking Chief *(to'oto'o)* has the duty of settling disputes within and between villages and putting motions before the village council. It might be said that he is the ruler of the village, but he may be overruled by the High Chief. The people of the village call the High Talking Chiefs the "difficult people," because no one may disagree with them except the High Chiefs. Even in these cases, the High Chief merely offers advice. If a High Talking Chief is wealthy he will, from time to time, roast pigs and prepare food for the High Chief, for which he receives gifts in return, as repayment *(lafo)*. If the High

Talking Chief wants fine mats for his daughter's wedding and gives the High Chief a pig, the High Chief must give him the equivalent in fine mats.

Whenever a visiting party *(malaga)* comes to the village the High Talking Chief serves as the village orator, and the prestige of the village is in his hands. It is his duty to deliver the official welcome of the village, and he must attempt to better the visiting Talking Chief in oratory. As a mark of office the High Talking Chief wears a large fly switch *(fue afa)* over his shoulder and carries a speaker's staff *(to'oto'o)*. On ceremonial occasions he must wear a tapa as a wrap-around skirt *(lavalava)*.

In local affairs, the High Talking Chief supervises the distribution of food at meetings of the village council. He announces what food has been brought by the individual chiefs and instructs the untitled men how to distribute it to the assembled chiefs. If a kava ceremony is held in the morning the second drink of kava goes to the High Talking Chief. If a second kava ceremony is held during the day, the High Talking Chief always drinks first.

The Chiefs of second and third rank have similar duties but different status.[1] They are not required to make speeches in the village council, but may do so. If the High Chief is not present at the council meeting, a second rank Chief acts as High Chief and sits at his post. If no second rank Chief is present, one of third rank substitutes for the High Chief. These Chiefs of second and third rank are permitted to carry small fly switches signifying only chiefly status. They may wear tapas at ceremonial occasions, but only the High Chiefs and High Talking Chiefs are required to do so. Most Chiefs of second rank have special posts in the council house while most Chiefs of third rank must sit between the posts.

Second- and third-rank Talking Chiefs carry messages between villages when untitled men are not available. They have fly switches of smaller size than those used in speech giving, but do not wear them on their shoulders. They have no speaking staffs but may use walking sticks. The lower rank Talking Chiefs traditionally give speeches in times of peace or at ordinary village meetings and ceremonies, while the High Talking Chiefs give speeches in times of trouble or on special occasions such as intervillage ceremonies and festivities. If a visiting party *(malaga)* arrives with only a second-rank Talking Chief as its speaker, a second-rank Talking Chief represents the host village in oratory.

Equal respect is shown chiefs of all ranks by their families. While much of a chief's time must be devoted to the village council and to village ceremonial and administrative duties, the chiefs are not considered to be above working the family land or joining into village cooperative activities. Many of the village chiefs are carpenters, boat-builders, or expert fishermen who engage daily in their trade. Chiefs who do not join in family agricultural work are considered lazy by the villagers. Holding a chief's rank does not entitle an individual to economic support by the family.

Every village of Samoa has its own village council *(fono)*. In nearly every village there are traditional divisions of chiefs who occupy certain sections of the council house and are designated by some such title as "the brother chiefs," "the four houses," the "cluster of chiefs," or by titles of local significance. The organization and functioning of no two village councils is exactly the same. Some, such as Faleasao, are ruled by a single High Chief of indisputable rank, while others have several High Chiefs of equal rank who share the control of the village. The relationship between Chiefs and Talking Chiefs also varies from one village to another. In some, Talking Chiefs speak for particular Chiefs; in others they represent divisions of Chiefs; in others they bear no relationship at all to individual Chiefs and merely speak for the village welfare as a whole. In some cases Chiefs have the right to double as Talking Chiefs, officially speaking for themselves, and are then known as Chief-Talking Chief *(tulafale ali'i)*.

The hierarchy of rank in Ta'ū village is founded in the tradition that tells of the early creation of the titles by the Tuimanu'a (King of Manu'a). These legendary accounts include details of early kings, the origins of villages, the composition of village councils, etc. This knowledge is passed down orally in families, but since about 1930 a certain amount of this material has been recorded in writing. It must be admitted that there is always the possibility of manipulation of legends in order to make them serve private ends, but this is probably nothing new. However, one of the methods of ascertaining where such manipulation has taken place is by comparing contemporary versions with those recorded by early travellers or missionaries.

Distinct from this traditional ranking, titles are also ranked at any moment in terms of personal achievement and circumstance. In certain cases a chiefly rank may be raised in the eyes of the village by an exceptional title holder. Acquisition of wealth and a display thereof, holding of a high government position, affiliation with a family of high rank through marriage, or exceptional ability and service to the village may often submerge the fact that a man holds a relatively low title and may put him in line for honors due chiefs of much higher traditional rank.

This is the problem the ethnographer must face in the study of Samoan political organization. Ascertaining the "correct" hierarchy of chiefs is made difficult by the fact that once a chief raises his own status through personal achievement, the Talking Chiefs who are numbered among his relatives attempt to raise his traditional status by modifying the village legends so as to make him appear traditionally more important than he really should be. One method of holding the margin of error to a minimum is to use several informants with different family affiliations. A comparison of these independent accounts with each other and with those in the early literature is the only satisfactory way to check data concerning traditional political organization. Observation may be used to describe the existing structure of the political organization, but not the traditional patterns of ranking chiefly titles that are more than an affair of the moment. Another valuable check was obtained by consulting chiefs of nearby villages who are more removed from the intrigues of the village in question.

The traditional aspects of village organization are of utmost importance in Manu'a, as tradition is often the only source for understanding special titles and alliances of chiefs. An example is the title *Vaimagalo*, shared by Soatoa and Galea'i. Its function can only be found in the legendary accounts of the difficulties between Ta'ū village and Fitiuta village factions of the King of Manu'a's family. Another title used to refer to High Chief Galea'i in the Fitiuta set of courtesy titles is *Pulefano* (representative to the court of Tuimanu'a) which also may be understood only from legendary sources of early village organization.

The King, Tuimanu'a, was traditionally paramount throughout the three component islands of Ofu, Olosega, and Ta'ū of the Manu'a group, and there is evidence that his sovereignty extended to other parts of Samoa. There is no record of anyone of kingly status having reigned in Tutuila, but two such sovereigns are known to have existed in Western Samoa. In Manu'a there are seven villages: Lumā, Si'ufaga, Faleasao, Fitiuta, Olosega, Ofu, and Sili. Each of these recognized a paramount Chief known as a "second to the king" *(fa'atui)*. Saotoa of Lumā, Lefiti of Si'ufaga, and Asoao of Faleasao were of such status. Beneath these were ranked the various Chief and Talking-Chief titles.

The organization of the twin villages of Lumā and Si'ufaga, constituting Ta'ū village are merely variations on a common theme of Samoan political organization.

Ta'ū, like many other villages of Samoa, has a traditional grouping of chiefs. First, there is the division of the village along descent lines into the "three houses," and second, certain of the higher ranking Chiefs of these "three houses" are designated the "brother chiefs" (*usoali'i*) and the "cluster of chiefs" (*pupuali'i*). The two highest ranking Chiefs of Ta'ū are those recognized as the head of *usoali'i* and *pupuali'i*. Both of these Chiefs, however, were ranked below the Tuimanu'a, or King of Manu'a, whose royal grounds were situated in Ta'ū village. The title of Tuimanu'a was abolished by edict of the American Government in 1904 when sovereignty was tranferred from the King to the United States of America.

Since the abolition of the Tuimanu'a title, the component parts of Ta'ū village, Lumā and Si'ufaga, have tended more and more to function as independent units. However, there is a great deal of evidence of cooperation between them. The councils of Lumā and Si'ufaga often meet as one in the "great council" (*fono tau faleula*) to discuss government business, and they also meet together to discuss laws that apply to the whole of the Ta'ū village. Many of the Lumā title holders live in Si'ufaga and many title holders of the latter village live in Lumā. All Si'ufaga titles may sit on the Lumā council, and all Lumā titles have the privilege of sitting on the Si'ufaga council. The two villages function as a single unit ceremonially, and one official listing of courtesy titles (*fa'alupega*) is used for both. Si'ufaga today has its own set of honorary titles, while Lumā uses a form of courtesy titles once employed for the combined villages in which references to the Tuimanu'a title are omitted. While Lumā and Si'ufaga have separate *aumaga*, the head of each *aumaga* is referred to as Silia, as was the one under the Tuimanu'a. Under the king, Silia was a very important title given to an untitled man of the king's family, but today it is strictly honorary and used to refer to the head of the *aumaga* on ceremonial occasions.

FONO DECISION-MAKING AND ORATORY

We have in Samoan culture what small group researchers refer to as a status leader situation where certain members of the council might, by virtue of their traditional rank, be expected to play a more important role in the decision-making processes and in the leadership picture than others. Although traditional rank is respected, it is only one element among many that must be considered in understanding village council decision making. The voices of men holding high titles will in certain circumstances carry more weight than those of the lower titles, but all ranks are given full opportunity to bring their opinions to the attention of the assembled chiefs. The main advantage in holding a high title is that it may mean that the individual will serve as the presiding officer in a discussion. This provides a better opportunity to place a particular proposition before the assembly and, while doing so, comment on its ramifications.

While status leadership is something the investigator must take into consideration, the participants themselves think of the decision-making process more in terms of a group function. That is to say, that village leadership is thought of as resting primarily with the group rather than with the status leader. It is impossible for any high-ranking individual to make a demand upon the village without first discussing the matter with the village council and obtaining its permission. In one very well known case, a village council objected to the autocratic behavior of the High Chief and sent a runner to all the surrounding villages and informed their councils that they no longer recognized the title of their paramount chief and had named another chief as their highest officer. When the officially deposed chief arrived at the next council meeting he found that his post was occupied and he had no alternative but to return home. The members of his extended family, upon hearing of the council action, threatened to remove his title, since they no longer had representation in the village council. To prevent this action the chief had to return to the council and ceremonially ask forgiveness by prostrating himself outside the council house with a finemat over his head until the council reinstated him to his official position.

When a village council decision must be made, the Talking Chiefs are responsible for passing the word and assembling the titled heads of families. The convened council is presided over by a High Talking Chief (*To'oto'o*) and it is he who states the issue to be decided.

The initial speech is made by a High Chief. It is noncommital and expository in nature and represents an attempt to clarify the issue without taking a definite stand. The participants of the *fono* interpret the speech as one designed to feel out public opinion on the matter.

After this opening statement chiefs of all ranks may express their opinions. Each speech represents the vote of the speaker, yea or nay, and serves the same function as a hand vote or ballot. After everyone who wishes to has spoken, a statement of concensus is made by the paramount chief of the village.

The opinions of the higher titles carry more weight than the lower ones. Four chiefs of high rank voting together would represent a majority opinion over six opposing chiefs of low rank. However, a council decision seldom involves such a division of opinion. Most decisions are, in effect, unanimous, for Samoan chiefs are masters of compromise. They alter and adjust a resolution until all seem satisfied.

The oratory that plays such a large part in decision making is seen by the Samoan as the normal procedure for determining action and therefore something apart from the art of oratory associated with occasions of high ceremony. True oratory is exclusively a Talking Chief's art.

Samoan speech-making is an art for both its own sake and the sake of the social structure it complements. The ability to speak well brings prestige to oneself and to one's family and village. The same talent, of course, is useful in the village council when there is a desire to persuade others to accept one's point of view, but the oratory that is most enjoyed, brings the most prestige, and attracts the most attention is that which occurs during the various phases of Samoan ceremonial life. Oratory is one of the few activities within Samoan culture where competitive behavior is not only tolerated but encouraged. This is best observed in the *fa'atau*, the traditional competition between village Talking Chiefs. This custom, still prevalent today, was described by Stair in his discussion of district meetings with several villages in attendance.

> Much stress was always laid upon the privilege of address-ing a public assembly, therefore when the time came for a particular settlement to address the meeting, the whole of the speakers stood up and contended amongst themselves for the honor of speaking on that day. Sometimes, and especially if the subject was important, the palm was quickly yielded to the speaker generally acknowledged to be the most effective, but on ordinary occasions they con-tended long for the honor. A quarter of an hour or twenty minutes was a very common time for a speech. They man-aged to speak in rotation, and although they might not be able to exercise the privilege very often, they all liked to assert their right to speak, and to exhibit their *to'oto'o lauga*, or orator's staff. [Stair 1897:85]

While it is undoubtedly true that in most cases everyone knows that one of the orators has been chosen beforehand to deliver the oration in contention, there are times, particularly in *malaga*-centered cere-monies, when the competition is genuine. The Talking Chief who delivers the major speeches will be rewarded by the *malaga* with gifts *(lafo)* of kava roots and bark cloth. The man chosen will be the one who, through clever use of words and allegorical references, con-vinces the others that he is the most able to represent his village with distinction in oratorical exchanges with the guest party's speaker. He must, of course, show the same brilliance of rhetoric as his *malaga* counterpart, and this often requires a particular talent or special style.

On especially important occasions, the *fa'atau* often takes two or three hours to conclude (a custom that has been of some annoyance to Western observers). Samoans on the other hand enjoy this game. They are amused by the clever arguments of thier own orators, and the visitors are flattered by the effort expended in choosing the most distinguished orator to address them.

Grattan, in commenting on the social function of this custom, sees first its complimentary aspect; that is, the privilege is worthy of only the finest speaker, and all are eager to receive that special honor. His second observation calls attention to a traditional value in Samoan culture—the importance of rank and its prerogatives. Grattan states: "An individual or family that neglects its privileges may find itself in danger of losing them. . . . Social and political precedence and recognition are dear to the heart of every Samoan, and no opportunity is lost for claims to status to be put forward or demonstrated, even though in the case of the *fa'atau* it may have been decided before the arrival of the visitors who actually is to have the honor of speaking" (1948:41–42).

With respect to the actual techniques employed in Samoan oratory, it should be noted that although there are individual differences in style, there is also a clear-cut pattern of acceptable rhetorical behavior. Speeches are given both within a council or guest house and out in the open, often on the village green *(malae)*. Normally, little movement or gesture is associated with the speech. Orations given outside are usually made in a fixed, standing position and seldom involve much body movement. The standard posture is one in which the orator sets his feet about twelve to fifteen inches apart, plants the pointed end of his six-foot orator's staff between the first and second toe of his right foot, and begins his speech with his head held high and his chest thrown out. The position of the staff is thought to be a carry-over from the times when a Talking Chief's staff was a spear and was held thus so it could be used readily if negotiations broke down. Although the orator may move the upper part of his staff back and forth to emphasize a point, to raise and use it in gesturing would be in exceedingly bad taste, for presumably this was a dangerous move in earlier days.

In addition to the *to'oto'o* (speaker's staff), the orator also has another significant badge of office, the fly whisk *(fue)*. All titled men have the right to carry a fly whisk, but the orator's whisk has a shorter and heavier wooden handle, and the whisk itself contains more and longer strands of sennit. The orator who gives a speech in a standing position normally rests the whisk on his shoulder and executes a significant set of movements before his speech begins. When the Talking Chief first takes his position to speak, the whisk rests on his left shoulder. If he then moves the whisk to his right shoulder and allows it to rest there, it is a sign that his speech will be short and informal. If he merely touches the whisk to his right shoulder and then returns it to his left, the assembled chiefs can expect a somewhat more formal and lengthy address. If, on the other hand, he touches the whisk to the right shoulder, then the left, and finally brings it to rest on his right, everyone prepares for a session of elaborate and formal rhetoric. The orator has indicated that he will exercise his maximum rhetorical powers.

Speeches presented within a house are made from a cross-legged sitting position. A few hand gestures are used, and the fly whisk is sometimes employed in a dramatic way. Often a swish of the whisk is used to emphasize a special point or to give the speaker a respite so that he may consider his next statement. He may rock back and forth slightly, but his general posture renders him more or less immobile.

The normal voice pattern in formal speaking is to start quietly and to increase in volume as the speech proceeds. This is particularly true of speeches inside the house. The initial phrases are often spoken in a whisper, and everyone must strain to hear what is being said. By the end of the speech the orator is nearly shouting. Phrases and sentences are often clipped, and special statements are frequently emphasized by raising the voice at the close of the thought. Individual orators have their own bag of tricks for holding attention and highlighting special points. A wise orator plays to his audience and alters his style in response to its moods.

Samoans have a strong faith in the magical power of words to charm, soothe, persuade, and arbitrate. This can be seen in their concept of "comforting words" at funerals, in their constant attempts to placate angry people through prolonged conversation, and in their attempts to influence elite ranks through the use of flowery phrases and courtesy references.

The general pattern of ceremonial oratory involves the principle of reciprocity. This, Keesing and Keesing observe, is characteristic of all relationships between Samoan people of rank. "Whatever is involved—goods, services, participation—a careful balance of give-and-take, of rights and obligations, of 'basic compensation' is maintained" (1956:86). Speeches of welcome must be matched by speeches of thanks, speeches of sympathy by those of appreciation, and speeches of apology by forgiveness. Oratory is an institution providing still another unifying bond between village and village, family and family, wronged and wrongdoer. It provides spice for commonplace lives and a demand for excellence in intellectual endeavor. It promotes respect for family and community identity.

Although Samoa is probably as traditional in its customs as any island group in Polynesia, it is also true that the era of classic oratory is passing. The legends, proverbial sayings, and *solo* (poetry), so important to the formal Samoan oration, are usually known only by a few of the older Talking Chiefs. For the young, the distinction of being an orator of ability runs a poor second to the prestige of being a good auto mechanic, taxi driver, or government office clerk. There were occasions, however, when tradition-minded young men approached me and asked if I had books of proverbs, *solo*, or myths they could use in developing oratorical skills and thereby be applauded by the older men of the village.

As one looks back over many centuries of great Samoan oratory, one cannot but be impressed by the fact that this institution has been a response to the Samoan's desire for social recognition and personal dignity. It has been satisfying avenue of activity in his quest for excellence. The gracious custom of honoring others through great oratory has brought equally great honor and community admiration for the Samoan orator himself. This is the essence of reciprocity—getting back the equivalent of the gift.

Samoan bride and groom

FIVE

Samoan Religion

CHRISTIAN MISSIONARIES

Samoans have been Christians for over 150 years. Samoa's first introduction to Christianity came from European sailors shipwrecked on Upolu several years before the first missionary arrived. Although the cargo of the wrecked vessel was seized by the Samoans, the crew was treated well and provided with food and shelter. In order to ensure their good treatment the captain advised the crew to turn missionary, setting an example for them himself. Although probably not very well-versed in religious knowledge, the captain nonetheless built several churches and established numerous congregations until forced to give up his newfound calling by the arrival of real missionaries.

The first bonafide Christian missionary to make contact with the Samoan people was John Williams, an ironmonger turned missions administrator. After building a 60-foot brigantine, "Messenger of Peace," in Rarotonga in only three months, Williams sailed for Samoa by way of Tonga in 1830.

In 1830 the Samoan archipelago represented a different mission field for the London Missionary Society than they had encountered elsewhere in Polynesia. Williams described the Samoan situation:

> The religious system of the Samoans differs essentially from that which obtained in the Tahitian, Society and other islands with which we are acquainted. There are neither

maraes, nor temples, nor altars, nor offerings; and consequently, none of the barbarous and sanguinary rites observed at the other groups. In consequence of this, the
Samoans were considered an impious race, and impiety
became proverbial with the people of Rarotonga; for when
upbraiding a person who neglected the worship of the
gods, they called him "a godless Samoan." [1839:464]

However, John Williams was wrong. The Samoans did have temples and they made offerings to their gods. While they did not have
bloody and "barbarous" ceremonies dedicated to deities, they were
not an "impious race." References to "godless Samoans" (Williams
1839:464) undoubtedly stemmed from ethnocentric perspectives
shared by pagan Rarotongans and Christians missionaries. Unfortunately, this concept of the "godless Samoans" has been passed on
and has even been quoted by modern anthropologists and historians
trying to explain the purported "success" of missionaries in the
spread of Christianity. However, Samoans were not godless, and the
Samoan mission was not particularly successful in achieving its cherished goals.[1]

The Samoans worshipped a single high god, Tagaloa, although
much like the Holy Trinity concept, the god had many names and
many manifestations. In fact, the Samoans tended to think of the
Tagaloa more as a family than as an individual; the polytheistic pan-
theons of eastern Polynesia were definitely missing in this Western
Polynesian culture. Samoans had no shortage of lesser gods, however. Missionary George Brown wrote:

No statement could be more contrary to the actual fact than
the assertation that the Samoans were a godless people, for
as a matter of fact, they worshipped in some form or
another a large number of gods, some of which were immediately connected with certain families. [1910:227]

Corroborating Brown's observation, George Turner, one of the
London Missionary Society's better scholars, devoted two entire
chapters in *Samoa: A Hundred Years Ago and Long Before* to enumerating
and describing household, war, and village gods. Noting 43 general
village gods and 22 "inferior or household gods," Turner explains that
this is only a fraction of the number actually acknowledged. The
highest level of Samoan god was *atua*, but Tagaloa was the sole
occupant of this status. Lesser spirits were known as *tupua* (local and
family gods) and *aitu* (demons and ghosts of the dead). Much of the
literature, however, lumps all village, family, and war gods together
under the common term *aitu* (spirit).

Although John Williams described Samoans as not having temples, priests, or offerings, Turner says:

> There was a small house or temple consecrated to the deity of the place. . . . Some settlements had a sacred grove as well as a temple where prayers and offerings were presented. [1861:240]

Temple paraphernalia observed by Turner included sacred stones, sacred drinking cups, and, in one case, a skull on a pole decorated with white streamers. One temple featured a conch shell in a basket suspended from the roof which was there for the deity to blow if he wanted the village to go to war.

Turner also wrote:

> The priests in some cases were the chiefs of the place; but in general someone in a particular family claimed the privilege, and professed to declare the will of the god. His office was hereditary. He fixed the days for the annual feasts in honor of the deity, received the offerings and thanked the people for them. [ibid.:241]

Margaret Mead records that Manu'ans recognized two types of priests: *taula aitu*—those who could converse with spirits or become possessed by spirits; and *va'a Tagaloa*—those who possessed power to make curses (1930:160). Williamson, on the other hand, cites four categories of Samoan priests: war godpriest, family priest, prophets, and sorcerers. He maintained that

> all the different orders of priesthood possessed great influence over the minds of the people who were kept in constant fear by their threats, and impoverished by their exactions. [1933:407]

He also claimed that at least one class of priests, *taula aitu,* qualified for their office by being malformed or because of some striking peculiarity in temperament of disposition. Hunchbacks and epileptics were often *taula aitu* because it was believed they were possessed by a spirit. These religious specialists were occasionally women, usually elderly, and sometimes epileptic.

It is true, however, that Samoans did not have the impressive stone altars, ceremonial courtyards lined with huge coral blocks, or the lithic images *(tiki)* of eastern Polynesia. It is almost pathetic to read of Samoans trying to demonstrate the rejection of their old gods, because they had no idols to topple or altars to destroy. Samoan temples looked too much like regular residences *(fale)* to make their destruction very dramatic. Rejection of old beliefs was difficult to demonstrate. Some deliberately ate totem animals *(etu)* and one recorded case reports the "drowning" of an old piece of matting which was purported to be the symbolic representation of a deity (Williams 1832). Equally unimpressive were the Samoan forms of ceremonial. Aside from the kava ceremony and certain first fruits observances, early missionaries were hard pressed to describe anything which they recognized as ritual.

> As far as I can gather there was no distinct form of worship in the general acceptance of the term. There was the element of fear, the desire for protection or for the acquirement of some desired object, but for all these application was to the priest and payment made to him and his directions accepted as the will of god. [Brown 1910:228]

This relative lack of rituals and structures associated with worship contributed to the "godless Samoan" impression that still colors descriptions of Samoan traditional religion. Thus Captain J. A. C. Gray suggests in his book *Amerika Samoa* (1960) that the Samoan's reaction to the events associated with the arrival of the "Messenger of Peace" shows their traditional religion played an unimportant part in their lives. He wonders, for example, why there was no reaction from the religious leaders to the "Messenger of Peace," bringing not only John Williams and mission teachers but also an influenza epidemic that took a great number of Samoan lives. Gray writes,

> . . . the Samoan's acceptance of this plague is evidence of the weakness of their religion, for no authoritative voice was raised to argue it was punishment for too ready acceptance of strange gods. [1960:36]

There are several weaknesses in this interpretation: It assumes Samoans would entertain the idea that gods punish wrong-doing. Samoan gods do not; breaches of proper behavior are punished by the village council. Even if there were reason to suggest that acceptance of foreign gods might bring punishment, it is possible that there was no authoritative voice to speak out. While there were family and village priests who interpreted the will of locally honored deities, there was no single religious leader who might have spoken for Samoa as a whole.

Finally, it would not have occurred to a Samoan that the influenza epidemic and the rejection of their traditional religious beliefs were in any way related. Their typical Oriental approach to religion would have led them to believe that the addition of another deity to their coterie of gods and spirits would merely result in making their lives fuller and richer, particularly in terms of material wealth, which seemed to be the new foreign god's forte. Samoans did not understand, as missionaries did, that Jehovah was a jealous god, for Polynesian gods did not have that attribute. There would have been little basis in their traditional concepts for believing that gods would be angry and send illness and death because of the acceptance of an additional deity. Gilson observes:

> A polytheistic and practical people, the Samoans were tolerant of the gods of other [people] and inclined to judge a deity at least partly in terms of the favours he lavished upon the living. [1970:72]

Believing in a positive correlation between supernatural power and wealth and abundance, Samoans had been greatly impressed with the high quality of the Westerner's material wealth, in the form of three-masted sailing ships, muskets, cannons, cotton clothing, and iron tools. They believed that the white visitors must have a superior god indeed. One native chief is recorded as saying:

> Only look at the English people, they have strong, beautiful clothes of various colors while we have only leaves, they have noble ships while we have only canoes. . . . I therefore think that the God who gave them all these things must be good, and that his religion must be superior to ours. If we receive this God and worship Him, He will in time give us these things as well as them. [Williams 1832]

Williams and other English missionaries used these Samoan anticipations to their advantage. On at least one occasion Williams is known to have told a Samoan chief that European vessels would not come to trade at Samoan harbors unless he and his people became Christians (Gilson 1970:23). The London Mission initially experienced considerable success throughout the islands, but their religious teachings were not accepted without a great deal of deliberation and debate. Before a community decided to join the *lotu* (church), a village meeting was called by the chiefs in order to explore the issue. Williams reports that deliberations were lengthy and insightful.

Some chiefs claimed that if all villages accepted the new religion, wars would be prevented. For some Samoans, the ceremonialism of the worship services was appealing. The Samoan love and appreciation of oratory brought a favorable response from those who enjoyed listening to the almost interminable sermons delivered by the mission pastors. Even today the role of substitute pastor is one eagerly sought by village Talking Chiefs anxious to exhibit their versatility and eloquence in the area of ceremonial and formal rhetoric. Many of the chiefs took a characteristic Samoan position in relation to the new religion—that acceptance or rejection be delayed until they knew more about it.

In the early years of Christianity's introduction into Samoa, the question of religion became a divisive issue in many villages. Many communities "held out" and were considered by other, converted communities as the "property of the devil." Antagonism between the "saved" and the "unsaved" often erupted into armed conflict that had to be quelled by the missionaries working in cooperation with village chiefs. After an initial period of apparent success there was also a great deal of back-sliding. The first formal mission station was established on the island of Ta'ū in 1837 under the supervision of a Rarotongan and a Tahitian mission teacher. By 1840 the London Missionary Society characterized the Manu'a group as one of its principal strongholds.

All of the early English missionaries seemed to be unable to separate their religious beliefs from their cultural values. John Williams, for example, believed that sloth was the deadliest of sins and saw it as a paramount responsibility to keep the people busy, partly to keep idle hands from devil's purposes and partly to ensure sizable donations to the church. In 1825 the native London Missionary Society congregation at Raiatea, in the Society Islands, was commanded by missionaries to build a larger church, although the one they had built five years earlier was more than adequate for their needs. Such demands were communicated to Samoans as well, and a church-building mania—still evident today—began.

The Samoans were quick to appreciate the new mythology taught by the mission teachers, the sermons, and the ceremonialism of the liturgy. The Bible stories were added to the oral literature and Talking Chiefs found new avenues for achievement—delivering sermons on Sunday mornings or serving as elders or deacons in the village church organization. In a culture where speech-making had traditionally accompanied any formal gathering, long sermons involving even a new set of gods and heroes was compatible with existing cultural forms. As an addition to the ritual of the kava ceremony the people now had communion, and they immediately took to the new symbols and trappings that adorned the church interiors. Generosity in gift exchange had always been an admired quality among Samoans, and Christianity provided the opportunity of acquiring additional respect from one's fellows by lavish giving to the church.

The proponents of the new god—Europeans or native mission teachers from Tahiti or Rarotonga—quickly impressed upon their converts the "Thou shalt nots" of the new religion. This was not novel either, for although *tapu* was not as strong a concept in Samoa as in eastern Polynesia, it was certainly recognized. Christian *tapu* priorities seemed to rest in the area of sex and family relations, and Samoans were directed to abolish such practices as polygamy, divorce, political marriages, marriages between Christians and non-Christians, adultery, premarital sex relations, lavish gift exchanges at marriages, the public test of virginity, and prostitution. Violation of any of the tenets of the church meant expulsion from membership. Somewhat less serious, but of great enough import to warrant special attention from missionaries, was the matter of nudity. New standards designated "full coverage" for women. For men, who normally covered what the missionaries considered the necessary areas in their everyday dress, special church dress of shirts, ties, and often coats was prescribed in addition to ankle-length wrap-arounds *(lavalava)* of cotton trade cloth.

Beyond the sphere of family life there was yet a greater list of *tapu* behavior. War and violence were forbidden except in defense of life or property. Consumption of liquor and kava and the use of tobacco was prohibited. There was to be no gambling, tattooing, bush medicine, or sorcery; and funeral feasts, which missionaries considered wasteful, were strongly discouraged.

In exchange for all these prohibitions the Samoans received literacy[2]; the idea of the dignity of work; new ceremonialism in the form of christenings, weddings, funerals, and Communion; new songs to sing with strange new harmony; and the promise of salvation in a hereafter which resembled, in some ways, the Pulotu that they had believed in for centuries. What Samoans probably expected, although the European missionaries were not aware of it, was that ultimately they would also acquire some of the white man's magic for getting material wealth.

In 1845 a seminary known as Malua College was established on the island of Upolu, and the London Missionary Society began training its own Samoan teachers and village pastors *(faife'au)*. The graduates of this school were supposed to be paid a salary of ten pounds a year, but good intentions soon outstripped the London Missionary Society coffers, and individual villages were made responsible for the support of the local pastor. This system still prevails.

INDIGENOUS BELIEF SYSTEM

In order to understand the nature of the Samoan religious system today, it is important to know something of the indigenous beliefs, as there are numerous survivals of those beliefs in contemporary Samoan religion. Traditional understandings have also led to reinterpretations of Christian doctrines.

While the names of a large number of supernatural beings are included in Samoan myths, their supreme god and creator was Tagaloa. Elsewhere in Polynesia this deity had a restricted sphere of influence, being primarily the god of the sea and fishermen. The Samoans believed in a Tagaloa family who lived on ten mountains which they referred to as *lagi* (heavens). The most important of the Tagaloas was Tagaloa Lefuli (unchangeable) who was also known by the names Tagaloa Mana (powerful) and Tagaloa Fa'atutupunu'u (creator). Within the Tagaloa pantheon were such deities as Tagaloa Pule (authority), Tagaloa Tetea (albino), Tagaloa Tula'i (standing), and Tagaloa Savalivali, the messenger of the gods.

Tagaloa was not worshipped, although the early literature implied that prayers were often offered and feast foods dedicated to him. Even today, references are made to the ancient gods during various phases of the kava ceremony. Tagaloa had no priests and whatever attention was paid to the deity was from family heads or orator chiefs whose religious office was a part of their normal role as titled elite.

Tagaloa, known as *atua*, was the highest of two classes of supernatural beings. Below Tagaloa was a class of national, village, and family spirits referred to as *aitu*. Most *aitu* were believed to be the spirits of dead ancestors and had only local significance for particular families or villages, but there was a large class of *aitu* that had national significance. Examples of the latter were Tuiatua, Sauma'eafae, Saveasiuleo, Nafanua, and Nifoloa. Some of these spirits are still revered, and older villagers often are able to identify sacred places or objects occupied by the spirits.

Tuiatua is believed to have a special association with the Manu'an village of Fitiuta, although he may travel about the entire Samoan archipelago. This is the spirit of a human being who once lived in Fitiuta on a section of land known as Mutie. One old chief maintained that he always knew when the spirit was present by the sound of his staff on the village path. Returning bonito boats dedicate their catch to this spiritual being.

Sauma'eafe also was once a mortal who also lived in the Manu'a island group. It is said that while still a girl she was stolen by *aitu* and changed into a spirit. Like other *aitu* she has the power to possess and speak through people.

Saveai'uleo is a spirit who presides over Pulotu, the realm of Samoan afterlife. His daughter, Nafanua, a kind of Samoan Joan of Arc, left Pulotu in mythical times to lead the people against an oppressive political regime. In a great battle in which her forces were victorious she wrapped coconut leaves about her body so the enemy would not discover her sex. After the battle she made the vanquished wrap the trunks of coconut trees with palm fronds, thereby symbolically designating her ownership of the land and its products. The practice is still followed today in the form of a charm *(tapui)* used by land owners to protect their coconuts from theft.

Nifoloa, the long-toothed demon, was a disease- and death-dealing spirit. One disease, which carries the name of the *aitu*, is still much feared throughout Samoa. It is believed that once one has contracted Nifoloa, the slightest scratch will produce an infection that is in most cases fatal.

All the above spirits are classed under the term *folauga aitu* and are believed to be capable of traveling throughout the Samoan chain. They are purported to be able to take the form of birds, fish, reptiles, or human beings, or remain invisible if they choose. They possess men and women and often speak through them and affect their behavior—a phenomenon which becomes a convenient rationalization for departures from prescribed Christian behavior.

There were also lesser *aitu* associated with only one village or one family. These often appeared to people in the form of birds, animals, or fish and were undoubtedly the basis for food *tapus* which have been interpreted as totemic observances. Little remains of these ideas today, but there are villages and families in Samoa who have traditionally refrained from eating particular land or sea creatures although they are not certain exactly why they are so restricted.

The kind of *aitu* that are universally accepted in modern Samoa are the ghosts of ancestors, sometimes benevolent, sometimes mischievous, and sometimes malevolent. They are believed capable of appearing in recognizable human form, but at night they invariably wear white. There are places traditionally recognized as gathering spots for such ghosts, and few people care to dally while passing such haunts. Almost without exception Samoans can relate eerie and often terrifying experiences they have had with these spirit beings.

According to common belief most *aitu* cause trouble only if their families are engaging in activities of which they do not approve or if they are the spirits of those who died in a distant village or country. The latter belief has led to some reticence on the part of the seriously ill to go to the hospital on Tutuila for treatment.

When *aitu* bring misfortune to families with whom they are displeased it is usually in the form of an illness known as *ma'i aitu* (spirit sickness) and involves the symptoms of delirium, chills, sleep-walking, and sudden, aimless running about. Village specialists in *aitu* medicine, known as *taulasea*, treat these spirit maladies with various leaf and herb concoctions. Recoveries may also come about as a result of a family changing its ways or reversing a decision that they believe might have precipitated the wrath of the spirit.

Numerous precautions are taken to protect against the possibility of contact with *aitu*. For example, a single house blind (*pola*) left up when all the rest are lowered is an invitation for a spirit to enter the *fale*. If two blinds on opposite sides of the house are left up *aitu* will invariably walk through the house, and sleepers lying in their path will wake up feeling sore and tired as if someone had walked over them throughout the night.

Even before the coming of the Christian missionary, Samoans believed in an immortal soul (*agaga*) which left the body at the time of death and journeyed either to Pulotu or to Fāfā. Pulotu was known as the "abode of the blessed." It was described to Charles Wilkes in 1839 as "an island to the westward," where "the spirit goes immediately after death"; a place where "it never rains," where people "eat and drink without labor," and where they are "waited upon by beautiful women, who are always young" and "whose breasts never hang down" (1845:132). While Wilkes was told that Pulotu was an island to the west, the more common belief was that it lay beneath the sea just beyond the end of Savai'i and was entered by way of two whirlpools—one for chiefs and one for the untitled.

Fāfā was the Samoan Hades, a place of dread and punishment ruled over by Ole Fe'e (octopus). Early literature tells us little concerning who was assigned to this afterworld, or why, and its location has been described merely as "westward of Savai'i." It is likely that after the coming of the missionaries Fāfā was quickly conceptualized as being identical with Satan's domain. Although souls were permanently committed to these afterworlds, they were apparently free to return on occasion to their earthly village homes where they would appear in ghostly form to family members or intervene in the lives of surviving kinsmen.

Mana and *tapu* seem strangely unimportant in Samoa when compared with eastern Polynesia. Samoans have always thought in terms of sacred *fono* (village councils) rather than sacred chiefs. Agricultural lands or fishing areas on the reef flat were (and still are) made *tapu* if there was danger of depleting resources when a large feast or celebration was anticipated, but these restrictions were imposed by the village council and not by an individual chief or by a deity. There were vague suggestions that a paramount chief had more *mana* than regular chiefs and that chiefs of any degree had more than untitled persons, but *mana* was only an important consideration where royal titles such as the Tuimanu'a or the Malietoa were concerned. The Tuimanu'a, for example, had to be served meals by his wife who had comparable *mana* or by serving people who had been ceremonially rendered immune to the force of his inherent power. Since no such title as the

Tuimanu'a exists today, and since most ideas of *mana* were associated with titles rather than persons, these concepts have now disappeared. In Western Samoa special precautions against the force of *mana* inherent in royal titles like Malietoa and Mata'afa have also become a thing of the past.

Among the survivals of indigenous belief in 1954 was the concept of *tapui*. This idea, originally noted by George Turner during his period of mission service in Samoa (1842–1859), involves what Turner (1884) calls a class of "curses" used as a protection for property. He lists eight such "curses" which might better have been labeled "protective charms." They are the sea-pike, the white shark, the cross-stick, the ulcer, the tic-douloureux, the death, the rat, and the thunder *tapui*. Over a hundred years later at least two of these—the sea-pike and the rat *tapui*—are still being used to protect property.

In the case of the rat *tapui*, a small coconut leaf basket filled with *vaofali* or *vaolima* weeds is hung on a coconut tree to protect plantation land from damage and theft. Violation results in damage being done by rats to the clothing, tapa, or fine mats of the guilty party. The sea-pike, or swordfish, *tapui* consists of half a coconut frond braided into a facsimile of a swordfish which, like the basket, is hung on a tree to protect agricultural land. The charm threatens the thief with impalement by the swordfish on his next entrance into the sea. The same general concept is retained in several new *tapui* which have been developed in modern times. Among these are the boil *tapui*, the hernia *tapui*, the general sickness *tapui* and the *tuia* (skin disease) *tapui*. Each of these charms threatens various forms of physical ailments if ownership rights to land or other forms of personal or family property are violated.

CONTEMPORARY SAMOAN RELIGION

Samoans are capable of compartmentalizing Christian and indigenous beliefs so that what appear to be contradictions in the two systems do not seem to cause any anxiety or conflict. Although nearly all modern Samoans identify themselves as Christians, there is still widespread knowledge of indigenous mythology and spirit lore. While Samoan Christians subscribe to the scriptural belief in a Heaven and a Hell, there are few Samoans who would not recognize the word *Pulotu* or have some knowledge of traditional beliefs concerning its characteristics. When I asked an elderly Talking Chief (who had just spent several hours describing the Tagaloa pantheon) if he believed in the veracity of the Book of Genesis, he stated that he believed every word of it. When he was asked how he reconciled this belief with the story of how Tagaloa had created the Samoan islands and its inhabitants, the Talking Chief replied that the story of creation as it appeared in the Bible explained the origin of the white man but that he was absolutely convinced that Tagaloa was the creator of the Samoan people and the islands they inhabited.

While the majority of Samoans are enthusiastic supporters of the modern Church, and church attendance equals almost 100 percent of villagers, European observers have expressed some doubt as to the depth and quality of Samoan Christianity. An example is found in the statement of a missionary quoted by Felix Keesing:

> I am afraid that from the Christian viewpoint the missions have been rather a failure in Samoa. Instead of accepting Christianity and allowing it to remold their lives to its form, the Samoans have fitted them inside Samoan culture, making them a part of the native culture. [1934:410]

Of course, the phenomenon of a particular culture "swallowing up" or reinterpreting a foreign theology so that it meets the needs of the society is not unique to the Samoan situation, and is hardly evidence of lack of depth and quality. Indeed, it probably has happened wherever Christianity has spread throughout the world.

Over the years any number of denominational groups have tried their hand at molding religious belief and worship in Samoa. The Wesleyan Mission, which is known as *lotu toga* (The Tongan Church), was established by Peter Turner in 1835, approximately a year earlier than the arrival of the first resident European missionaries of the London Missionary Society. Wesleyan native teachers began working in the Manu'a Group as early as 1828, but their effect was minimal. More effective was the London Missionary Society convert named Hura who was shipwrecked on Ta'ū Island sometime during the 1820s. With great zeal and a portion of the Tahitian Bible he managed to salvage, he immediately set about instructing the people of Ta'ū in the new religion.

Roman Catholic Marist missionaries arrived in Samoa in 1845, but most of their influence has been confined to Savai'i, Upolu, and Tutuila. The Manu'a group has remained fiercely loyal to the London Missionary Society from the very beginning. They have tolerated the few Roman Catholic families who live among them and have permitted occasional visits to their villages by priests, but there are no Roman Catholic houses of worship in Manu'a nor any other evidence that the Roman church has had much success in terms of converts.

Mormon missionaries began working on Tutuila in 1888 and on Ta'ū

Island in 1904 but found a mission field that was far from fertile. Elder Workman, first Latter Day Saints missionary in Manu'a, after a period of three months, complained of strong opposition by chiefs and even the Tuimanu'a. Meetings, he claimed, were broken up and those in attendance were fined or otherwise punished. In 1954 Mormon missionaries had been stationed in Fitiuta for several years, but their work had generally met with little success. Other denominations such as Nazarene, Seventh Day Adventist, Four Square Gospel, and several varieties of Pentecostal churches have sent missionaries to American Samoa, but as of 1954 none of these had carried on any proselytizing in the Manu'a group. Margaret Mead found a Bahai unit in Ta'ū village, however, when she revisited the locale of her *Coming of Age in Samoa* study in 1971.

Church membership in American Samoa remains dominantly London Missionary Society, with approximately 76 percent of the population. Roman Catholics make up 13 percent; Mormons make up 6 percent; Wesleyans 3 percent; and all others 1 percent. While accurate statistics did not exist for Manu'a in 1954, this area contained a higher percentage of London Missionary Society members than the average.

The church started by native teachers of the London Missionary Society in 1830 is known today as The Congregational Christian Church of Samoa. It has seven districts in Western Samoa and one in American Samoa. The church is self-governing and self-supporting. Although it is a member of the International Congregational Council and the World Council of Churches, there are no European or American church representatives in residence in Samoa. The church today sends its own missionaries to Niue, the Gilbert, Ellice, and Tokelau islands, and to New Guinea.

Although there is a church organization that encompasses the entire Samoan archipelago, each individual village church enjoys a great deal of autonomy. Native pastors *(faife'au)* serve and are supported by the community.

The ministry is the highest calling in all Samoa, and the village pastors are the most respected and influential of men. No religious leader under the ancient Samoan religion ever equalled the paramount position of the village pastor *(faife'au)*. Many of the decisions of the village council may be clearly traced to his wishes. While clergy may not hold chiefly titles, the village pastor is paid greater honors than are accorded any titled chief, regardless of rank. When he attends a village council he sits in the end of the house, the seat of honor, and drinks first kava, also the position of honor. Village visitors are often quartered at the pastor's house rather than the house of the High Chief, which was formerly the place to entertain those of high rank.

The pastor and his family are completely supported by the village; various families take turns providing their daily food. After every community fishing party, one of the first shares is set aside for the pastor. Much of the village and intervillage cooperation is directed toward church projects—thus, the cutting of copra for church revenue is a joint project of the villages of Lumā and Si'ufaga. The church choirs of the two villages are composed mostly of the formal organizations of untitled men (*aumaga*) and young women (*aualuma*) of the villages, and the weekly choir practice is the most anticipated social event of the week for the young people. A single church building serves these villages, which collectively make up the village known as Ta'ū, and its unifying effect cannot be too highly stressed. The ultimate in cooperation is achieved within and between the two villages in the fund raising, building and dedication of new church property. Their latest project in 1954 was the construction of a house costing $17,000 for the village pastor.

The church not only unifies adjacent villages like Lumā and Si'ufaga but is instrumental in uniting all of Samoa. At a church dedication attended in Fagasā on Tutuila, villages from all over American and Western Samoa attended and gave large gifts of money for the financing of the completed church. The Manu'an village of Fitiuta donated $2,000 to the church dedication, and the Fitiuta chiefs and untitled men rehearsed a lengthy original dedication song for better than a month and presented it at the church dedication.

The village church organization consists of a group of elders, deacons, and the *Ekalesia* (ecclesiastical membership). Elders and deacons are invariably titled individuals, and such offices are important to personal and family prestige. As in many Protestant church organizations, elders are the decision-makers and supervisors of spiritual affairs, and the deacons are the keepers of the church treasury and administrators of church property.

The members of the *Ekalesia* make up the preferred membership roll of the church. These are the people who have undergone a period of instruction called the *Sāiliili* and consequently adhere to a specific set of beliefs and code of behavior. In addition to the requirement of attending church regularly, they are forbidden to drink alcoholic beverages, attend movies, or participate in European-style social dancing. Their lives must be beyond reproach morally, and they are expected to give sizable donations to the church on a regular basis. Members of the *Ekalesia* (which include the elders and deacons) are the only ones permitted to partake in Communion when it is served on the first Sunday of every month. Any violation of the behavioral code of the *Ekalesia* results in the offender being removed from membership. Reinstatement comes only after an additional period of instruction and the permission of the entire membership.

Samoan churches are European in architectural design with cement or limestone walls, corrugated iron roofs, and elaborate folk-art interiors involving wood inlay designs and windows with stained-glass panes. Altars are often draped with appliquéd or embroidered hangings and decorated with artificial flower arrangements and religious pictures of conservative European style. Most churches have pews, a Communion table (used mostly for collection of the church offering), a pulpit and an altar. Ventilation is poor and most sanctuaries are uncomfortable, as the architecture is ill-suited to the tropical climate (one of the more necessary items of church-going equipment is a coconut leaf fan). Early missionary accounts speak of construction of churches which replicated the Samoan *fale*, but evidently as the new religion grew in favor, the prestige of European style churches also increased and soon the English country church design, often with a touch of Spanish influence, became standard in every Samoan village.

SUNDAY IN SAMOA

On Sunday in Ta'ū village, the church bell rings at about 5 A.M. Even at this early hour there is activity in the village. Because Sabbath cooking must be completed before daybreak, many young men and women are already busy preparing the day's food. For others, the bells represent early announcement of the first church service of the day, which will take place at 6 A.M. There will be sufficient time to open the large wooden trunks that hold Sunday clothing, to select the proper attire, and press out the wrinkles with a charcoal-heated iron; there will be time to eat cold cooked taro or a cooked green banana and still be punctual for the early church service. Attendance at this service is light—the majority of worshippers prefer the 8 A.M. service. In the 30–40 minute interval between services the village choir congregates in the *fale* of one of its members and runs through a last-minute rehearsal of the morning choral selections. Their main rehearsal takes place earlier in the week. In most of the *fale* in the village the church-goers wait until the last minute before putting on their Sunday best so that it will not become wrinkled in the humid heat of the morning. Young women carefully dress their hair in braids and pin to their heads low-crowned, wide-brimmed coconut hats. Everyone carries a coconut frond basket to hold a Bible and a hymnal. The chiefs wear white *lavalavas*, shirts, cotton coats, and solid black ties.

Untitled men often leave the coat at home and occasionally sport a flowered or striped tie. Unmarried women wear a knee-length cotton frock (usually white), but married women find it proper to wear a *pulatasi*, a two-tiered costume consisting of an ankle-length *lavalava* overlaid with a thigh-length cotton dress, all in white.

At approximately 7:45 A.M. the church bell rings again and the church procession begins. Whole families emerge from their household dwellings and walk leisurely in single file along the path that separates the village from the sea. As the families enter the church the members disperse, the women filling in the right side of the sanctuary, the men the left, and the children taking seats in the middle. On the left and right sides at the front of the pulpit is a section reserved for the choir. This is also the location of a small pump organ that is often played by the choir director who conducts and plays simultaneously.

At the back of the children's section two elderly men station themselves. Equipped with canes, they are there to maintain order among the youngsters who are prone to forget church decorum. Whispers or nodding heads are often responded to with a gentle but unmistakable rap on the skull by one of the elderly monitors.

The service begins with a hymn and a prayer followed by a responsive reading from the Samoan Bible. A hymn which follows this reading is more in the form of an anthem, and this is the choir's opportunity to perform. The words are often direct translations of traditional Protestant hymns, but the melodies are frequently different. Harmonically, Samoan church music differs little from Western religious music, but the tonal quality and musical style are uniquely Polynesian. The women sing in high nasal voices, while the men carry the lower parts with full, deep tones. The female voices carry the melody and the male voices provide a moving bass line which complements and yet provides a contrapuntal contrast with the lead voices. Few Samoans read music, and hymnals do not include musical notation. Most melodies are traditional and familiar to everyone. The ability to sing in three-part harmony seems to come easily to Samoans, although the indigenous music of this area did not feature harmony. Traditional chants of various kinds were characterized by a narrow range in melody, carefully enunciated texts, and well-coordinated unison rendition.

Samoan church music, highly influenced by European modes in its structure, differs greatly in performance in that it tends to be joyful, rhythmic, and loud. More likely than not it resembles the vocal music used to accompany the Samoan dance, the *siva*.

The morning sermon is the highlight of the service. Rich in parables and Old Testament biblical history, the sermon stresses proper be-havior, piety, and the wages of sin. In a society which has developed oratory as its highest art, the minister is valued for his rhetorical skill and style and for the content of his message. Sermons are normally lengthy and are concluded with a prayer. When the final hymn of the morning ends and the worshippers close their hymnals, the deacons station themselves at a long table in front of the Communion rail and begin the reading of the church roll. When each family name is called, a representative of that family comes forward and lays the morning offering (money) on the table. The amount is observed by a deacon, recorded in a book, and announced to the congregation. In a status-oriented society like Samoa, where generosity is praised, Sunday morning offerings are substantial.

After the service, families return home and quickly change into less elegant attire and prepare to eat their morning meal that was cooked before daybreak. The *matai* of each family does not share this meal, for he and the other *matai* of the village gather in the *fale* of one of their number, eat together, and discuss things trivial and profound well into the afternoon.

Sundays are for rest and relaxation. The women of the village take long strolls with neighbors, children go down to the beach and play in the surf, and elders take long naps, sit quietly, or carry on lengthy conversations with friends or family members. No work is done, and the village remains quiet and lethargic.

The church bell tolls again at 4 P.M. announcing the afternoon service. This service is much like the morning one, but it attracts fewer worshippers and those who do attend are more informally dressed. Men arrive in shirt sleeves and women wear simple flowered dresses. There is a noticeable absence of teen-age children at this service, for they have one of their own two hours later.

The evening is again the time for strolling and conversation, for a cool bath, and an early retirement. For most, the new work week will begin before dawn with a journey to the plantations high on the slope and a morning of cultivation before the advent of the noonday heat.

Dance group made up of untitled men

SIX

The Life Cycle

INFANCY & CHILDHOOD

Most Samoan babies are delivered in village dispensaries by Samoan medical practitioners or by registered nurses. In the more remote areas, midwives operate with the sanction of the Public Health Department. Newborns are nursed whenever they cry; they are fed only milk for four or five months, at which time solid food is introduced, though breast-feeding will continue for 8-24 months. The process of weaning involves removal of the child from the mother for three or four days, at which time water in a cup is given in place of breast milk. If the child, upon being reunited with his mother, still demands the breast, she will smear her nipple with lime juice until the infant loses his taste for it.

At age 4 to 6 months, the child's mother will leave it in the care of an older sibling or a grandmother so that she may resume her work on the family plantation. The child may be left as long as eight hours a day, and will be fed by its caretakers. While baby bottles and powdered milk are now found in most Samoan villages, this is a recent development. In 1954, nourishment for small infants during the mother's absence consisted mostly of solid food. Since babysitters were in some cases young children, they were often careless about making sure that their charge ate properly. Malnutrition and other complicating diseases, which until recently took a great toll on Samoan babies, is very likely directly attributable to this irregular and haphazard pattern of feeding.

73

In 1954, Samoan babies were often wrapped in several layers of cloth (more than necessary in this tropical climate) but they wore no diapers. The mother merely cleaned up the child and the floor mats after each elimination. At one year of age, when an attempt at toilet training begins, the child is put outside the house each time it begins to eliminate. If that doesn't work, the child may be spanked. Young children are bathed daily in fresh seepage water on the beach or in tubs of cold fresh water.

Although children stand at about seven or eight months, few start walking before one year of age. Children are encouraged in their efforts to walk by adults who take their hands to support them. Slow walkers are dealt with in a somewhat indelicate way. The child may be buried in the sand of the beach up to the top of its legs and then after a few minutes violently jerked out. Another remedy for slow walking involves taking the child out into the lagoon, swinging it over the water, and occasionally allowing its legs and buttocks to strike the surface.

About the time of the Samoan child's first birthday it is trained to fetch things and to sit down while inside the house. To stand inside the house (and have one's head as high or higher than chiefs') is considered very bad manners. They are also taught at this time to remain quiet (again to show respect for elders and chiefs), and to avoid the sleeping mats of their parents. Samoan youngsters begin talking at eighteen months, but they are not expected to know proper kinship terms or proper salutations until they are about 12 years old.

Corporal punishment is administered to children as early as one year of age and it can be severe. It can take the form of slapping the buttocks, legs or face or whipping the child's lower extremities with a broom or belt. Mothers do most of the punishing, but fathers occasionally administer belt whippings.[1] Children are often shouted at when they are disobedient or are told that the spirits will "get" them. In some cases, disobedient children are forbidden to play on the village green with the rest of the children.

Samoan children appear to learn the value system more from older siblings (who do most of the babysitting) rather than from adults, but much is learned from watching adults and attempting to imitate their behavior. As the children grow older they quickly learn that there is a rigid status system to a large extent based on age, but which also has to do with sex roles and family leadership. For example, a very small child is fed on demand, but once it is weaned it is the last to eat. The *matai* eats first and age determines the order in which the others are allowed to eat. Children also learn that they owe respect to those older and more important than them (the ones who eat first), and that their commands must be obeyed.

Until the age of four, there is little difference in the care and training of Samoan boys and girls. After four years, however, patterns of labor differentiation start to emerge. Girls begin to help feed the younger children and to perform many of the simpler household tasks. While boys are usually free from household duties, they may be asked to collect coral pebbles for the house floor, to carry pails or kettles of water, or to feed the chickens or pigs. Girls as young as six or seven may be entrusted with the care of younger brothers and sisters, sometimes on a rather long-term basis. Their charges must be protected from other children, entertained, and kept from disturbing others.

By the time Samoan children are seven or eight years old they have been exposed to most of the household chores. Unlike Western cultures, there is no carefree childhood without responsibilities. Because Samoan children are increasingly given more and more adult responsibility, the transition from childhood to adulthood is a smooth and unbroken one. A child is permitted to undertake any work it feels capable of doing, even very dangerous things like wielding a bush knife or an axe.

Boys have more play activities than girls, because they have more freedom and time to play. Girls are more frequently tied down with the time-consuming responsibilties of babysitting. Boys' games are mostly competitive games of athletic skill. When they have the opportunity, girls play more at singing and dancing, or they often engage in a Samoan form of hop scotch or marbles. There are no games that demand high degrees of abstraction, such as chess. The children are also great spectators of adult activities such as ceremonial singing or dancing, and they love to observe village celebrations involving feasting or the entertainment at parties for important guests (*malaga*).

Play activities of children can be vigorous and rough. There seems to be no shame for a child who cries in front of the other children, and in any group of active playmates there is usually one who is crying, often because they have been deliberately struck by another child. When this happens no mother will ever come to soothe him. There seem to be no best-friend relationships among these younger Samoan children. Children of both sexes play together until they are six or seven but brother–sister avoidance regulations will separate them into boy's groups and girl's groups by the time they are approaching puberty.

COMING OF AGE

As Samoan girls approach puberty they are given more and more responsibility in the home. The tasks they are assigned are more difficult and require more skill, but it is at this time that they are relieved of their baby-tending chores. The babies will now be turned over to younger siblings to watch. Boys, by the age of twelve, have learned fishing techniques; they are becoming proficient in agriculture and the preparation of food, and they can handle an outrigger in rough water.

Several events in the life of a Samoan adolescent male may be considered as constituting a rite of passage. First, there is the matter of circumcision, which in some cases is performed by a native specialist *(tufuga)*. Although many Samoan boys have been circumcised in the European manner, many others prefer the traditional operation, which is seen as more of a mark of bravery. Another rite-of-passage milestone is entrance into the *aumaga*, an event which takes place at about age 16 or whenever the young man finishes his schooling. Finally, there is the matter of acquiring the traditional Samoan tattoos on the upper legs, buttocks, and lower back. A number of young men never undergo this very painful and dangerous ordeal but those who do (and there is a revival of the practice in recent times) display their body decorations with pride.

The following account by a Samoan informant describes the life of an untitled man.

> While the young man is at home, he must continually ask his *matai* (family head) how to do many things, such as: the *fa'alupega* (courtesy titles) of the village; the exact turn of each chief to take his kava cup; the exact time which each chief may make his speech in the village or in the district meeting; the genealogy of the family and also the lands of the family.
>
> It is necessary to cook the food every day for the chief's meal *(sua)*. Every night, he must get coconuts to satisfy his chief's thirst. So that he can cook every day, he must work very hard in the plantations (taro, banana, coconut, breadfruit, etc.) so that he will get as much as he wants for his chief—both to feed him and also to supply food offerings by his *matai* for the village. If he is zealous in doing all these things, he will be known as a good young servant.
>
> If there are many young untitled men of the family, one of them is the head of them all (this is the *matai taule'ale'a*). His duty is to ask their *matai* what work is to be done for the day. So, every young man must obey him. He allots the daily tasks. This allotment must be changed every day so that each young man may take his turn in doing each task—cooking food, fishing, working in the fields. He must supervise and see that all duties are performed. He must lead in the work in the plantations, fishing, cooking

and also in feeding fowls and pigs. If he has a wife, he must instruct her to go to the wife of her *matai* to get her orders for the day about weeding taro, mulberry, sugar cane and other fields, and all women's tasks. She must take care of all the lavalavas of the unmarried young men of the family and look after the wives of the young men of the family.

Every young man looks forward to the day when he will have a title, but it cannot be said that the untitled men are envious or covetous of the position of family head. They strive to work diligently and faithfully for the family and wait patiently for the time when they will be chosen for a family title. When an untitled man is elevated to titled status, much of the menial labor of the Samoan young man is left behind, but he now has new responsibilities to his family and to the village. The following passage from Copp describes a *matai*'s adjustment to his new titled status:

And so I got to be *matai*. And I can't go often now and play cricket with my boy-gang or sing love songs along the road by the moonlight. And also, when a happiness-time is in the village, I can't sing and dance any more like I used to make them laugh, but I have to sit in my place and watch the company of young men sitting there in their own place and doing everything.

And I'm sorry for this. But I'm glad too. Because now I am a real family head, and I can sit with the other chiefs in the meeting *fale* and give my opinion too and have my share of food. And I am leaving now the heaviest work of a young Samoan boy, serving for everything, when it is hot or when it is raining cold, and keeping on in doing all things even when he is too tired, because this is his special duty. [1950:173]

The counterpart of the *aumaga* is the *aualuma*, the organization of unmarried women. This group no longer functions in the traditional manner. In times past a girl would enter at fourteen or fifteen and the young women would live together in a house known as the *faleaualuma*. Their main duty was to serve and chaperone the village ceremonial princess, the *taupou*, but they were also called upon to undertake village work projects such as mat-making or tapa cloth manufacture. Today the organization is composed of unmarried girls, fifteen and older, widows of all ages, and, in many villages, the wives of untitled men. *Taupou* now are appointed to serve temporarily on ceremonial occasions, and therefore they no longer need hand-maidens or chaperones. And villages no longer have *faleaualuma*.

Aualuma still undertake community work projects, however; they prepare group dances to entertain visiting groups *(malaga)*, and they undertake fund-raising projects to aid the church.

SEX, COURTSHIP AND MARRIAGE

Sexual activity for Samoan males begins before a boy enters the *aumaga* and traditionally has involved an intermediary *(soa)* who approaches girls, argues his friend's case, arranges a rendezvous, and stands guard to report if the girl's brothers approach. *Moetotolo,* or "sleep crawling," is still found, and it is recognized as a form of illicit sexual behavior bordering on rape. Here a boy will enter a girl's house at night and attempt to have intercourse without revealing his identity. This reportedly only occurs when a boy cannot find a consenting partner.

Homosexuals are accepted without stigma or ridicule, but prostitution is looked upon very negatively. Prostitutes are found almost exclusively in larger port towns, and their customers are mostly tourists and crew from docked freighters.

Samoan men marry at about twenty-five years old and Samoan women at about twenty. Generally, both have had numerous affairs and flirtations by this time. A certain amount of sexual freedom is enjoyed by Samoan young people but probably no more than is characteristic of their counterparts in the United States. Unwed mothers face very little stigma, and their offspring are welcomed into the family. Some of these children will be legally adopted and, if they are boys, this will greatly improve their future chances of acquiring a family title.

When the formal announcement of a forthcoming marriage is made, the families of the boy and girl begin to prepare for the wedding and the ceremonial visit *(nunu)* for the exchange of wedding gifts. The girl's family prepares fine mats, barkcloth, sleeping mats, and food and the boy's family collects money, food, and wraparounds and dresses for the girl and her family. The following account, given to Copp by a Samoan, clearly illustrates the elaborate preparation for the wedding of a High Chief.

> For our share of the wedding food we had sixty big pigs, and as the nowadays custom is, my father had two hundred dollars American. And he got this two hundred dollars, some from the Bank of American Samoa where he owns an account, and some for selling copra to the trader, and the rest from the others in our *aiga,* or family, in that

place. . . . And after he gets married with that virgin girl *(taupou)* her own *aiga* will give plenty of *mea alofa*, or love gifts, with her, fine mats, and tapa-cloths, and lavalavas. And then my father will share out these gifts for all the helping people in his own *aiga* by money or food, and so everybody will come out even. [1950:142][2]

During the traditional fourteen-day engagement period, letter invitations to the wedding feasts are sent to friends and village chiefs. Wedding dresses are also prepared. The girl's family prepares a dress to be worn at the wedding ceremony, and the man's family prepares a dress for her to wear at the festivities that follow. No prewedding feasts are given for, or by, the groom.

On the day of the wedding, the bride and groom, accompanied by a wedding party *(aumea mamae)* composed of from four to forty of the man's and woman's best friends, go to the district judge where a civil marriage ceremony is performed. After the civil ceremony, the bride, groom, and wedding party proceed two-by-two to the village church where they enter by the front door and go down the aisle. Here the families of the bride and groom have assembled to observe the sacred ceremony which follows the usual Protestant ritual.

Following the church ceremony the wedding party and relatives proceed to the wedding festivities. Both the bride and groom's families may give separate feasts, but usually they combine and give one large one. After dancing, eating, and speech-making by Talking-Chiefs of the bride's and groom's families, the wedding festivities are over and the two families go to their homes to prepare the goods to be used in the wedding exchange *(nunu)*. The reciprocal exchange may take place at the same time, or one family may wait as long as two or three years to return gifts of equal value. Of the many gifts exchanged, the bride and groom seldom receive more than sleeping mats with which to set up their home.

In rare cases, the wedding festivities include a defloration ceremony. While this is forbidden by Government law and frowned upon by the church, it has been occasionally practiced. Formerly it was always performed on a *taupou* and frequently on other girls as well. Such a ceremony, which took place in Lumā village in 1952, was described by an informant as follows:

> The ceremony took place in the evening following the marriage ceremony. The blinds of the house were up so that the whole community could watch. In this case, the husband of the girl did the actual defloration (traditionally it was performed by a Talking Chief of the groom's family). She came to him with a white lavalava on, put her hands

on his shoulders and spread her legs. The fingers were
inserted and the white bark cloth (wrapped around them)
was red. The girl allowed the blood to stain the white
lavalava. This lavalava was displayed in front of the house
for many days.

The intrigues that often accompany the defloration suggest the
society's attitude toward sexual freedom. While proof of virginity at
marriage is appluaded by the families of both the bride and the
groom, informants state that many a girl has been saved embarrass-
ment by the substitution of a membrane containing animal or chicken
blood for that normally produced by a broken hymen.

On the wedding night the groom takes his bride to the house of his
family. The couple sleep in the same house with the rest of the family,
but the family hangs up a curtain to separate them from the others.
According to Mead (1930:96), old custom dictated that initial consum-
mation of marriage take place behind a tapa curtain immediately
following defloration.

In addition to the conventional form of marriage there is also
elopement (*avaga*). A man and woman may simply run off to the bush
and live together for a period of a day to a week. A couple may elope
because the woman finds herself pregnant and fears her family will
not permit marriage with the man. Elopement is often precipitated by
disapproval of the match by the woman's family, and the returning
couple usually must face their anger. Both the man and woman may
be beaten, and in some cases the woman's hair is cut off by her family
as a mark of disgrace. Usually, however, after much recrimination, the
family becomes reconciled and prepares for a wedding ceremony.
This ceremony invariably follows elopement, and serves to soothe the
tempers of the families involved.

Marriage in the Samoan family is based upon a consideration of
compatability, ability to have children, ambition, and, contrary to
some observers (e.g. Mead 1928:104–105), in many cases, a certain
amount of love and affection. While many men speak with great
affection of their wives, the relationship between spouses on the
surface appears very cold. Husbands and wives rarely appear together in public. In church, the men sit on one side and the women
on the other. They walk to church separately and on Sunday evening
go for walks separately. The only close relationship between spouses
is in the home.

Because Samoan houses have no partitions, sexual intimacies often
have to take place while others are sleeping in the same room. While
some couples have intercourse every night the average seems to be
about three to five times per week for couples of child-bearing age.

However, the frequency of intercourse is limited by the fact that husbands sleep apart from their wives while they are pregnant.

A wife's most important role is that of child-bearer. Large families are always desired, for they ensure a labor force to work the family land and promise a leisurely old age for the parents. Pregnancy, which is recognized by the cessation of menstrual flow, is surrounded with a myriad of taboos. A pregnant woman must not eat by herself. This is to prevent her from eating selfishly *(nanoa)*. It is believed that a woman guilty of this will give birth to a child with a birthmark with long black hairs growing out of it, like the hide and bristles of a pig. Again she may not drink from the eye at the top of a coconut, but must have the top of the coconut broken open. If she breaks this taboo the child will be born with a round pursed mouth. Nor may she drink from the spout of a tea pot or coffee pot, lest the child be similarly deformed. She must not cut food that she is holding in her mouth, or the child will be born with a hare lip *(laugutu motu)*. She must not steal and eat anything from anyone's land, nor go too near the fire, or her child will be marked by skin blemishes.

Sterility is not common in women, but when found, the cause is recognized to be physiological. Barren women are not treated in any special fashion, although barrenness is generally considered unfortunate and believed by many to be the result of promiscuity. One woman laughed at the idea of frigidity, but men stated that frigidity often produces family tensions, and that either husbands or wives may be responsible.

No contraceptives are used, and many Samoans expressed surprise that such a thing existed. The very idea of contraceptives seemed strange to informants who live in a culture where the more children a couple have the better off they will be in old age. Abortion *(fa'apa'u)* does occur when an unmarried pregnant woman feels that the man responsible for her condition will not marry her, or that family censure will be severe. In the case of married women, abortion is practiced by those who wish to have no more children or who fear the process of childbirth. Massage *(fōfō)* is believed to be an abortifacient as is the insertion of a rolled tapioca leaf in the vagina.

Manu'ans recognize a common law union *(fa'apouliuli)* wherein a man and woman live together without being officially married. The birth of children to a union like this does not necessarily force a wedding ceremony. A man and woman living under these circumstances may worship, but are barred from church membership. The term for common law marriage also applies to a relationship where a man and woman are not living together but the man is responsible for all of the woman's children. Unmarried adults of either sex are rarely found in Manu'a. Only one unmarried woman over thirty years of age, an albino, was encountered in Ta'ū village.

Residence may be with either the husband's or the wife's family. At marriage the young couple usually is given a small sleeping house (*fale o'o*) on the household village land. Since most Samoan men are untitled when they marry, they continue to carry out their obligations to the family head of their own or their wife's family, depending on residence.

Whether the Samoan bride moves in with her husband's family or remains at home her duties as the wife of an untitled man are much the same. She must help work the family plantation, assist in carrying home the produce, care for the smaller children of the family, sweep the pebbled floor of the house every day, roll up the sleeping mats and fold up the sheets every morning, see to the drying of copra and mat materials, make wrap-arounds and shirts and dresses from trade cloth, and weave new floor mats, sleeping mats, and blinds. She must direct the smaller children in bringing water or carry it herself, care for the family chickens, aid in the family cooking, and contribute to the family fare by reef fishing. Nearly every morning the wives of the untitled men, and often the wives of chiefs as well, will be seen sitting in the shallow water near the beach doing the family washing. There is little leisure time for the young married woman of the village, and only on Sunday will a short afternoon nap give her a brief release from the duties of the household.

In the flow of family life, certain conflicts arise that can be settled only by one member leaving the group. According to government records, adultery is the most common ground for divorce in Manu'a (cruelty and desertion are also grounds). Being caught in an adulterous act is considered worse for a woman than for a man, and it often involves physical punishment of some type. Today, a husband does not go to the village council to have the offender punished as described by Turner in 1861, but he may file a case against the guilty party in the district court. A case of adultery involving the wife of a pastor, doctor, or teacher is considered a village affair, and the village council imposes a punishment, because the pastor, doctor, and teacher are considered the "sacred children" (*feagaiga*) of the village.

Adulterers often flee into the bush for one or two days. If a married woman wishes to marry another man, elopement (*avaga*) is the surest method of forcing a divorce. When the couple returns from the bush they go to the mayor (*pulenu'u*) for protection. Divorce almost always follows, and the man is expected to marry the woman with whom he elopes. In rare cases if the wife were just having an affair, and if the husband feels that she is a good wife, he may take her back.

Divorces are relatively easy to obtain, involving a fee of $25 and either proof or admission of guilt. However, according to the census made in the restudy, there have been very few divorces in Ta'ū village, and almost none among the chiefly class. Children of the divorced couple remain in the household where they had been residing and are visited infrequently by the parent who has found residence elsewhere.

MIDDLE AND OLD AGE

During middle age, women often attain a great deal of prestige in the village. As wives of chiefs, they hold important positions in the Women's Committee and have a good share of the responsibility for civic projects. The Women's Committee, composed of (1) wives of Chiefs and Talking Chiefs (*faletua ma tausi*), (2) wives of untitled men (*ava a taulele'a*), and (3) unmarried girls and widows (*aualuma*), is a group dedicated to civic welfare projects. In Ta'ū village it raised the money for the pastor's new house, and it maintains a welfare fund that is used to purchase new equipment for the dispensary. The women of this committee aid the village nurses in child clinic programs and stand ready to assist the village medical personnel in times of epidemic. It is often called upon by the village council to make mats for the pastor's house or to watch over land that has been tabooed for some future use.

If a visiting party (*malaga*) comes to the village, the women give the welcome ceremony (*aiavā*), bringing kava roots for presentation to the chiefs and providing a feast for the group. While the basic organization of the traditional *aualuma* is reflected in the new women's organization, its function and structure has changed a great deal. The church has destroyed the sanctions that once maintained the *aualuma*, but it has enlarged the group, channeled its activities into philanthropic projects, and produced a group that functions ceremonially but yet contributes to a greater extent to village welfare.

In Manu'an society prestige increases with the advancing years. The aged are respected for their wisdom and knowledge of Samoan tradition, and they are often called upon to give advice in the family and in the village council. It is the duty of the children to care for their parents when they are old. Parents come before wives in priority for care, and if there is a shortage of food, the elderly are fed first. Generally the sons provide food and money for the care of their parents, but parents may be taken in and cared for by their daughters. Having raised a large family, the old women are believed to be entitled to duties involving less physical labor. A great share of their time is occupied in tending the small children, weaving mats and blinds, or making thatch and *tapa*. They are responsible for very little of the cooking or laundry.

Old chiefs spend many hours conversing with one another, but elderly women usually work with the younger members of their family. Old men have less to do than old women, but they may often be seen assisting the older women in household tasks such as weeding, or making blinds and thatch. It is not unusual to find an elderly grandfather taking a turn at caring for the small children. In any household the major producers of sennit are the old men, who roll and braid the fibre while they pass the time of day with their friends. Old people are a definite asset to the household, for they discharge many of the menial tasks about the house that the younger, more active members of the family find tiresome.

One of the most important functions of the old men is that of educating the younger men in Samoan tradition. The *fa'asauga* is a meeting of old men of the village to discuss Samoan myths, legends, and customs. While participation in these discussions is restricted to chiefs, the young men of the village may sit outside the house and listen. Similar discussions are held within the family to acquaint the young men with family history and genealogy.

The ritual burning of the candle nut for tattoo pigment still lies with the old women of the family, but since very little tattooing is done these days, the custom is rapidly passing. The same may be said for the profession of midwifery which was formerly in the hands of the older women. The old women of the village are still storehouses of knowledge concerning the medicinal properties of herbs, and many of the specialists in massage (*fōfō*) belong to this age group.

Old people sleep more in the daytime than do other adults but seldom go to bed any earlier. Indeed, many of the meetings of older chiefs take place in the evening and extend far into the night.

DEATH

Statistics were not available for Manu'an life expectancy in 1954, but from observation of the age at which adults died, it seemed comparable to the ages of death for adults in the United States. Once past infancy and childhood, during which mortality is high, people attain fairly ripe old age. The average age of adult deaths would probably fall in the range of about 60 to 65 years. In a village census nine individuals (2.5%) gave their age as over 70.

Dying men and women sometimes refuse to go to the hospital in Tutuila, believing that if they should die away from home their spirits will be troubled and cause the family harm. When a person dies in the home all blinds are immediately raised and a boy of the family is sent running to toll the death on the bell of the village church. The body is prepared in full view of concerned friends and bystanding children. It is dressed in white clothing and placed on a mattress or on a pile of sleeping mats covered with a white sheet at the north end of the house. The female branch (*tamasā*) of the family takes its place behind the body to watch over and care for it until it is placed in the grave. The village pastor is usually in attendance to do what he can for the mourning family. Grief is not excessive and there appears to be no retention of the former practices of bruising one's head with stones, cutting oneself with sharp objects, or cutting one's hair.

As soon as the news of a death reaches the village, the choir calls a rehearsal to prepare for their visit (*leo*) to the home of the deceased. Within four or five hours of the death, the choir arrives, dressed entirely in black, and is seated in the house. After singing a few opening hymns, a speech for the dead (*lauga i maliu*) is given by a choir member, usually a Talking Chief, selected by the choir leader. If a family head has died the speaker should be a titled man, but if the deceased is an untitled man, the speaker may be untitled. While the village choirs are composed of both men and women, only men may deliver these speeches, which are intended to console the family, particularly those who are caring for the body. In reply, an appointed member of the deceased's family, who is usually a Talking Chief, gives a speech of thanks to the choir for conducting a *leo* to honor the dead person. After the exchange of speeches, another hymn follows, and the choir departs.

As long as the corpse remains within the house (seldom more than 24 hours), the women of the house never leave. They are forbidden to sleep, and if one of them should fall asleep, as a mark of her neglect, ashes are placed on her forehead which cannot be washed off until after the funeral. From time to time throughout the night young men come in and play guitars and sing to help the relatives stay awake.

Soon after news of the death, friends of the family and relatives from other parts of the village begin to arrive with gifts of trade cloth, tapa, and fine mats. While the funerals for untitled and titled men are roughly the same, the death of a chief often brings upwards of forty or fifty mats, which are displayed on the mosquito netting wire strung about the house. One large and particularly valuable fine mat (*afuelo*) hangs behind the body, and after the funeral it is given to the female relative who cares for the corpse.

In cases of childbirth where there is a question of saving either a mother or a child, the mother is always saved. Whenever a woman dies with her child still unborn, the fetus is removed and put in a separate grave. A doctor or Samoan medical practitioner, if available, or in isolated places, the woman's husband, incises the abdomen and removes the fetus. It is believed that the mother and her child must be separated or their spirits will not rest and will cause the family trouble.

Whenever death results from a very serious illness, the family head or another male family member incises the abdomen of the corpse after it has been placed in the grave. This cutting *(fa'apoi)* is to stop the disease, so that the illness will be taken away by the spirit and not bother the family further.

The family head selects the spot for the grave, which is always dug on the land of the household. When the family head dies, the spot is chosen by another influential titled relative of the family. The grave is dug by family members aided by friends, or, if for a chief, by other village chiefs who receive a payment *(lafo)* for their labors from the family after the funeral. The body is carried to the grave by members of the choir or of the household, and laid to rest carefully wrapped in the sleeping mats, sheets and *tapa* that the body was displayed upon. Goods such as dishes, pipes, or other personal belongings are often interred with the body. Graves are dug in two levels and the corpse is placed at the bottom. A large piece of galvanized iron sheet is placed over the lower level, and large stones are piled upon this metal partition. This is done because of the generally accepted belief that the spirit will return to wander among the living if it is not properly secured in the grave.

A Christian funeral service, as found in American stateside Congregational churches, is performed by the village Samoan pastor with the village choir in attendance. After the pastor has thrown three handfuls of sand into the grave, all relatives and mourners near the grave who want to may do likewise. The grave is then filled with sand and, in the case of an untitled person, is left without any marker except a bouquet of flowers and perhaps some coral slabs set on edge.

The death of a Samoan woman is marked by funeral rites similar to those of an untitled man. A very old and respected woman may be honored at death by the bringing of many fine mats, but nothing like those that would be presented at the death of High Chief. Like the grave of an untitled man, the grave of a woman is marked by coral slabs, decorated with flowers for a year, and then forgotten.

In the case of a High Chief or High Talking Chief, a grave marker *(tia)* is built. This is a large cairn of round stones usually constructed in the form of a pyramid, although recently these have been cubical in shape and made of concrete.

During the funeral services, the more distant relatives of the deceased cook the food *(lauaua)*, which is distributed immediately after the funeral. Special shares of pork, chicken, fish, and vegetables are set aside for the village pastor and food is given to the relatives and friends of the deceased, and in some cases to every household in the village. Special care is taken to reimburse the donors of fine mats and *tapa* with food or goods of equal value. Payments *(lafo)* to individuals who aided in the funeral proceedings are made, and the ceremonial distribution of fine mats is begun. These fine mats will be held within the family for use as gifts when other members of the village die. Proxy burials are the same as described above except that an insect or other creature, which represents the returned soul of a person lost at sea, is buried in the place of the corpse.

A period of mourning is observed for approximately a year, at the end of which the family calls an official end to mourning. During that year the grave is decorated every day with flowers. After a number of years the coral slabs that mark the graves of untitled men and women sink into the ground and become covered with sand, and the graves become indistinguishable, only the grave-markers of the High Chiefs remaining.

Interviewing in Ta'u Village 1954

SEVEN

The Factor of Change

Few areas of the world offered as controlled a scientific situation for a restudy as did Ta'ū village in 1954. The Manu'an group enjoyed a high degree of isolation; European influence had been minimal; the culture was traditionally conservative; and documentary literature covering material and nonmaterial culture was quite complete. Early in the restudy it was recognized that the greatest difficulty in any test of reliability of earlier research was whether recorded differences were due to the processes of cultural change or to other personal and methodological factors. This problem is magnified when the intervening period between reports has been great or when the culture has been subjected to a great deal of European contact. H. A. Powell, who restudied Malinowski's materials in the Trobriands, felt that the intervening period of approximately 36 years between the two studies was too great for him to be successful in evaluating Malinowski's materials. He states:

> I do not think that such a recheck, as a main aim of research, could be undertaken after the lapse of so long a time. The difficulty of deciding whether apparent discrepancies were due to cultural change, to inaccurate recording or interpretation of material, or to what extent the personality factor was responsible, seem to me to be magnified the longer the interval between original investigation and recheck, although I am aware that techniques exist whereby these factors can to some extent be taken into account. [Personal correspondence, 1955]

89

This problem was minimized somewhat in the case of Manu'a because of its relative isolation, and because of the basic conservatism of the Samoan culture. As Mead observed:

> Given no additional outside stimulus or attempt to modify conditions, Samoan culture might remain very much the same for two hundred years. [1928a:273]

It can truly be said that no additional outside stimulus to cultural change existed in 1954 in the Manu'a group that was not present at the time of Mead's study in 1926. As at that time, the U.S. Government continued to govern the island group according to the following section of the Legal code:

> *Sec. 2.* Samoan Customs and Local Regulations: The customs of the Samoans not in conflict with the laws of American Samoa or the laws of the United States concerning American Samoa shall be preserved. The village, county, and district councils consisting of the hereditary chiefs and their talking chiefs shall retain their own form or forms of meeting together to discuss affairs of the village, county, or district according to their own Samoan custom . . . The village councils may enact village regulations concerning matters of a strictly local nature to the extent otherwise permitted in this Code. [Code of American Samoa 1949:1]

No other island, or group of islands, in Samoa (with the exception of Swain's Island, which is privately owned) was as isolated as the Manu'a group. There were no permanent white residents on any of the three islands of Manu'a, and no government salaried workers, aside from native doctors, nurses, and school teachers. County chiefs, clerks, and village officials, who received monthly salaries so small that they were insufficient to support them, were local inhabitants who had limited contact with the outside. Government officials visited the islands from time to time, but seldom stayed more than a day or two in any one village. There were no permanent public works laborers or stevedores. There was no dock in Manu'a, so that landing of passengers and freight from the inter-island schooner had to be made by long boats which negotiated the dangerous reef passages. The only commercial contact with Pago Pago took the form of shipments of foodstuffs to individual families or to Toaga Sotoa, the keeper of the only store in Manu'a.

Missionary activity was also negligible in Manu'a. Mormon missionaries from the United States often resided in Fitiuta village for several months at a time, but their influence was not greatly felt since they had direct contact only with the three Mormon families in that village. At the time that my 1954 study was being concluded, one of the Mormon missionaries was attempting, without success, to establish a Boy Scout troop in Fitiuta. One Catholic priest visited the Manu'a group about four times a year for a week at a time, but his influence extended to only about a dozen families in the entire group. Otherwise, the pastors were Samoans.

Two Navy Pharmacist Mates representing the government department of Health were stationed on Ta'ū and Ofu islands in 1926 during Mead's study, but were withdrawn in 1951. Their influence has been greatly felt in the realm of modern medicine. Daily sick calls, conducted by native nurses and doctors, are well attended, and childbirth in the home had almost completely disappeared, except in the village of Fitiuta, where a medical practitioner was not in attendance. Even here, however, most children were delivered by visiting Samoan nurses. In spite of the long residence of medical practitioners in the Manu'a group, there was still widespread suspicion of many aspects of Western medicine. "Bush medicine," as practiced by recognized specialists, was still largely employed.

With the exception of Pharmacist Mates, there were no servicemen on Manu'a during World War II despite the thousands of American service personnel stationed on Tutuila. A few of the young men of the villages of Manu'a went to Tutuila as laborers because of the wages offered by the Naval Government, but generally the Manu'a group did not suffer from the problems connected with the influx of easy money as did the rest of Samoa.

The Samoan native governors had been important in influencing the lives of the Manu'a people. Each of the three districts of American Samoa was administered by a native governor of high hereditary rank. The first governor of the Manu'an district was the deposed King of Manu'a, the Tuimanu'a. Following his death the position passed to the Tufele family and was held by three successive Tufele titleholders. The first was a member of the Navy Fita Fita Guard stationed in Pago Pago; the second was educated in Hawaii; and the third spent about 10 years in the United States. Two of these native governors are known to have instructed the Manu'a people to maintain their own ways as the only road to their salvation. Since Mead's time the only documented changes away from traditional customs effected by these governors have been the abolition of costly funeral feasts and the introduction of new agricultural crops, mainly cocoa.

Navy retirement checks and government service allotments affected very few people in 1954. The major source of income was the production of copra. Annual reports for the period 1944–54 reveal that

Manu'a produced approximately 85 percent of the copra in American Samoa. During and shortly after the war, Manu'a produced almost all of the copra of the area, though it comprises less than 30 percent of the arable land and only 17 percent of the population.

In Western Samoa the greatest agents for change have been individuals of mixed parentage. Constituting approximately 5 percent of the total population of Western Samoa, they have been accorded "white status" by the government courts, providing they can prove literacy. They have become the major land holders and entrepreneurs of the area. In American Samoa, as in Western Samoa, those of mixed parentage operate the major private business enterprises of the area, but governmental laws restrict their ownership of land. They constitute approximately 10 percent of the population, but are almost entirely in residence on the island of Tutuila.

In Manu'a, individuals of mixed parentage constituted less than 1 percent of the total population and were spurned, rather than looked to, for guidance, with the possible exception of Toaga Sotoa, the store keeper, who enjoyed a certain amount of prestige in the village of Ta'ū because of her useful role.

The fact that Samoan culture has remained minimally affected in its basic structure in contrast to the rest of Polynesia has often been remarked by students of Polynesian culture. Thus, Oliver states:

> Samoa presents a radically different picture from the usual South Seas spectacle of native peoples cheerfully and unknowingly losing their identity and their heritage in a setting of successful and expanding economy established and controlled by white men . . .
>
> To the scientist they provide a fascinating and almost unique example of Polynesians surviving the strong impact of western civilization without changing their everyday lives and without losing their numbers, their strength, their dignity, or their zest for a good fight. [1951:158]

Mead, in a similar vein, characterized the Samoans as possessing "all the strength of the tough willows, which bend and swing to every passing breeze, but do not break" (1928:495). It is this flexibility and sensitivity to minute change which has proven to be a highly conservative factor.

Peter Buck feels that

> The pleasure derived from the exercise of native institutions is perhaps the most important factor that has led to the persistence of Samoan customs and helped them to resist the disintegration that has taken place in other parts

of Polynesia. The Samoans are thus more conservative than other branches of their race and their satisfaction with themselves and their own institutions makes them less inclined to accept the change that foreign governments consider would be of benefit to them. Their viewpoint is bounded by their own immediate horizon. The Samoans are self contained. [1930:5]

Keesing also comments on the conservatism inherent in the social structure, religious organization, material culture, and economic pattern, stating that much of this conservatism is due to the fact that "leadership continues to lie with the old, who are often torpid and conservative, and there is no encouragement of innovation or outlet for youth's enthusiasm within the native group" (1934:479).

Another student of Samoan culture, Reverend J. D. Copp, suggested to Stanner that:

Samoan custom now serves as a "refuge" from the conflicts of choice and judgment resulting from Western contacts. That is, he postulated a fear of "change," and a belief that change is "wrong," as elements integral in the fa'a Samoa tradition. Against this are now ranged the material attractions, the manifest superiorities, and the greater power of the West; its divided Christianity, antagonistic secularisms, and now-exhorting now-scolding Governments; the fascination of new ideas, the trade cycle, the clash of sovereignty, internal social shifts, and much else there is no need to list. All these, it was suggested, sowed in Samoan minds the fear that "non-change" was also "wrong." The consequence was a conflict of choice, of great poignancy and irresolubility. In such circumstance fa'a Samoa remained not only deeply "right" but also became a place of refuge. Fa'a Samoa was "home." [Stanner 1953:315]

My 1954 restudy confirmed the stability of Samoan culture and the fact that the rule of the Samoan society lies in the hands of the titled men. Titles are conferred only in later life and therefore are held by a more conservative element of the society. Maintenance of position involves extensive ceremonial exercise, thus perpetuating the body of ceremonial lore and practice. The younger men of the group have little voice in community planning or politics and are completely subservient to the older titled men. The untitled men are considered the servants of the chiefs whom they must please in order to qualify for titles themselves. A young man in Manu'a may gain recognition only by being a better servant than other young men of his status, or by showing an interest in the ceremonial and traditional aspects of

Samoan life. Much of the ceremonial life carried on by the chiefs gives validity and importance to their positions, and young men who seek other kinds of recognition can find it only outside the society, thus leaving the traditionally minded behind. Rebellion from accepted ways is impossible, since the pressure of the village organization is too strong. The council of chiefs is the executive, legislative, and, to some extent, the judicial body of the village, and stands as a strong force opposing cultural change. The Manu'ans' satisfaction with the traditional way of life was repeatedly noted by observers, even after only a short period of residence within the society.

Of course, there were changes in Manu'an culture between the 1920s and 1954, but these had been so slight, and new traits had been so well incorporated into Manu'an culture, that they were all but inconspicuous.

From an analysis of changes in Samoan culture as described by (1) nineteenth-century observers and by (2) Mead, Buck, and their contemporaries, it can generally be stated that those elements of aboriginal Samoan culture which had disappeared were those that clashed with government or missionary policies. Where direct pressure from the American government had been exerted, conflicting Samoan cultural patterns had tended to wither away. Judiciary powers of village councils had been curtailed, sovereignty of district chiefs had been overthrown, and European medical practices had been accepted by the people.

Other changes were documented in the area of material culture, but generally, European goods had been added to the traditional artifacts, except in a few cases where the new had replaced the old. These substitutions involved such things as trade cloth for daily clothing, metal knives and adzes, spear heads, weapons, fishing line, certain types of nets, etc., but much of this replacement had occurred prior to 1900. On the other hand, iron roofs, which were occasionally seen in the villages, had not replaced the traditional thatch as the preferred form of roofing. Longboats (whaleboats) were being used for local transport without replacing the traditional bonito boat or the dugout fishing canoe. European foods had been added to the diet but had not replaced traditional fare. Dishes and metal pots were in use for cooking, but they had not reduced the pattern of cooking food on hot stones wrapped in breadfruit leaves or the use of wooden food bowls (*tanoa*). European cigarettes were smoked, but they had not replaced native grown tobacco. Silk and satin were used for ceremonial dress, but barkcloth and fine mat clothing were still a mark of prestige on ceremonial occasions. Despite the introduction of cocoa growing, there was no neglect of the traditional crops such as coconuts, yams, taro, breadfruit, and bananas. It was apparent that in their material culture, the people of Manu'a were evidencing an ability to accept desirable Western innovations without losing their cultural identity. It was also apparent that in those areas of culture where outside influence had been most effective, innovation had been an additive rather than a substitutive process.

Some difficulty was encountered in determining the amount of change from the nineteenth century by reading of Mead's accounts. Although she states in *Social Organization of Manua* that her emphasis was "upon cultural dynamics, the study of social processes rather than description of cultural traits" (1930:7), many evidences of acculturation were not recorded, and the work contains accounts of contemporary society juxtaposed with reconstructions of the culture as it existed a century earlier. A similar situation was encountered in *Coming of Age in Samoa*, where behavior patterns derived from "months of observation of the individuals and of groups, alone, in their households, and at play" (1928a:264) were presented in such a way that, by implication, they appear in a traditional culture setting unaltered by historic change. Samoan culture as it actually existed in 1925–26 is discussed systematically only in Appendix III of that work (1928a:266–277). Here she notes that the following innovations had taken place since the mid-nineteenth century, when missionary accounts described the traditional culture:

1. A thorough entrenchment of Christianity as the religion of the people.
2. The development of copra as a cash income crop.
3. The establishment of a network of Manu'an government officials such as a district governor, county chiefs, county judges, mayors, and village policemen.
4. The establishment of a government court system thereby limiting the judicial powers of the village council, eliminating the life and death powers of family heads, and outlawing blood revenge in the settlement of disputes and differences.
5. The development of the military (Fita Fita Guard in Tutuila) and the ministry as prestige occupations.
6. The establishment of government schools with European patterned curriculum.
7. The alleviation of exclusive control of building by craftsmen through the introduction of superior European tools.
8. A softening of the moral code.
9. A decline in the importance of tattooing.
10. The elimination of long canoe voyages.

11. The change from chewing to pounding in the preparation of kava.

The discussion is very incomplete as regards acculturative influences of which she no doubt was aware. The principal aspects of acculturation that had already occurred but which seem to have been neglected or underemphasized in Mead's work are:

1. The importance of Christianity in marriage and funeral ceremonies.
2. The effect of Christianity on the social and political life of Manu'a.
3. The disintegration of the *taupou* system including the disappearance of a permanent society of unmarried women *(aualuma)*.
4. The importance of government schooling in altering the patterns of enculturation within the home.

CHRISTIANITY

Church and civil ceremonies at marriages and funerals have been documented by Keesing, who states that in 1930 all Samoan pastors were authorized to perform marriages, government registry of marriages, having been required as early as 1904. He further states,

Along with church and civil sanctions, the wedding dresses, rings and cakes, now more or less adopted from Western culture, are found the old celebrations at which mats and other goods are exchanged between the families. Similar blendings of custom are found in connection with birth and death ceremonies and at many other points in Samoan life. [1934:412]

The influence of the church on the social and political life of Samoa is also noted by Keesing:

In social life the church still forms the essential stabilizing, regulating, and integrating force: sanctioning the old kinship and *matai* systems together with traditional customs, providing new outlets in place of those passing or passed—opportunities for assembling and engaging in cooperative activities, means of self expression and competition as in singing, giving, church going, and the like—and making adjustments and fusions between the old way and the new. [ibid.:412]

These influences were not innovations introduced after Mead's investigation, for in 1929 the Samoan district of the London Missionary Society was well enough organized so that control of local affairs could be placed in Samoan hands, with but one white missionary representative (a co-treasurer) sitting on the district mission council.

TAUPOU SYSTEM

Keesing also writes that, by 1930,

> The *taupou* system, by which the ceremonial life of each community revolves around the person of a village virgin, is passing: chiefs who are entitled by tradition to the honor of having a *taupou* find the entertainments connected with the position too costly; again, due to the breakdown of the older order, the marriage of such maidens has lost its former value in securing political alliances and economic and ceremonial advantages; the missions have discouraged the custom as heathen, preferring the unmarried girls and unattached women who formed in the old days the *taupou's* entourage *(aualuma)* and slept together in her house, to live at home or in the pastor's house; the old women find guarding and caring for her a burden. [ibid.:142]

The society of unmarried and unattached girls and women *(aualuma)* has already all but disappeared as a formal institution. [ibid.:144]

Mead's definition of the *aualuma* as the organization of unmarried girls past puberty, wives of untitled men, and widows (1930:31), indicates that its breakdown had already begun. Traditionally, the *aualuma* was composed of only "single ladies," (Pratt 1862:76) and the inclusion of wives of untitled men suggests a movement toward the Women's Committee which Grattan states came into being in Samoa about 1928 (1948:11). At any rate, Mead's description of the *taupou* system (1928a:42–53) is not characteristic of Ta'ū village, the village principally discussed. Here the existence of an official and permanent *taupou* title passed with the death of the last King of Manu'a *(Tu-imanu'a)* in 1909.

EDUCATION

Formal government education is described by Mead as imparting hazy English, part singing, cricket and other games, and elementary ideas of hygiene, with the most promising students being selected to become nurses, teachers, and Fita Fita guardsmen. The principal effects were reported to have been the breaking down of "barriers

between age and sex groups and narrow residential units"
(1928a:272). Actually, the influence upon Samoan life was considerably more penetrating, involving interference with enculturation in
Samoan family industries and in some cases the loss of traditional
techniques. A school was established in Manu'a as early as 1904, this
being one of the conditions demanded by the chiefs who signed the
deed ceding their islands to the United States. In 1911 the Governor of
American Samoa issued a regulation making compulsory the attendance at school of every child between the ages of six and thirteen for
at least four days a week during the school year (Keesing 1934:425).

The annual school report of 1926 (Ta'u School) gives the following
picture of Manu'an education.

Grade	Enrollment
Chart	132
Primer	38
First	13
Second	21
Third	7
Fourth	4
Fifth	4
Total	202

Course of Study

Chart (started at five years of age)—reading, phonics, numbers (count to 50), conversational English, music.

Primer—Reading, phonics, numbers (count to 100 by 1s,
2s, 5s, 10s; subtract, add, divide, multiply), conversational
English, hygiene, music, spelling.

First—Same as above only more advanced content.

Second—Same as above only more advanced content.

Third—Reading, phonics, arithmetic, English, Geography,
hygiene, music, spelling, sewing.

Fourth—Same as above. Wider and more advanced content.

Fifth—Reading, phonics, arithmetic, English, geography,
hygiene, music, spelling, sewing, manual training.

A comparison of school records for 1925–26 and 1954 reveals a
progressive extension of facilities to include grades up to the ninth
grade and a broadening of curriculum at all grade levels. The marked

segregation of boys and girls in play groups observed by Mead (1928a:59) could not be confirmed by this restudy. This is undoubtedly due to the influence of the school environment which Mead felt was breaking down the barriers between age and sex groups. This trend was also observed by Keesing who writes of the school situation that "distinctions are not drawn between the sexes, giving the girls a place they never took in earlier days" (1934:434).

Something of the effect of compulsory education upon the life of the Samoan family may be sensed in the following statement of a Samoan recorded by Keesing:

> Education is creating an ignorance of *fa'a Samoa* (Samoan custom) since the whole of our customs are bound together in one sheaf we fear that too much education will destroy us. [1934:437]

The removal of children from the home is deeply felt, and was responsible for initial hostility toward the schools. Keesing notes that although parents could be fined for keeping children home from school, they often did so to aid in plantation or household work or to assist in family ceremonials (ibid.:435–436).

RECENT WINDS OF CHANGE

While Manu'a is definitely the most culturally conservative area in American Samoa, changes continued to take place between the time Mead concluded her study and the beginning of mine in 1954. The following are areas of Samoan culture which have been changing since Mead observed Ta'ū village cultural behavior in 1926.

Economic Trends

In recent years the tendency has been toward a greater share of economic independence for nontitled members of the family. Records of copra receipts over an eight-year period from 1946 to 1954 show an increasing division of income among the various biological families comprising the household group, in place of turning over all family income to the family head who provided for family needs. Fita Fita Guard pensions and allotment checks from Samoans in the armed forces are also economic innovations allowing increased use of imported foods and other trade goods and making possible greater displays of wealth for the enhancement of family prestige.

Concerning such displays Keesing reports,

In 1924 the Manu'a people proposed the abolition of "death feasts," a custom calling for feasting and the accumulation of property, and when the other districts proved conservative they actually imposed it upon themselves independently. [1934:342]

While all funerals I observed in Manu'a were followed by a feast and an exchange of property, there was nothing of the traditional dispersement of wealth which often amounted to thousands of dollars. This custom, which led to complete impoverishment of families, was done away with at the direction of District Governor Tufele before I arrived in Ta'ū.

Behavioral Avoidance Patterns

The strict avoidance patterns for brothers and sisters as described by Kramer, Turner, Mead, and others have generally been softened since the 1920s. While definite avoidance patterns were observed in this restudy, they were by no means as strict as those recorded in the earlier literature. A similar observation was made by Grattan:

> The position at the present time is that in some families the rule is still strictly enforced; in others much less regard is paid to it. Everywhere, however, it is still considered particularly improper for brothers and sisters to make doubtful remarks in each other's presence. This, although it may be said that personal standards in family relationships are now in many cases much more lax than they were formerly, is the only significant remaining aspect of this custom at the present day. [1948:174]

Taupou System

The period since the investigations of Mead, Buck, and Keesing has seen the complete breakdown of the *taupou* system in Manu'a. In 1954 Fitiuta had no permanent *taupou* whatsoever, and numerous informants testified to the fact that not even a Tufele *taupou* had existed in eight to ten years. In Ta'ū village only the Tuimanu'a was allowed a *taupou*, but following his death a number of chiefs—Soatoa, Alalamua and Lefiti—attempted to justify establishment of *taupous* with titles other than the traditional Samalaulu. Similarly, several of the higher chiefs attempted to establish *manaia* titles other than the traditional Solia. None of these attempts were successful and there has been no attempt to establish a permanent *taupou* in Ta'ū village since about 1925. Temporary *taupous* function only on rare occasions. The disappearance of a permanent village *taupou* has all but eliminated the organization of unmarried girls *(aualuma)*, which traditionally functioned as her entourage. While the organization was definitely on the decline in the 1920s, it functions today only as a component part of the Women's Committee which includes all village women.

Tattooing

In 1925–26 Mead reported that "untattooed boys were not allowed to make the kava" (1930:124). Due to the use of the word "were" in the sentence it cannot be definitely established whether this prohibition existed in 1925–26 or in the past. However, in 1954 the practice of tattooing had fallen away to such an extent that such a regulation would hardly have been possible. None of the higher status members of the society of untitled men *(aumaga)* were tattooed, and the wringing of kava by untattooed men was often witnessed.

Traditional Religious Beliefs

Certain bonito fishing prohibitions were reported to have existed in Manu'a in 1925–26. These included (1) never taking food in a new bonito boat, (2) pouring water over the catch before women could touch them, (3) abstinence from sexual intercourse on the night before bonito fishing (Mead 1930:124). Additional taboos are listed by Buck to include (4) wearing nothing on the head, (5) wearing nothing above the waist (1930:520). While informants stated that all of these prohibitions were formerly adhered to, few if any, were in force in 1954.

In describing religious aspects of Manu'an culture, Mead states that the village of Ta'ū showed veneration to the owl *(o le lulu)* (1930:195) but investigations into supernatural lore failed to provide confirmation. Informants had never heard of any special veneration of the owl, and it plays little part in their mythology. However, Turner reports that the owl was sacred in Western Samoa where it was the reincarnation of a war god.

Further comparison of religious beliefs is difficult because much of Mead's account is a reconstruction of indigenous religion; actual traditional beliefs held in 1925–26 are infrequently mentioned.

Children's play group

EIGHT

Assessing Margaret Mead

Although I differ with Mead on several issues, I would like to make it clear that, despite the greater possibilities for error in a pioneering scientific study, her tender age (twenty-three), and her inexperience, I find that the validity of her Samoan research is remarkably high. Differences between the findings of Mead and myself that cannot be attributed to cultural change are relatively minor, and in most cases involve not differences in data but in interpretation. The most important thing to emphasize, however, is that I confirm Mead's conclusion that it was undoubtedly easier to come of age in Samoa than in the United States in 1925. This involved not only analysis of the Samoan material, but an investigation of what life was like in the United States in 1925. This is a small detail Derek Freeman has overlooked.

What I did find in an exhaustive review of Mead's writings on Samoa was that the culture was not quite as simple as she would have had us believe. In other words, she often over-generalized, a common failing among novice fieldworkers. I could not agree with Mead on the degree of sexual freedom supposedly enjoyed by young people on Ta'ū, but I am sure that she had greater rapport with teenagers than I (and probably Freeman) did. However, there was considerable evidence in the form of illegitimate children and divorces with adultery as a ground to indicate that a fair amount of premarital and extra-marital sexuality existed.

I also saw the culture as considerably more competitive than Mead did. I sensed a great preoccupation with status, power, and prestige, and on more than one occasion I observed very competitive verbal contests between Talking Chiefs for the purpose of enhancing their own or their village's prestige. I felt that Samoans loved to display their abilities, but in general one was respected more for modesty than for conceit, and it was better to have someone else praise one's abilities than to do it one's self. I also observed that in interpersonal relations, particularly in romantic alliances, Samoans played for somewhat higher stakes than Mead indicated. I never saw the society as inflexible nor the Samoans as aggressive as Freeman characterizes them. Actually, I saw the society as one in which people went to extremes to avoid conflict and to arrive at compromises. Village council decisions always had to be unanimous, and village council meetings sometimes went on for days until a decision satisfactory to all was reached.

Turning specifically to the problem that Mead was concerned with, salient characteristics of Samoan culture (particularly in Ta'ū) which contributed to a more tranquil passage through adolescence than was characteristic of the U.S. in 1925 are:

1. The structure of the household is such that there are a number of adults who may both discipline and reward the children in that residence unit. This results in a diffusion of authority *and* affection, making individual parent-child relationships less intense and stressful. Where a child identifies with a number of "parents," personal attachments do not become so strong that psychological disturbances accompany the death or divorce of a given parent. In matters of discipline it is difficult for a child to direct resentment against any single individual, since a number of people punish him when he misbehaves. Because of this lack of strong personal attachment with certain individuals, the child is more flexible in his adjustment to new situations. A perfect example is the widespread custom of adoption. Here children often leave the home of their biological parents and go to live with family friends or relatives. They do so without apparent difficulty and they function as regular members of the new household. Another significant feature of the Samoan family situation is the large number of children found in any residential unit. Contrary to the condition encountered in most European families there is a complete absence of complications arising from sibling order and only-child situations.

2. Age segregation is almost completely absent in the household, and this facilitates greater communication across generations.

3. Children are more readily exposed to the facts of life in regard to sex, death, childbirth, and family leadership responsibilities, and this knowledge prepares young people for adult experiences, roles, and obligations.

4. There is no dichotomy between a child's world and an adult world. Coming of age involves assuming family chores and responsibility whenever the child is physically and mentally able. Full responsibility for caring for siblings often begins as early as five or six years of age, and many adolescents are functioning as adults in agricultural work, fishing activities, and household tasks long before such weighty responsibilities would be thrust upon an American child. While some observers emphasize the oppressive work loads forced upon teenagers, in this relatively bountiful environment few put in a forty-hour week or are required to work beyond his or her capacity.

5. Flexible residence patterns permit young people to flee to households of kinsmen when difficulties in parent–child relations develop. While Freeman maintains that this does not happen in Samoa (1983:204), I have known several such cases in Ta'ū village.

6. Life is simpler, and there are fewer decision-making dilemmas in Samoa than in the United States. Samoa in 1954, and therefore certainly in 1925, presented fewer careers among which to choose, fewer alternative life-styles, and fewer conflicting moral and ethical codes. In Mead's Samoa nearly all young persons grew up knowing that they would spend their lifetimes as farmers or farmer's wives; most men knew if they worked hard for their family and their village that someday they would acquire a chief's title and be responsible for a village household unit. In all Ta'ū island villages there was but one sanctioned denomination (London Missionary Society), and church membership and attendance was nearly compulsory because of social pressure. However, Manu'an culture, as observed in 1954, was not completely free of conflicting doctrines, ideals, or Western influences. The factor of European education had complicated the picture, and young people found themselves confronted with the choice of remaining within the society and following traditional custom, or leaving Manu'a to find work in the urban areas of Samoa, Hawaii, or the United States where they could utilize their education. This trend was observed as early as 1930:

> The finished human products of Malifa and Poyer (missionary schools) must be pictured as facing not a world of economic and social life in which they win or lose by their own striving, but either a Samoan society of devious or traditional paths in which they must traverse to gain ultimate honour and prestige,or a white and mixed-bood society in which they have the status (and in large measure the stigma) of "semi-educated native," "Europeanised Samoan." Only by going overseas is there escape, and freedom of opportunity, but so far this has involved a lonely venture, experiences of racial discrimination, a hard eco-

nomic struggle, unfamiliar climatic conditions, and a sense of exile that almost inevitably leads to a return and a surrender to Samoan circumstances. [Keesing 1934:436–447]

7. While young children were punished for misbehavior, and often severely, but for relatively few offenses—usually for making noise or standing up in the house when chiefs were seated—no Samoan child was ever forced, as a child might be in America, to finish dinner, to go to bed at a particular time, or to keep from fighting with siblings. Most punishment is directed toward smaller children with the idea that it will make them learn proper behavior. I have never seen an adolescent struck by a parent nor even severely lectured for misbehavior. Expectations in intergenerational relations are clear, and there is little in the way of challenges to authority. By adolescence, Samoans have learned to regulate their own conduct, and there is little testing of the limits of sanctioned behavior. If limits are violated, punishment is expected and not resented. Even then the offender seldom feels the brunt of the full penalty for this violation. As in all other corporate decisions compromise takes place so that the punishment is softened. As Bradd Shore has noted, "There is among Samoans a stress on the maintenance of interpersonal harmony, at least in its external manifestations" (1982:117).

8. The amount of sexual freedom allowed Manu'an girls also may contribute to the lack of trauma in adolescence. Premarital relations were tolerated by the elders and an unwed mother faced only the short-lived anger of her parents and brothers. As Mead says, "Sex activity is regarded as play; as long as it remains informal, casual, meaningless, society smiles" (1930:84). The fact of being an illegitimate child was soon forgotten by the village, and the child took its place in the household with all the advantages and opportunities of the legitimate children. On the other hand, in American culture, which denies normal heterosexual outlets, young people may be forced, through anxiety during the dozen odd years between puberty and marriage, into less preferred patterns of sexual behavior.

SAMOAN–AMERICAN COMPARISONS

Ta'ū village is extremely isolated. In 1954 it represented something of an untouched, traditional environment, thereby making growing up somewhat easier to accomplish than in the more acculturated villages like Pago Pago or Leone on the island of Tutuila. George Irwin, a teacher in Western Samoa during the 1940s and early 1950s, reports a coming of age situation much like that which I (and Margaret Mead) observed in Manu'a. He writes in *Samoa—A Teacher's Tale* as follows:

In their treatment of children the Samoans anticipated by centuries the teachings of modern psychology. There are no problem children in their Islands because every child is accepted by his village for what he is. He may be good at singing, finding things, telling lies, throwing stones, or nothing in particular. It makes no difference, he is accepted; his opinion is considered. He may even make momentous decisions for himself. If he is unhappy at home, custom permits him to take his little bundle of mats to his cousins' *fale* and live with them. Perhaps it is because of their uninhibited childhood, the love and security they share as children, that the Samoans are such gay, singing people.

There are no restrictions on the free development of personality, no insistence on conformity, yet the children delight to conform. They take pleasure in being one of a group, especially a uniformed group, and saying multiplication tables, singing, dancing, eating, and praying together. [1965:89]

Compare this tranquil milieu with the U.S. culture that Margaret Mead was familiar with. Joseph Folsom's book *The Family*, published in 1934 (and undoubtedly researched about the time Margaret Mead was observing and writing about adolescent behavior in the South Seas) describes American patterns of discipline as follows:

Children are disciplined and trained with the ideal of absolute obedience to parents. Corporal punishment is used, ideally in cold blood. [1934:21]

And in regard to adolescent and young adult sexual behavior he writes:

All sexual behavior on the part of children is prevented by all means at the parents' disposal . . . For the sake of prevention it has been usual to cultivate in the child, especially the girl, an attitude of horror or disgust toward all aspects of sex. [ibid.:23]

Premarital intercourse is immoral though not abhorrent. . . . Violations are supposedly prevented by the supervision of the girl's parents. [ibid:25]

Illegitimate children are socially stigmatized. . . . The chief stigma falls upon the unmarried mother, because she has broken an important sex taboo. [ibid.:10]

Willystine Goodsell, in her book *Problems of the Family*, portrayed the stigma of illegitimacy in 1928 America as follows:

> Harsh and condemnatory as the traditional attitude of society to the unmarried mother has been, it has not been so crushing as the treatment meted out to the illegitimate child by its parents and by society. . . . He is frequently deprived of a mother's care as well as of the care and support of his father; . . . He labors under hampering legal and social disadvantages. In most states, the illegitimate child can inherit from the mother, but not from the father; . . . his birth record discloses the fact of his illegitimate birth, if not specifically, yet by implication; and since this record is more often than not open to public inspection it may be maliciously used against him. [1928:254]

Goodsell not only faults the hardness of the American code of morality but points to the inadequacies of the American family in 1928 and to the less than satisfactory physical circumstances associated with this society making a hasty and somewhat inadequate adjustment to urban living. Of the family milieu she writes:

> That the home is not successfully meeting either the demands of society or the deepest needs of its members is evidenced by the prevalence of juvenile delinquency and crime, by outbursts of suicidal mania among youth, by the establishment and spread of child guidance clinics, juvenile courts and the probation system. Unsuccessful functioning of the family is further revealed by the alarming growth of mental and nervous diseases, culminating in nervous breakdowns. [1928:420]

Regarding the difficult physical environment in which American adolescents were force to come of age, Goodsell adds:

> The conditions of modern life in our huge urban centers are so complex that both the child and his parents find difficulty in adjusting to them. Homes consist of a few or many rooms on "shelves" of tall apartment houses. They bear not the remotest resemblance to the original homes of man—simple huts in the open, with wide stretches of earth, air, lake and river around them. Although life was laborious in some early societies, it was simple and relatively without strain. At present, both adults and children in our large cities live under conditions of hurry, noise, competition and nervous tension. [ibid.]

PORTRAIT OF A VILLAGE

One source of difference between Mead's publications and the restudy concerns the presentation of data concerning village life in the chapter "A Day in Samoa" in *Coming of Age in Samoa*. Mead's picture of a noisy, busy village with young men shouting to one another as they go to and from the plantations was not observed by me, nor do such actions on the part of young men seem characteristic of a Samoan village, where part of the respect shown to chiefs includes not disturbing them with undue noise. Prohibitions against such noise in the village are well-documented by Kramer (1941:101–102). Nor were Mead's descriptions of the awakening village muting the sound of the breaking surf confirmed by this research. In the morning the village was deathly quiet, and people moved about like shadows, performing their morning tasks. Many times on awakening, the Samoan members of our household were found to have completed many of their chores.

While nearly all of the activities described in Mead's "A Day in Samoa" were witnessed during my five-month stay in Manu'a, not all of them are typical of a single day. Although the compression of typical activities into a typical day is an accepted literary device, it tends to distort perspective on the tempo of village life. After having been immersed in Mead's account, it came as a surprise to find Ta'ū not a bustling village, but one almost deserted during the daytime. People went off one by one to their occupations by way of the rear path of the village. One or two girls were observed fishing on the reef, unless the tide was very low, when perhaps a dozen women engaged in the task. Only one house was begun during five months of this research; the bonito boats did not go out a single time; the society of untitled men *(aumaga)* danced for visiting maidens only two or three times; and pigs were cooked only on infrequent ceremonial occasions. Mead's typical day, therefore, presents a composite picture, but one which is not representative of actual conditions to be encountered on any given day.[2]

THE LIFE CYCLE

In 1930 Keesing recorded that "matters connected with childbirth remain almost entirely in native hands. There are many Samoan woman skilled in midwifery by Samoan methods, though on the whole these are crude and responsible for no small proportion of the mortality among infants and women" (1934:390). In 1954 childbirth took place almost exclusively in either of the two Manu'an dispensaries, where mothers were attended by trained Samoan medical practitioners and nurses. In isolated villages such as Fitiuta, trained nurses delivered children. In rare cases, deliveries were made by midwives who had been authorized for such service by government medical personnel. This development in public health services has without doubt been responsible for the reduction in infant mortality. Government records establish a 100 percent increase in survival of young children in 1954 over 1925–26. Mead wrote that "actual age can never be determined in Samoa" (1928a:263); however, complete records of Manu'an births dating back to 1904 were discovered in the government archives in 1954 and have been utilized here.

In 1925 Mead recorded: "For the birth . . . of a baby of high rank, a great feast will be held, and much property given away" (1928a:20). In 1954 the pattern had changed to include feasts for children of untitled fathers, and informants maintained that while a feast was traditionally given for only the first child, the births of all children were celebrated.

Mead reported that the umbilical cord was traditionally buried "under a mulberry tree to ensure her growing up to be industrious at household tasks" (in the case of a girl) or was "thrown into the sea that he [a boy] may be a skilled fisherman" (ibid.). The 1954 practice was to bury the cord near the church to ensure pious qualities in the child.

There has been increasing disregard for the traditional pattern of birthing in the mother's village—government birth records show that in 1926, 77.8 percent of children were born in the village of the mother's family; in 1954 the percentage of matrilocal births had fallen to 56.2 percent indicating that the custom had nearly ceased to exist.

The duration of infant nursing was recorded by Mead to be as long as two or three years, but it was found by others to be approximately one year, and Susan Holmes (1951:14) sets the maximum at twenty months. In *Coming of Age in Samoa*, Mead reported that "food is . . . masticated by the mother and then put into the baby's mouth on her finger" (1928a:21). This practice was not observed in this restudy, and there is reason to believe that premastication has disappeared in most of Samoa. Susan Holmes records that on the rather isolated island of Manono this type of infant feeding was strongly disparaged by district nurses and had been given up by most Samoan mothers.

Another aspect of child care described by Mead which was not corroborated by this restudy concerns the use of wild orange juice for bathing babies. Mead states that infants were "bathed frequently with the juice of a wild orange and rubbed with cocoanut oil until their skins glisten" (1928a:22). The application of coconut oil is common even today, but the use of juice of the wild orange for bathing was not observed, and informants, when questioned, knew nothing of its use.

Observation of the activities of older children revealed other differences between Mead's account and the restudy. In regard to play activities Mead writes that Samoan children "never make toy houses, nor play house, nor sail toy boats" (ibid.:230). Children were repeat-edly observed sailing self-manufactured boats, and Brown records that children constructed toy houses in their play activities (1910:59). In response to my observations about playtime activities Mead wrote

> My statement (quoted by Holmes, 1957, p. 219) that: "Samoan children never make toy houses, nor play house nor sail toy boats" was an accurate statement of my very elaborate and careful observations on Ta'u in 1925–1926. I had stated the time and place of observation, but I did use the word Samoan where, of course, Manu'an would have been more accurate. The fact that children constructed toy boats in 1954 is a valuable point, possibly of social change. But after the experience of three restudies of the Manus village of Pere (in 1953, 1964, and 1965) I would never again use a negative of this sort. Dr. Schwartz and I have esti-mated that it might take continuous observation over thirty years to exhaust a repertoire of small, sporadically used customs, many items of which informants would com-pletely disown for most of that period. Only comparative work over a very long period, in different villages, makes it possible to establish even the knowledge, to say nothing of the practice of episodic activities like children's games.[1969:225]

Shortly before puberty the Samoan boy submits himself to circum-cision. Although Mead's accounts maintain that "always an even number of boys went together to be circumcised" (1930:41), Turner states "two or three would unite and go" (1884:81), and Kramer records that the number can be five (1941:104). While Kramer and Turner deal mostly with Western Samoa, Manu'an informants con-sulted also failed to confirm Mead's statement.

In the discussion of adolescent sex activity and courtship, Mead reports that a girl's first partner in sexual relations was usually a much older man (1928a:88). Impressions gained in this restudy pointed rather to school mates and boys of the girl's own age as initial partners in sexual activity. Mead further states that the conventionalized desig-nation for clandestine meetings of young people after dark is "under the palm trees" (ibid.:92), but informants consulted in the restudy never had heard of this and maintained that the correct phrase was "go to meet the girl" *(alu i le teine)*.[3]

The intermediary is an important figure in all courtship activities. Mead records that "if marriage results from his ambassadorship, he receives a specially fine present from the bridegroom (ibid.:90). Infor-mants stated that this was not the custom, and was not observed during the restudy.

LANGUAGE

Differences were also found in the use of greetings or salutations. Mead describes Ta'ū villagers going to the beach in the morning shouting *Talofa! Talofa!* to one another (1928a:14). The greeting *Talofa*, which means "hello" in Samoan, was never used in greeting a member of the same village. It was rather used for strangers or Europeans, while fellow-villagers used other forms of greeting among themselves. If they did exchange greetings, all Ta'ū women and untitled men would say *ua e sau* (you are coming) while titled men would greet each other in the morning with *sautia mai* (you come with the dew).

The accounts of Mead and the restudy also vary in regard to the recording of a number of proper names and terms, notably the following:

Mead	Restudy	Meaning	Corroboration of restudy found in
Lapui	La'apui	'Fitiuta Chief'	Kramer (1941)
Sae	Sai	'Ofu chief'	Kramer
Tuleisu	Tuileisu	'supernatural channel guardian'	Kramer
Malemu	Malemo	'Olosega chief'	Kramer
Talolo	Ta'alolo	'food giving ceremony'	Grattan (1948) & Pratt (1862)
Laloga	Lalaga	'to weave'	Pratt
Mapu	Maupu	'division of Fitiuta chiefs'	Churchill (n.d.)
Vaitoilau	Vaito'elau	'west wind' or name of fono	Kramer
Ali	Ale	'Fitiuta chief'	Churchill
Taapi	Ta'ape	'Olosega chief'	Churchill
Salaese	Salelesi	'Upolu jester'	Kramer
Fa'ava	Faiava	'to marry'	Pratt

While I am certain that Margaret Mead had some competence in using the Samoan language some of the above may be due to an unfamiliarity with nuances in the language such as her ignoring the glottal stop in La'apui and Ta'a'lolo (which is not always easy to hear in conversation) or it may be due to carelessness in recording. The dedication in Mead's book *Coming of Age in Samoa* is to the girls of Ta'ū village and is in Samoan but unfortunately it contains numerous language errors. While Mead may not have been completely fluent in the language, I know that she could communicate effectively since I have heard her use the language in conversations with Samoan speakers.

KINSHIP

Considerations of social organization reveal that Mead's section on kinship terminology in *Social Organization of Manua* records that *tamasa* (sacred child), designating sister's child, was "known in Manu'a but not in use" (1930:131). I found *tamasa* the most common term used to designate this relationship. Other differences between Mead's and my own presentation of kinship terminology results primarily from the greater number of kinship terms and reciprocals recorded in the restudy.

There is an informal and formal set of kinship terms used in reference, the former used within the family, being classificatory; the latter, used to make relationships precise to outsiders, descriptive. In direct address only personal names are used, except for a *matai* who is always referred to by his titled name, his personal name being used only to distinguish one title holder from another.

Classificatory

Within the family the following set of terms is used when referring to family members. Ego refers to all men of his father's or grandfather's generation as *tamā* (father), and to all women of his mother's or grandmother's generation as *tinā* (mother). All men and women of the father's generation refer to ego as either *atali'i* (son) or *afafine* (daughter). All males of male ego's generation are referred to as *uso* (sibling of the same sex), and all females as *tuafafine* (sibling of the opposite sex, male speaking). All females of female ego's generation are referred to as *uso* (sibling of the same sex), and all males are referred to as *tuagane* (sibling of the opposite sex, female speaking).

Descriptive

The following is a list of the more formal terms used to make relationship references prescise when speaking with persons outside the family (m.s. = man speaking, and w.s. = woman speaking). Terms which corroborate those recorded by Margaret Mead in *Social Organization of Manua* are indicated by an asterisk. Discrepancies are footnoted. Mead's list was somewhat incomplete.

1. *tamā moni*—blood father (m.s. and w.s.).*
2. *tama moni*—own child (m.s. and w.s.).*
3. *atali'i*—son (m.s.).
4. *afafine*—daughter (m.s.).
5. *tamā fai*—adopted father (m.s. and w.s.).*

6. *tama fai*—adopted child (m.s. and w.s.).*

7. *atali'i fai*—adopted son (m.s.).

8. *afafine fai*—adopted daughter (m.s.).

9. *tinā moni*—blood mother (m.s. and w.s.).*

10. *tamatama*—son (w.s.).[1]

11. *tama teine*—daughter (w.s.).[2]

12. *tinā fai*—adopted mother (m.s. and w.s).*

13. *tamatama fai*—adopted son (w.s.).

14. *tama teine fai*—adopted daughter (w.s.).

15. *uso*—brother (m.s.).*

16. *tuagane*—brother (w.s.).*

17. *tuafafine*—sister (m.s.).*

18. *uso*—sister (w.s.).*

19. *'o lo'u uso matua*—older brother (m.s.).*

20. *'o lo'u tuagane matua*—older brother (w.s.).*

21. *'o lo'u tuafafine matua*—older sister (m.s.).

22. *'o lo'u uso matua*—older sister (w.s.).

23. *'o lo'u uso laititi*—younger brother (m.s.).*

24. *'o lo'u uso laititi*—younger sister (w.s.).*

25. *usa tinā*—much older sister (w.s.).*

26. *tamā o lo'u tamā*—father's father (m.s. and w.s.).

27. *atali'i o lo'u atali'i*—son's son (m.s.).*

28. *afafine o lo'u atali'i*—son's daughter (m.s.).*

29. *tinā o lo'u tamā*—father's mother (m.s. and w.s.).

30. *o le atali'i a la'u tama*—son's son (w.s.).

31. *o le afafine a la'u tama*—son's daughter (w.s.).

32. *tamā o lo'u tinā*—mother's father (m.s. and w.s.).

33. *tama a lo'u afafine*—daughter's son (m.s.).*

34. *tama a lo'u afafine*—daughter's daughter (m.s.).*

35. *tinā o lo'u tinā*—mother's mother (m.s. and w.s.).

36. *tama a la'u tama*—daughter's son or daughter (w.s.).[3]

37. *tamāfai*—father's brother (m.s. and w.s.).

38. *atali'ifai*—brother's son (m.s.).

39. *afafinefai*—brother's daughter (m.s.).

40. *tamāfai*—mother's brother (m.s. and w.s.).

41. *atali'ifai*—sister's son (m.s.).

42. *afafinefai*—sister's daughter (m.s.).

43. *usotinā*—mother's sister (m.s. and w.s.).

44. *tei*—sister's son (w.s.).

45. *tuafafinetamā*—father's sister (m.s. and w.s.).

46. *tei*—brother's son (w.s.).

47. *tei*—brother's daughter (w.s.).

48. *atali'i o le uso o lo'u tamā*—father's brother's son (m.s. and w.s.).*

49. *afafine o le uso o lo'u tamā*—father's brother's daughter (m.s. and w.s.).*

50. *atali'i o le tuagane o lo'u tinā*—mother's brother's son (m.s. and w.s.).

51. *afafine o le tuagane o lo'u tinā*—mother's brother's daughter (m.s. and w.s.).

52. *toalua*—spouse (m.s. and w.s.).*

53. *tane*—husband.

54. *avā*—wife.

55. *to'alua a le uso a lo'u tamā*—father's brother's wife (m.s. and w.s.).

56. *atali'i o le uso o lo'u to'alua*—husband's brother's son (w.s.).

57. *afafine o le uso o lo'u to'alua*—husband's brother's daughter (w.s.).

58. *tane a le tuafafine o lo'u tamā*—father's sister's husband (m.s. and w.s.).

59. *afafine o le tuagane o lo'u to'alua*—wife's brother's daughter (m.s.).
60. *atali'i o le tuagane o lo'u to'alua*—wife's brother's son (m.s.).
61. *to'alua o le tuagane o lo'u tinā*—mother's brother's wife (m.s. and w.s.).
62. *tama a le tuafafine a la'u tane*—husband's sister's son (w.s.).
63. *tama a le tuafafine a la'u tane*—husband's sister's daughter (w.s.).
64. *'o le tamā o la'u tane*—father-in-law (w.s.).*
65. *'o le tamā o la'u avā*—father-in-law (m.s.).*
66. *'o le tinā o la'u tane*—mother-in-law (w.s.).*
67. *'o le tinā o la'u avā*—mother-in-law (m.s.).*
68. *tuagane o lo'u to'alua*—wife's brother (m.s.).
69. *tane a lo'u tuafafine*—sister's husband (m.s.).
70. *uso o lo'u to'alua*—wife's sister (m.s.).
71. *tane a lo'u uso*—sister's husband (w.s.).
72. *uso o la'u tane*—husband's brother (w.s.).
73. *to'alua o lo'u uso*—brother's wife (m.s.).
74. *tuafafine o la'u tane*—husband's sister (w.s.).
75. *to'alua o lo'u tuagane*—brother's wife (w.s.).

76. *to'alua o le uso o la'u tane*—husband's brother's wife (w.s.).
77. *to'alua o le tuagane o lo'u to'alua*—wife's brother's wife (m.s.).
78. *tane a le tuafafine a la'u tane*—husband's sister's husband (w.s.).
79. *tane a le uso o lo'u to'alua*—wife's sister's husband (m.s.).
80. *tane a le tuafafine a la'u tane*—husband's sister's husband (w.s.).
81. *tane a le uso o lo'u to'alua*—wife's sister's husband (m.s.).

General Kinship Terms

82. *ulu matua*—oldest son.[4]
83. *tausoga*—half brothers or sisters.[5]

A brother refers to a brother with a different mother but the same father as *usoilamā* or *tausogaitamā*.

A brother refers to a sister with a different mother but the same father as *tuafafineitamā* or *tausogaitamā*.

84. *ga'au*—all the children of a union.[6]

[1] Mead recorded *tama tane*
[2] Mead recorded *tama fafine*
[3] Mead recorded *'o le tama o si'au tama*
[4] Mead and Kramer recorded "first born."
[5] Mead and Pratt recorded *uso taufeagai*
[6] Mead recorded "only child."

POLITICAL ORGANIZATION

A large share of the differences between Mead's accounts and those of my restudy which are not readily attributed to change are factual inaccuracies on Mead's part in the sphere of political organization, particularly those having to do with political alignments and relative statuses of chiefs.

The twin villages of Si'ufaga and Lumā, collectively known as Ta'ū, boast two sets of High Chiefs, the "cluster of chiefs" *(pupuali'i)* and the "brother chiefs" *(usoali'i)*. The former, located in Si'ufaga, look to Lefiti

as their paramount chief, while the latter, located in Luma, claim
Soatoa as its highest chief. Concerning the personnel of these groups,
Mead states that Lefiti is no longer an *usoali'i*, but detailed investigation of this point shows that he never was an *usoali'i*. Tradition has it
that the "cluster of chiefs" *(pupuali'i)* division and the Lefiti title as its
head was established by Tuimanu'a Salofi, the twenty-fifth Tuimanu'a. Calculating on the basis of the usual twenty-five years per
generation, the genealogy of Manu'an kings places Salofi's reign at
about 1650. Accordingly, Lefiti had been a member of the "cluster of
chiefs" for about three hundred years when the title was first created.
Six titles are recognized to be members of this "cluster of chiefs":
Lefiti, Moliga, Fua, Fasua, Leasau, and Nua. Although Mead states
(1930:194) that the title Fua had been dropped from the list, all
informants consulted gave six titles as comprising the group. The title
Fua (or Ali'ifua) was not occupied in 1954, but it is officially recorded
with the government, and the man who last held it died in approximately 1947.

Mead reports that the "brother chiefs" *(usoali'i)* of Ta'ū village are a
group of lesser officials who sat in the "unnamed, undistinguished
section" (ibid.) of the *fono*. Elderly informants who served under the
Tuimanu'a regime maintain that the posts on the right of the King
were those of the "brother chiefs," and those on the left, those of the
"cluster of chiefs." Distinguishing one group as superior does not
seem justified from observations of the council in session, or by the
fact that the post of the King is today occupied by either Lefiti or
Soatoa. Each of the two groups is honored in its own section of Ta'ū
village, and there is no indication of one being superior to the other
when they meet in the village councils.

Mead also says that two of the "brother chiefs," Levao and Faaee,
had the right to function as both High Chiefs and Talking Chiefs
(tulafale ali'i) (ibid.). Informants Soatoa, Su'afo'a, and Ili insisted that
the title Levao did not carry that power, and none of the chiefs of Ta'ū
village had ever heard of any such title as Faaee. A subsequent
perusal of government records, where all recognized titles must be
recorded, revealed that there had never been such a title in Ta'ū
village during the period that registry of titles was required, 1908–
1954. It was generally agreed that the only High Chief-Talking Chief
(tulafale ali'i) who has ever functioned in the Ta'ū council was Asoao, a
High Chief of Faleasao, an adjacent village which occasionally met
with the Ta'ū village council.

Mead's section on Ta'ū village organization lists official *taupou* and
manaia titles for the Lefiti and Soatoa families which are different from
the traditionally recognized Ta'ū titles of Samalaulu and Silia. Al-

though no *manaia* title except Silia appears in any of the early literature, Mead reports the *manaia* of Lefiti to be Timale and that of Soatoa
to be Vaimagalo. Extensive discussion of this point with village chiefs
established that Timale was never a Si'ufaga *manaia* title, but rather the
personal name of a boy of the Lefiti family who in the 1920s headed
the village *aumaga* by virtue of his family head's paramount title; as
aumaga leader he was referred to ceremonially as Silia. The title
Vaimagalo is an honorific one shared by Soatoa himself and Galea'i of
Fitiuta and refers to their function as peacemakers between the villages of Ta'ū and Fitiuta. Mead further states that the title Vaimagalo
was shared by Lefiti. However, the sanctions supporting the
Vaimagalo relationship concern the myth describing the stealing of
the Tuimanu'a crown from Fituita and the establishment of the throne
of Manu'a in Ta'ū village, and thus reach back into Manu'an oral
history to a period when the title Lefiti had not yet been created.

In describing the paramountcy of the Tufele title Mead holds that
the term *Afioga* was used before Tufele's name, *Afioga* is a courtesy
term corresponding to "His Majesty," and should be used only for a
very high chief or King. While "Afioga Tufele" appears in Mead's
version of the Fitiuta courtesy titles, it is not found in Kramer's
version of these titles recorded in 1902. In Kramer's accounts the term
Afioga appears only in connection with the King of Manu'a (Tuimanu'a), and Churchill writes, ". . . in Manu'a there is but one *Afioga*
and this is Tuimanu'a" (Churchill n.d.:1020).

Fitiuta

The relative status of the two top High Chiefs in the village of Fitiuta
was a very controversial subject in 1954, and I believe that Mead's data
in regard to this situation are open to question. Since the removal of
High Chief Tufele from the Manu'an District governorship in 1948
there has been a decline in the prestige of the once paramount Tufele
title and a corresponding rise in that of the Galea'i title. This was
prompted by Tufele's fall from power, coupled with the strong personality of Galea'i who held the important government position of
Manu'a copra agent in 1954.

Although Mead records that there has been "an unquestioning
acceptance of the Tufele title as having been the high title of Fitiuta for
hundreds of years" (1930:197), there is reason to believe that the
Galea'i title is traditionally one of the highest on the island of Ta'ū
(Williamson 1924:49), and very likely the highest in Fitiuta. But due to
various circumstances his prestige has long been overshadowed by
that of Tufele. After the removal of Tufele from the district gover-

norship the position was awarded to Lefiti, now the paramount chief of Ta'ū village, but because of his lack of leadership qualities he has never attained the status of the Tufele title holders.

It is only fair to reveal, however, that Mead, after reading statements in my restudy concerning relative ranks of chiefs, responded as follows:

> Reliance on Samoan informants, either in the 19th century or the 20th century to establish such matters as relative rank of titles and the various prerequisites and prerogatives of rank, seems to me, in the light of all the Samoan materials, unjustified. In 1926 informants did not even agree when they were selected from different neighboring villages, and inquiries on Tutuila provided quite different *fa'alupega* for Manu'a from those provided by contemporary Manu'ans. [1969:224]

Other Political Issues

Mead reports that one family head had his title taken from him because he was too old, but informants insisted in 1954 that titles are never taken from an individual because of old age. A thorough investigation of this point was made, but informants maintained that families could remove a title only if its holder was excessively cruel or if he was absent from the family for an extended period. Court files of title disputes confirmed their statements.

Considerations of the society of untitled men *(aumaga)* also illuminated differences in the two accounts. According to Mead, "When a boy is old enough to enter the *aumaga,* the head of his household either sends a present of food to the group, announcing the addition of the boy to the number, or takes him to a house where they are meeting and lays down a great kava root as a present" (1928:76). It was found that chiefs seldom visit meetings of the untitled men's society, and that although a young man must bring a present of food to his initial *aumaga* meeting, it is his own gift and not that of the *matai,* and that the presentation of the kava root is made to the village council rather than to the untitled men's society. The *matai* accompanies the boy to the village council and presents the kava root so that his son will have village recognition when he joins the group of untitled men. Kava is recognized as a chief's drink only, and kava drinking in groups of untitled men is rare. It is not surprising, however, that such minor inaccuracies appear in Mead's account, as the group excludes women from its regular sessions, and information of this type would have to be obtained exclusively from interview.

Discrepancies between what I found and what Mead recorded in regard to village political structure and relative ranks of chiefs indicate, I believe, the great difficulty Mead encountered in trying to establish rapport with the titled ranks. Because she was a young woman, she was not permitted to attend official village council meetings, and judging from my own difficulties in gathering traditional data of a political nature, the chiefs probably did not consider it worth their time to reveal relatively esoteric and complicated information to a young woman who was spending most of her time associating with teenage Samoan girls. While I was perceived as a person of chiefly status because of my university affiliation, my marital status (married with a child) and the fact that I was male, I still found investigation of political matters laden with pitfalls. I had the advantage, of course, of being in a position of checking on an earlier investigator and therefore being able to immediately identify problem areas by the different facts that were presented to me, and this signaled a need for more intensive investigation utilizing many informants or even government records if possible. It is also only fair to remind the reader that Franz Boas specifically recommended that Mead not produce a general ethnography of Samoa but to investigate a specific problem area—the trauma (or lack of it) associated with adolescence. *Social Organization of Manua* is therefore by Mead's own admission a "by-product, an extra dividend" (1969:228) of her Samoan experience. This is the only work in which she describes particular village structures and hierarchies.

ETHOS

While my restudy tends to confirm Mead's general thesis that it was (in 1925–26) easier to come of age in Samoa than in the United States and that the difference could be explained in terms of different cultural environments, there were also some interpretations by Mead that I could not support. These areas of disagreement might best be labeled quarrels over ethos, i.e., value dispositions.

Those aspects of Samoan behavior and ideology that Mead and I interpret differently are:

1. Amount of "specialized feeling" in Samoan human relations
2. Degree of crisis in human relations
3. Competitive spirit
4. Sex activity data
5. The *mafaufau* concept

Mead's statements concerning a relative "lack of specialized feeling" which results from "diffusion of affection in the household"

(1928a:210) were confirmed in parent-child relations and have previously been cited as a factor in the lack of psychological disturbance in adolescents. While this is valid with regard to parent–child relationships, Mead's extension of the "lack of specialized feeling" to relationships between lovers and between spouses was not confirmed by personal observation. Such statements as "The Samoan girl never tastes the rewards of romantic love as we know it" (1928a:211), "Marriage was regarded as a social-economic matter, seldom grounded upon special affection" (1930:44), or "casual sex relations carry no onus of strong attachment, . . . the marriage of convenience dictated by economic and social considerations is easily born and casually broken without strong emotion" (1928:210), seem to be generalizations which overlook many important exceptions.

Custom dictates that displays of affection between spouses and between lovers not take place in public, but expressions of love and affection were often observed in the families of informants, and many of these same people spoke of feelings for their wives that involved much more emotional depth than mere compatibility or economic convenience. The folklore of Manu'a contains notable examples of fidelity and expressions of deep emotional attachment between spouses and between lovers. One example is found in the saying *O le ua na fua mai i Manu'a* ('The rain comes from Manu'a') which explains the ubiquitous rain clouds over Manu'a as the tears of a wife forcibly separated from her husband.

Mead's statement that romantic love does not exist in Samoa (ibid.:211) overlooks those cases of extreme attachment for a particular husband, wife or sweetheart which end in suicide. Informants reported that in about 1951 a girl of the Tauala family of Ta'ū ate poisonous seaweed *(matamalu)* because she could not marry the man she desired. Copp presents a similar incident. His principal character in *Samoan Dance of Life* recounts,

> My Auntie died because she ate some *matamalu*. This is like a red jelly, and it spreads across some of the coral under the water . . . We think she did it because she was jealous. We heard stories that her husband was making sexes with village girls. [1950:30]

Another instance of this was encountered in Tutuila in September 1954, when a young woman, formerly of Manu'a, was brought into the hospital after having eaten *matamalu*. She informed the attending staff that she had attempted suicide because she had heard that her husband was unfaithful to her, and she did not care to live under such conditions.[4]

Closely related to her concept of "lack of specialized feeling" in human relationships are Mead's statements concerning the lack of crisis and deep conviction in Manu'an culture. In *Coming of Age in Samoa* Mead writes "Samoa is a place where no one plays for very high stakes, no one pays very heavy prices, no one suffers for his convictions or fights to the death for special ends" (1928a:198). Many family problems, of course may be worked out simply—a child can run to the home of another relative; a quarreling husband and wife can separate—but not all Samoan problems are so easily solved. The records of suicides because of an unfaithful spouse or unrequited love, and instances of violence arising from religious intolerance do not quite confirm Mead's view.

An incident that occurred in Manu'a in October 1954 illustrates the Samoan capacity for strong feeling. A man trying to take his child out of the home of his estranged wife and back to Tutuila was driven off by the woman with drawn knives and a gun. Serious conflicts between villages are infrequent but not unusual. Government anthropologists in Tutuila have been summoned in the middle of the night to settle differences between two outlying villages before violence begins.

Mead's statement that "To go faster than one's age mates or one's fellows of equal rank, is unforgivable" could not be confirmed. Ability in formal education is always acclaimed, and the educational achievements of a child are celebrated on a small scale within the family. As early as 1934, Keesing recorded, "Still another typical characteristic emerging in schooling is the competitive spirit" (1934:436). This spirit of competition in educational affairs is definitely subject to change, but competitive behavior and efforts to gain praise through excelling one's peers is believed to be one of the traditional aspects of Samoan culture.

It was a common experience to have the best carpenter, the best coxswain, and the best dancer pointed out and praised for their ability. Mead herself says that in learning to dance "The little children are put out upon the floor with a minimum of preliminary instruction. The child who performed best at the last party is hauled forward at the next. This tendency to give the talented child another and another chance is affected somewhat by rivalry between relatives who wish to thrust their little ones forward" (1928a:112).

Moreover, the whole pattern of oratory is based upon a competition between Talking Chiefs in order to win prestige both for the orator and for the village or family he represents. Very early in this restudy, informants of the village of Ta'ū pointed out a young man who, despite his youth, was the best orator in the village. Several of his stirring orations were later heard. Because of his brilliance in oratory, this young man, although only a third rank Talking Chief, represented his village in place of the High Talking Chief in all matters of high ceremony. According to Mead's interpretation such a man should have been labeled *tautala* (presuming above one's age). However, the phrase is only used to describe an individual who represents himself as capable of something that is beyond his ability.

As noted earlier, rank is of utmost importance, and many chiefs twist and fabricate legends in order to raise their position within the hierarchy of chiefs. In view of Mead's long discussions of competitiveness in the village political organization of Manu'a, it is surprising to find that she characterizes Manu'an culture as one where competition is disparaged and played down. Rank and prestige constitute the focal point of Samoan culture, to which all other aspects of life are secondary in importance. Every installation, wedding, and funeral of a chief affords an opportunity to gain prestige and raise one's relative position within the village through the display of wealth.

While I became aware that there were some angry parents and *matai* when a female relative became pregnant out of wedlock, I also was aware that there was a goodly number of illegitimate children in the village who suffered no stigma because of their birth status. I knew that *matai* were often fined by the village council when an unmarried family member delivered a child, but I also had been present at beach gatherings of young people and had observed them slipping off two by two to enjoy the romance of a moonlit night under the palm trees. In comparison to other Polynesian peoples I found Samoans very conservative in regard to sex—at least in regard to talking about it. While I had trouble getting my Samoan informants—even close friends—to talk about sex my colleagues who have worked in Eastern Polynesia maintain they had trouble getting informants to stop talking about sex. While Samoan society certainly did not sanction sex outside of marriage, I did not find Samoan young people puritanical or sexually inhibited.

Finally, because of the importance Mead places upon the concept of *mafaufau*, the meaning of this term was thoroughly investigated. She states,

> Individuals are said to have *mafaufau* (judgment) or lack of it. Judgment is a quality which Samoans conceive to develop just as skill in swimming or facility with oratorical phrases must be developed. The child is born without it and as the social pattern impinges more and more upon its developing consciousness, it acquires judgment—judgment about etiquette about matters of sex, about participation in group activities. [1930:81]

Informants with whom this term was discussed did not consider it an overly important aspect of individual behavior, and their answers concerning it were hazy, and not specific. Many were not certain that *mafaufau* should be translated "judgment" at all, replying that it meant merely "to think." This is the translation that appears in Downs' (1942) dictionary *Everyday Samoan*. The Samoan Bible, which serves as perhaps as good a Samoan dictionary as can be found, equates the word with "to meditate" and in II Chronicles 30:22, with "skill."[5]

"Judgment" in the passage "teach me good judgment and knowledge" (*Psalms* 119:66) is translated as *fa'autauta*. Actually, *mafaufau* is a verb rather than a noun.

MEAD'S RESPONSE

When my dissertation was completed and I had received my doctorate in anthropology from Northwestern University, I sent Mead a copy of the paper I had developed for presentation at an annual professional meeting. This paper, based on my dissertation, summarized the discrepancies and confirmation I had arrived at in my restudy of Samoan behavior and ethos. The paper also included statements that I believed explained many of our differences. I had long considered Oscar Lewis's criticism of Robert Redfield's work (after Redfield's death) unethical and counterproductive, and I did not want to be accused of the same kind of behavior in regard to Mead's work. After digesting the discussions of the methodology and the differences in data and their interpretation which constituted the restudy, Mead was at first extremely hostile. But in time she tempered her opinion and on several occasions we conferred at some length about Samoan culture at annual professional meetings and at a day-long session at Wichita State University during the early 1960s. Her general attitude toward my study and toward restudies in general was clearly spelled out in a letter to George N. Appell (a student of Derek Freeman's) in 1968 and in a special chapter titled "Conclusion 1969" which was appended to the second edition of *Social Organization of Manua* published by the Bernice P. Bishop Museum in 1969. The letter to Appell, a copy of which was sent to me, read as follows:

> I would say that the best person to do a restudy—where the aim is to add scientific knowledge of a culture—is the person who did the original study. No restudy is any better than the original study—in its restudy aspects.
>
> I believe that if the main aim is method, rather than ethnographic content—and I am not sure that devoting a

whole field trip to the criticism of inevitably outgrown methods is worth it—then it should be done entirely blind, but with a courteous letter to the original field worker stating the new field worker's intention. This should not be complicated by requests for help, unless a new design is made. I consider Lowell Holmes' restudy design, taking the older material on Ta'ū, Samoa and his own and bracketing my field work in between, was a most ingenious one, and one that might well be replicated.

I consider the sort of thing that Oscar Lewis did in Tepoztlan in criticism of Redfield's work, was wasteful, breaking the first requirement that a restudy should be based on what the original field worker did do, not on what he didn't.

Anthropologists should be trained to be able to resist mythology, white folklore and nativistic vilification of their colleagues who have worked in the same field in the past. This is becoming a more important issue all the time.

I have had no direct contact with Derek Freeman's work as he seems to regard statements made 44 years after an event as more accurate than mine—using the fact that I deliberately altered details to give anonymity as an indication of inaccuracy.

Margaret Mead's final chapter in the reissue of *Social Organization of Manua* in 1969 was essentially a set of "reflections" on later theoretical work on the Samoans by Derek Freeman, Melvin Ember, Gloria Cooper, and me. Her responses to my restudy include the following statements:

> Since Lowell Holmes constructed his doctoral dissertation (1957) as a restudy of work done by Buck and myself, it would be churlish not to comment upon it. His methodology device was ingenious; the search of the literature and old government documents to establish a 19th century base, his own observations and inquiries in 1954, informed, of course, by both the 19th century materials and the materials of the 1920's, with the degree of agreement between his observations and the 19th century records serving as a test of reliability of observations made in between. Ingenious as this method was, reliance on Samoan informants, either in the 19th century or the 20th century to establish such matters as relative rank of titles and the various prerequisites and prerogatives of rank, seems to me, in the light of all the Samoan materials, unjustified. [1969: 233–224]

In regard to the personal equation, i.e., the status of the observer and its effect on rapport, Mead commented:

> Holmes also comments on the disadvantages of a woman's attempting to study Samoan political organization and on the fact that I must have relied on informants. I did, of course, completely rely on informants; I have repeatedly documented my disapproval of members of either sex altering their sex role in studying a culture. What I assembled was the formal ethnography which could be obtained from informants—who often gave constructs of what should have been the case without even any reference to what was claimed by other informants—plus the observations on the ethos of formal gatherings to which I had access, in visiting other villages, I had the status of a visiting *taupou*, a status which by definition, I never could have in Ta'ū. [1969:224–225]

In regard to the matter of Samoan mildness and the manner in which Samoans responded to insults and interpersonal crises, Mead commented:

> Holmes' questions about ethos raise a question about Samoan character which I have found to be least well accounted for by any of my Manu'an field research; this is the violence with which Samoans respond to certain kinds of insult. Holmes discusses the suicide of a girl who was not permitted to marry the man she desired as a matter of romantic love and also cites Copp's book (1950) which I felt, when I read it, was out of key with the material I had collected. . . . There was also the whole question of the virginity of the *taupou* and other girls of rank, and the savagery with which earlier reports said delinquents had been punished. The kind of absolutism which severely punished a girl who was revealed at her defloration ceremony not to be a virgin seemed incompatible with the mildness and low affect of the people as I knew them.
>
> There is a serious problem of reconciling these contradictions between the mildness, the willingness to gloss over and compromise, which I found in Manu'a and other records of historical and contemporary behavior. I see, at present, only two possibilities. Manu'a in 1925 might have represented a special variation on the Samoan pattern, a temporary felicitous relaxation of the quarrels and rivalries, the sensitivity to slight and insults, and the use of girls as pawns in male rivalries.
>
> The other possibility is that to the young girl, herself either a virgin but not a *taupou*, or experimenting quietly with

lovers of her own choosing, uninvolved in the rivalries that
were related to rank and prestige, moving gently, unhur-
riedly toward adulthood, the preoccupations of the whole
society may have seemed more remote than they would
have appeared from any other vantage point. And this is
the vantage point from which I saw it. [1969:226–228]

Recalling the strong identification she made with the adolescent
girls of her study, the fact that she was alone and therefore highly
dependent on their friendship and the fact that she was about their
size and looked about their age, Margaret Mead suggests that perhaps her close rapport with her subjects distorted her perspective on
the greater society—particularly certain aspects of its overall ethos.
She concludes the chapter with the challenge that ironically sent me
to study her work in the first place. She writes, "We have too few
cases where we can compare the consequences of sex, age, and
temperament in the observation stance of any observer" (1969:228).
Stating that *Social Organization of Manua* was really a byproduct of her
adolescent girl study, Mead labels it "an extra dividend" which "after
forty years makes it possible to read new materials on Samoa with
enthusiastic interest." "Hopefully," she writes, "we will soon have
some sophisticated microcultural studies: Gloria Cooper's on para-
linguistics [which has never been published]; and Derek Freeman's
proposed intensive attention to early experience" (1969:228).

But of course we now know that Freeman did not go to Samoa to
study "early experience" of Samoan children but to study the compe-
tency of Margaret Mead as a fieldworker and as a theorist whose
"absolute cultural determinism" would render, for his purposes, her
conclusions unacceptable.

NINE

Psychometric Assessment

In a paper in Francis Hsu's *Psychological Anthropology* (1972), Donald Campbell writes about my restudy of Margaret Mead's Samoan research:

> [It] is quite conceivable that there are some aspects of culture, including its overall pattern or ethos, that are so abstract or indirectly inferred that intersubjective verifiability is lost. If this is so, then until corrected, these aspects cannot become a part of science, and we, as scientists, should concentrate on those aspects upon which we can get agreement . . . If, as Mead has said, "in the matter of ethos, the surest and most perfect instrument of understanding is our own emotional response" (Mead and McGregor 1951:300), and if agreement in such emotional response is lacking, or can be disparaged as merely a shared ethnocentric reaction to a novel culture, then ethos may indeed be beyond the realm of scientific study. This lack of intersubjective verifiability is not inevitable however. Its presence or absence should be studied in Mead's own terms, with the precaution of involving observing anthropologists from differing cultures. It is also possible that science can make explicit the existence of abstract general themes in culture through formal combinatorial analysis of more concrete data. [1972:444]

Much of the difficulty concerning the "true" or "real" character and ethos of Samoan society involves a somewhat subjective analysis of situational behavior as observed or as it is described in the literature. With no scientifically reliable methods for measurement or observation as might be found in the hard sciences, ethnocentrism and personal bias are highly likely to influence the observer's descriptions of temperament and normative behavior.

Keesing (1934) describes the ethnocentrism which has dominated the white man's perceptions of Samoan character from the very beginning. He writes:

> The records give many frank statements of what different whites think of the Samoan faults. . . . These, however, are always evaluations made according to white standards which are very different from those of the Samoan. . . . The Samoan, it is said, is not straightforward; he indulges in "diplomacy" and "intrigue;" he is "cunning" and "ungrateful," and with few exceptions cannot be trusted; he tells what he thinks his hearers want, always willing to please; he deceives freely and cheerfully, making truth or falsehood subject to expediency; . . . he is mentally "childlike," yet his savagery is just under the surface and violent passions are easily aroused; he is assertive and boastful, yet a coward except in a crowd; . . . Among outstanding traits, these critics say are the selfishness and jealousy of the Samoans among themselves. [1934:27–28]

It is interesting to note, in the light of the Keesing discussion, that characterizations of Samoans by Derek Freeman in his book *Margaret Mead and Samoa* do not vary a great deal from those of earlier observers whose impressions were highly subjective and markedly different from later more professional observers. Freeman, who admittedly rejects relativistic thought as either a philosophy or as a tool of research, finds Samoans "jealous" (1983:149,156,243), subject to volatile and "uncontrollable anger" (ibid.:219), "ungovernably proud" (ibid.:156), "maladjusted" and subject to "psychopathological states, suicides, and other violent acts" (ibid.:216), "stubborn" (ibid.:222), extremely competitive, to the point of physical violence (ibid.:149), prone to lying (ibid.:223, 290), undemocratic (ibid.:274), and obsessed with a desire to demonstrate masculinity through surreptitious (*moetotolo*) or forcible rape (ibid.:245).

Ronald Rose, author of *South Seas Magic* (a book that Freeman selectively quotes from to substantiate his own view of Samoan personality), also notes the ubiquitous conflict between cultural systems and how it affects descriptions and interpretations of indigenous behavior. He writes

> Anthropologists are fond of telling the story of the government official who was asked to report briefly on the man-

ners and customs of the native people in his area. His report said simply: "Manners none, customs beastly."

He, of course, was applying his own standards to the native people. (If he could have known their judgment of him by their standards he might not have been so supercilious). The trained and experienced field worker suffers the same faults as this administrator—the difference is in degree only, not in kind. No matter how firmly we attempt to discipline ourselves in making judgments on a different culture, our own culture remains as a sort of final determinant. We take over a frame of reference: this is inevitable. We cannot assess people or things without making comparisons.

What we need to realize is that our standard is not necessarily the ideal, that it is, like the many others that exist, a working compromise with life. It is not final and it is not always good. [1959:82]

Descriptions of modal personality traits may also be influenced by the personality of the observer as well as the nature of the cultural system from which he or she comes. It is understandable that some of the anthropologists who have reviewed the Freeman book have stated that they think it tells us more about Freeman than about Samoa, and one wonders if the following statement by Felix and Marie Keesing might explain the great discrepancy between the interpretations of Freeman, a New Zealander now living in Australia, and those of the American observers such as Mead, myself, Bradd Shore, Paul Shankman, Melvin Ember and Martin Orans. The Keesings observe:

The New Zealander correspondingly tends to be critical of the image which Samoan traits convey to him e.g., the stress on hierarchy, the flair for dramatic display, ceremoniousness, and circumlocution, the emphasis on group-responsibility, with externalized shame-sanction, and suppressive (group-regulating) controls. [1956:305–306]

The Keesings also remind us that the New Zealand administration in Western Samoa has never permitted any Samoan government employee to wear trousers and that "most New Zealanders avoid easy comradely behavior with Samoans, both in and out of government, and keep a considerable social distance" (1956:193). Americans, on the other hand, are described by the Keesings as having less of a colonial mentality. They suggest that the American–Samoan relationships are marked less by a concept of "social distance," and more by a "colleague" relationship.

Given the problem of ethnocentrism, the possibility of varying

national attitudes between people like Freeman and American researchers, personal bias, and less-than-precise methods of documentation, a number of interested scientists have turned to psychometric
analysis to provide a more scientifically valid and reliable profile of
Samoan character.

PERSONALITY STUDIES

Although generally unrecognized, an impressive volume of research
in recent years has been devoted to Samoan personality and culture.
As a result, it is possible to establish a psychological profile of the
Samoan people that is without parallel in Oceania.

At least fifteen "students of personality" have directed their attention to the Samoan culture. They have utilized a broad range of
methods: folklore and literature analysis; projective, verbal, and nonverbal testing; observation and interview; controlled laboratory observation; personality inventories; value schedule analysis, among
others. The following is a survey of several studies that together, it is
hoped, will establish a Samoan personality profile, and throw some
light on the Mead/Freeman controversy.

Mead

The earliest anthropological analysis of culture and personality in
Samoa, and probably in the whole world, was Mead's problem-ori-
ented study of 30 adolescent girls carried out in Ta'ū village, American Samoa, in 1925. Her study involved no psychological testing,
although several intelligence tests (color naming, rote memory for
digits, digit symbol substitution, word opposites, and ball and field)
were administered. Depending mainly on participant observation and
interview (including collection of life histories), Mead noted the following as salient influences shaping Samoan juvenile behavior: (1) a
lack of deep feeling or involvement between relatives or peers; (2) a
liberal attitude toward sex and education; (3) a lack of conflicting
alternatives regarding ideology, political doctrine, morality, and oc-
cupational choice; and (4) a lack of emphasis on individuality. The
Samoan female adolescent was relatively free from tension, emotional
conflict, or rebellion; values were strongly situational rather than
individualistic. Mead saw Samoans as apathetic and submissive to the
aggression of others, unwilling to invest heavily of themselves in any
interpersonal relationship, and general casual in their attitude toward
life.

Mead discovered that numerous fixed relationships exist (associated with age, sex, and status) and that these are defined by the social structure. In all these relationships there was an elaborate pattern of appropriate behavior, with little freedom of choice. What choice was possible seemed to be the freedom to reduce interpersonal conflict by fleeing it. Thus, Mead states

> Choice is possible among homes, among teachers, among lovers; but the consciousness of personality, the attitudes necessary to make such choices significant, are lacking. So that the freedom in personal choices operates mainly in reducing the poignancy of personal relations, the elements of conflict, the need for making painful choices. . . . The individual need commit no murder, need not even muster up a fine rage to escape from a disagreeable situation—he simply slips out of it into the house next door. Such a setting does not produce violent, strikingly marked personalities; it is kind to all and does not make sufficient demands upon any. [1928a:494]

Torrance and Johnson

Creativity and original thought was the topic of research conducted by educational psychologists E. Paul Torrance and R. T. Johnson in 1962. Testing the hypothesis that original thinking is associated with cultural discontinuities (in education, sex roles, and independence), the researchers used three verbal and three nonverbal tests (Picture Construction Test, Incomplete Figures Test, and the Circle Test) with a sample of 1000 Western Samoan school children; comparisons were made with similar samples from Australia, Germany, India, and the State of Georgia in the U.S. All samples showed a continuous growth in creativity from the first grade through the sixth, but Samoan children ranked lowest in original thought at all levels. In an effort to explain low creativity scores in Samoa, the investigators pinpointed the following societal values as determinants of Samoan behavior: (1) the emphasis on remembering well; (2) acceptance of authority hierarchies; (3) submission to authority; and (4) doing nothing until told to do so.

Torrance and Johnson's general conclusion was that, to increase Samoan originality, cultural discontinuity must be introduced, but this would have to be done at the risk of producing undue personality conflicts, and making coming of age in Samoa a somewhat more traumatic phenomenon.

Gardner

Louise Gardner (1965) approached Samoan character through interview, observation, and analysis of responses to a modified *Kluckhohn*

Value Schedule, and a projective picture test of her own design. Working with 30 children and 30 adults in the Western Samoan village of Gautavai in 1962, she focused particularly on enculturative influences, attempting to understand what attitudes and values were held in common by both children and adults and what values would be likely to change as Samoan children matured. Results of her study were reported in terms of the Florence Kluckhohn categories of Relational, Activity, Time, Man–Nature, and Human Nature orientations.

The Samoan personality profile drawn from her data reveals a people who are present- or future-oriented, prone to see themselves in subjugation to, or in harmony with, nature, and viewing societal members as "good" or "neutral," while seeing outsiders as potentially "evil." Orientations were toward achieving familial (both lineal and collateral) goals and well-being rather than individual satisfaction, and toward "doing" (i.e., accomplishing goals measurable by societal standards) rather than "being" (i.e., spontaneous expression of impulses and desires).

Garsee

Jarrell W. Garsee, a missionary to American Samoa turned social scientist, tested observational generalizations about the nature of Samoan values and behavior with the help of Gordon's Survey of Interpersonal Values, assessing what he considered to be a particularly relevant dimension of Samoan personality—Conformity, Recognition, Independence, and Benevolence. It was Garsee's hypothesis that Samoans would score high on Conformity and Benevolence and low on Recognition and Independence. One hundred thirty-one students (85 boys and 46 girls) in the senior class at the High School of American Samoa were tested in 1965, and tests were compared with respect to differences in sex, academic program (i.e., academic, commercial, or technical), and test language (whether they took an English or a Samoan version).

Garsee contended that the results confirmed his own observations as well as those of a number of other anthropologists. The tests showed Conformity and Benevolence to be most valued, with Recognition valued the least. Comparison with norms for a Japanese college student sample showed Samoans to be relatively similar to them on Recognition, Independence, and Leadership, while comparison with American norms revealed that these are precisely the areas where Samoans and Americans are farthest apart.

Holmes and Blazer

In 1962 I tested 68 senior students (29 female and 39 male) at the High School of American Samoa. The instruments used were the California

Test of Personality, the Edwards Personal Preference Schedule, and the Rogers Test of Personality Adjustment. The tests were translated into the Samoan language and altered slightly to make them more relevant to Samoan culture. The tests were administered by a Samoan teacher who also provided personal and attitudinal information on each of the subjects. I was aided in the analysis by Leland K.Blazer, who used the material as the basis of a Master's thesis in 1968. Of the three tests, the Edwards test presented a profile which most nearly squared with my impressions gained through long-term participant observation in the culture. All three tests produced data compatible with the view of Samoan personality as summarized by the following characteristics: *Strong tendencies* toward (1) Deference, i.e., doing what is expected and accepting others' leadership; (2) Order, i.e., enjoying organization; (3) Abasement, i.e., being timid in the presence of superiors; and (4) Endurance, i.e., keeping at a job until finished. On the other hand, comparison with American norms revealed Samoans to be *weak in tendencies* toward (1) Autonomy, i.e., being independent of others in decision making, (2) Dominance, i.e., directing the actions of others, (3) Exhibition, i.e., being the center of attention, (4) Aggression, i.e., getting angry or disagreeing with others, (5) Achievement, i.e., doing one's best to be successful, and (6) Heterosexuality, i.e., relating socially and sexually to the opposite sex.

Vinacke

William Vinacke, a psychologist, consulted Mead's publications resulting from her 1925–26 research, Cook's Samoan Rorschach studies, Copp's novel, *Samoan Dance of Life*, Samoan proverbs and folktales, and a number of biased and questionable missionary accounts, in order to arrive at an armchair analysis of Samoan personality. His conclusions, often highly subjective and ethnocentric, were that, by and large, Samoan character is a "remarkably tempered organization" with "few dominant or extreme characteristics" (1968:32).

Hypotheses, which folklore analysis proved "more often correct than erroneous," were that dominant motivation themes in Samoan culture include sex, avoidance of humiliation, abasement, affiliation, deference, succorance, and play. Pronouncing Samoan personality to be essentially flaccid, Vinacke credited three main cultural features as influential: (1) mild pressures and demands imposed upon individuals during development; (2) influences operating at one stage usually being mitigated at another stage of development; and (3) a relatively strong guarantee that needs will be satisfied. He also states that there is "little evidence of deep hostility, strong aggressiveness, fearfulness, or anxiety in relations with other persons" (ibid.:21).

Maxwell

Robert J. Maxwell (1969) carried out a twenty-two month research project, inspired by the theories of Hans Eysenck, in the village of Vaitogi, American Samoa, in 1965–66. With a sample of 52 male Samoans he tested, for the first time in a nonindustrial setting, Eysenck's theories concerning extroversion–introversion behavior.

Believing that Samoans are extremely extroverted, but uncertain whether or not extroversion takes the same form in Samoa that it does in other societies, Maxwell's sample was studied for extrovert–introvert characteristics through (1) fellow villager rating, (2) objective tests, e.g., Spiral Aftereffect, Block Sort, and Vigilance Test; (3) questionnaires; (4) projective tests, e.g., "crisis-scene ink drawings"; (5) life-record data; and (6) participant observation.

While Maxwell's Samoan data do not tend to support Eysenck's theories about extrovert–introvert behavior, Maxwell believes his study does support two propositions: (1) that Samoans are, on the whole, an extroverted population; and (2) that Eysenck's theory has cross-cultural generality.

Maxwell acknowledged major methodological errors. These included using questionnaires in a culture where the investigator claims there is a great tendency for prevarication; use of tests of dubious validity; and the lack of controlled conditions, which probably would have been insisted upon in a test of Eysenck's theory in a laboratory. Maxwell characterized the extroverted Samoan (in his opinion, the modal type) as stronger-tempered, more prone to engage in fighting, more sexually active, less temperate, and more likely to steal than introverted Samoans. It was also concluded that extroversion decreases with age.

Holmes and Tallman

The influence of cultural change on Samoan personality (a factor generally ignored by Derek Freeman) may be gleaned from the research of Gary Tallman (a former Wichita State University graduate student) and me. In 1974, high-school students in American Samoa were once again tested with the Edwards and California tests of personality for the purpose of comparison with the 1962 sample (see "Holmes and Blazer" above). The period from 1962 to 1974 had been one of great cultural change. Twenty-six consolidated elementary schools and three high schools were built, and educational and entertainment television was inaugurated at a cost of better than three million dollars. A tourist hotel was built on the shores of Pago Pago Bay, and airport facilities were improved.

While a tuna fish cannery had been built early in the 1950s, a second cannery was established after 1962, and by 1970 the Samoan labor force processing tuna numbered close to 1,100 people. In addition to this industry, other types of enterprises—a watch factory and a dairy products plant—were drawing more and more Samoans away from subsistence agriculture and into wage labor. By 1970 the wage-labor force in Samoa totaled 4,939, the largest share (3,515) being government employees—teachers, health-service workers, public-works employees, and clerical workers in a variety of government agencies.

In 1974 the sample consisted of 31 male subjects on the Edwards test and 47 subjects (29 females and 18 males) on the *California* test. The tests were given again in the Samoan language (now a problem for some acculturated Samoans) and administered by a Samoan high-school teacher.

Scores on several of the variables on the Edwards and California tests indicate that the Samoan modal personality was changing in a direction that stressed modern traits more and traditional traits less. In the 1974 sample, the means of the Edwards test variables of *abasement, order, dominance, aggression,* and *heterosexuality* all show independence from the 1962 means, as measured by the *chi*-square. In addition, these and five other variables—*exhibition, autonomy, affiliation, succorance,* and *endurance*—are closer to American norms.

On the California test the variables of *personal adjustment* (a composite score) and *sense of personal worth* show independence between the 1962 and 1974 means, and at the same time are closer to American norms. Eight more—*self-reliance, sense of personal freedom, feeling of belonging, withdrawing tendencies, school relations, nervous symptoms,* and the remaining composite scores, *social adjustment* and *total adjustment*—are closer to the American norms, although there is not an independent difference between the 1962 and 1974 means.

In general, the Samoan scores on the California test have decreased in the area of social relations and increased in the area of personal relations. A similar trend could be inferred from the movement of the Edwards variables. *Abasement* and *order,* traits which were conceivably important in maintaining the traditional society's political and economic processes as mediated through the kinship structure, are lower and closer to the American norms.

Despite this trend toward more Western tendencies, the data also indicate a large degree of persistence of traditional traits in the Samoan personality. While the aforementioned variables on the Edwards test have moved closer to the American norms, they still remain in nearly the same rank-order of scores. For instance, *abasement* remains the highest score in both the 1962 and 1974 samples, while *dominance* and *aggression* remain in about the same positions at the lower end of the rank order. This is also true of most of the variables on the Edwards test, which we consider the more valid of the two tests. In the case of the *deference* and *nurturance* variables, there is a movement away from the American norms in the 1974 sample.

The Tallman (Holmes, Tallman & Jantz, 1978) analysis established that there had been both change and persistence in the Samoan modal personality in the 12-year period from 1962 to 1974. Change is most likely due to an adaptation to Western influences, since the majority of variables have moved in this direction. The persistence may also be considered a type of adaptation to changing conditions, in which traditional traits have found an increased usefulness in new situations.

The many evaluations of Samoan character, utilizing a great variety of diagnostic tools, produce a profile of Samoans very much at odds with that put forward by Derek Freeman. They are strongly supportive, however, of Margaret Mead's conceptualizations. While there is always the possibility that individual test instruments may not be cross-culturally valid (an objection Freeman has made in personal correspondence with me) it is believed that the personality research described above presents a relatively consistent picture of Samoan behavior and constitutes valuable evidence in establishing a scientific, bias-free representation of Samoan ethos and of Samoan personality proclivities.

Derek Freeman's objections to the lack of cross-cultural validity of the test instruments is amusing in light of his absolutist interpretations of mental illness. In 1962 Freeman strongly criticized M. J. Herskovits when the latter complained that "the terminology of psychopathology has been readily applied to these [West African] states of possession . . . but in these Negro societies the interpretation given behavior under possession—the meaning this experience holds for the people—falls entirely in the realm of understandable, predictable, normal behavior" (1949:67). To this Freeman responded, "To assert . . . that behavior is normal because it is set in a cultural mold, is to say no more than it is shared and accepted by the members of the culture concerned, but dereistic thinking and irrational behavior are not one whit the less dereistic because they happen to be shared and accepted" (1962:273). In other words, one need not take cross-cultural differences in perception into consideration in the interpretation of normal or abnormal behavior. Why then must we reject the findings concerning personality traits if an instrument developed in one culture is being used to diagnose personality in another?

TEN

Assessing Derek Freeman

THE SAMOAN RESPONSE

While anthropologists usually maintain that the group being studied is perhaps least able to be objective about its own cultural behavior and its motivations, the responses of Samoans to *Margaret Mead and Samoa* are worth consideration. Two weeks after the publication of a review article of Freeman's book in *Newsweek*, Fetaui Mata'afa, wife of the Prime Minister of Western Samoa, responded with a letter to the editor which stated, "Neither Margaret Mead nor Derek Freeman represented our ancient land, its customs or its way of life. Both anthropologists missed the subtlety of behavior in a Samoan. . . . My country is not perfect, but it is neither the permissive society of Margaret Mead nor the polluted populace of Derek Freeman" (*Newsweek*, 28 Feb. 1983). This was followed in the same issue by a letter from Lelei Lelaulu, who bitterly asked: "Are we Samoans now to be known as a nation of sex-starved, suicidal rapists? I much prefer my previous reputation as a free-loving orgiast." He then suggested that anthropologists should come and study the tribal tensions and sexual neuroses on the island where he now lives—Manhattan.

On Febuary 7, 1983 I received a letter from Mulima Afoa of Costa Mesa, California, stating that he had read my book, *Samoan Village* (1974) and Mead's *Coming of Age in Samoa* and was "delighted" with both, but was "very dismayed and surprised" about what Freeman was saying about Samoans in his new book. He asked how he should go about protesting Freeman's allegations.

Reporters from the *Wall Street Journal* and *Life* magazine apparently convinced their editors that covering the Mead/Freeman controversy required a visit to Ta'ū village, and upon arrival they interviewed elderly people who had allegedly been in contact with Mead in 1925–26. Most of them disagreed with much that Mead had written, although few had actually read *Coming of Age in Samoa.* One man, Napoleone A. Tuiteleapaga, is definitely known to have had close ties with Mead as both informant and interpreter. He is quoted in the *Wall Street Journal* article (14 Apr. 1983) as saying, "Margaret Mead was 100% right in her book." And in an interview in the *Samoa News* (11 Feb. 1983), published in American Samoa, he stated, "She got to know people well and wrote an accurate analysis of what she saw. Why didn't these anthropologists condemn Mead's book when she was alive? I'll tell you why, they waited until Mead is gone because they knew she knew what she was talking about."

On the other hand, *Life* reporter Elizabeth Owen quotes Le Tagaloa Leota Pita (Western Samoan Parliament member) as stating, "Freeman makes us human, Margaret Mead makes us unreal—angels and puppets" (*Life,* May 1983), and she records United States Congressional Representative Fofo Sunia as saying, "I think Mead went too far—Samoans aren't without troubles—but Freeman is too dark, too simple."

In correspondence with the editor of *Anthropology Newsletter* in April 1984, protesting the treatment his book had received at the business meeting of the annual convention of the American Anthropological Association, Derek Freeman wrote:

> Albert Wendt, the distinguished Samoan scholar, poet and novelist, who is Professor of Pacific Literature in the University of the South Pacific, and whose knowledge of Samoa certainly surpasses that of Professor Holmes, has written (*Pacific Islands Monthly,* April, 1983) that, in his view, my book, is "the most important study" of the Samoans "made this century by a non-Samoan," and has described it as being "a devastating refutation" of the conclusions reached by Margaret Mead in her *Coming of Age in Samoa.*

Wendt, who is generally supportive of the Freeman study, makes what I believe is a very significant comment concerning Freeman's objectivity in relating to Samoans. He writes in *Pacific Islands Monthly:*

> He [Freeman] has a deep love and respect for us. This I think helps to explain his almost obsessive quest to correct what he deems was the wrong Margaret Mead did to us.

Perhaps he has not felt at home in his own society, and in understanding us hoped he would find a people to belong to, to champion, to be needed by. The condition of the outsider is one I know well. [1983:12]

Although in the *Anthropology Newsletter* communication Derek Freeman leaves the impression that Wendt is *totally* supportive of his refutation of Mead, this is not the case. In Wendt's *Pacific Islands Monthly* article, from which Freeman quotes the Samoan novelist as describing *Margaret Mead and Samoa* as the "most important study of Samoans made this century by a non-Samoan," there is also the following observation:

The easily discernible flaws in Freeman's book stem mainly from its polemical form. To prove Mead wrong, some of his claims tend toward exaggeration and idealisation. (This idealisation is also perhaps the result of his profound trust in us).

For instance, he is correct in stating that we place a great priority on female virginity, we institutionalise it in the *taupou*, we forbid pre-marital and extramarital sex and promiscuity, but institutionalise bravado and machismo.

In sexual matters, Mead erred far too much on the side of free love and promiscuity, while Freeman errs on the side of sexual purity, strictness, and abstinence. "Ask the sailors" Freeman says rhetorically. Meaning: sailors know that Samoa is (and was) far from being a promiscuous port. But I know that sailors know that with the right approach and persuasion—the right dollar value—all ports (including Samoa) will open up. Admittedly some ports are easier than others. Even in the 1920s Samoa wasn't anywhere near "all virginity," as it were. [1983:14]

And in regard to Freeman's statement that Albert Wendt's "knowledge of Samoa certainly surpasses that of Professor Holmes," I would respond that Wendt might very well be more knowledgeable, but perhaps also more biased concerning his own society than someone like myself who has devoted much of his professional career to studying Samoan culture from the perspective of a scientifically trained outsider. However, the Freeman book is more than just a treatise on Samoa and Samoans; it is a judgment of Mead's methods and of Boasian anthropology in general, and in these areas I believe I exceed both Wendt and Freeman in my knowledge and understanding. In setting up Wendt as an authority Freeman ignores both time and place in believing that a young man born and raised in Western Samoa (who was just finishing his university training in New Zealand a year after my second field trip to Tutuila and Manu'a) has some special knowledge of what happened on the isolated island of Ta'ū some 39 years earlier just because he was born a Samoan.

THE ANTHROPOLOGY COMMUNITY'S RESPONSE

Some anthropologists have described the Mead/Freeman controversy as the most important anthropological debate in 100 years. A few have lamented the fact that it has invited indictments of anthropology as a "soft science," while others maintain that it is good for the discipline to review and analyze its theoretical foundations from time to time. The controversy has certainly resulted in considerable heat and perhaps some light. The titles of review articles alone bespeak the amount of ingenuity inspired among anthropologists because of the question. Consider, if you will, the following: "One Man's Mead" *(New York Times Book Review)*, "A Controversy on Samoa Comes of Age" *(Science)*, "Brouhaha among the Breadfruit" *(Nature)*, "The Coming of a Sage to Samoa" *(Natural History)*, and "Margaret and the Giant Killer" *(The Sciences)*. It is little wonder that anthropologist David Schneider of the University of Chicago, in his review in *Natural History* (June, 1983) writes: "Instead of a scholarly book of significance, the book is now a media event."

It is doubtful if any anthropology book to date has created such a media circus or produced such a media hero. It is also doubtful whether any academic press ever mounted such a campaign of Madison Avenue hype to market its products. Under the circumstances it seems reasonable that David Schneider should muse "I do not know whether the publisher should take the responsibility for this [the manner in which the book has been promoted] or whether the author shares a large part of that responsibility by virtue of the inflammatory statements he has made to the media" (ibid.). And Laura Nader asks, "Why did a university press lend its credibility to a zealous treatise published about 40 years too late with quotes on the dust jacket by well-known men who could not adequately judge the book's content?" *(Los Angeles Times Book Review,* 10 Apr. 1983). To all of this, Joy Pratt, director of publicity at Harvard University Press, responds, "Academics don't understand publishing. We have a responsibility to make money and generate sales for books as well as publish books with something important to say" *(Chronicle of Higher Education,* 11 May 1985). But does that responsibility include such questionable tactics as circulating bound page proof to sympathetic and somewhat biased academics and to media people more than two months before the book's announced publication date? And does that responsibility include flying this book's controversial and quarrelsome author half way around the world to appear on talk shows such as the Studs Turkel Show, the Phil Donahue Show, and the CBS Morning News? It is not surprising that Harvard University Press' actions prompted a special news article in the *New York Times Book Review* titled "The Making of a Celebrity" (6 Mar. 1983). It describes Freeman's trip from Samoa, his whirlwind TV tour of the United States, and contends: "Because Harvard is used to publishing scholars, not celebrities, it hired a New York public relations firm to handle Mr. Freeman's bookings."

After the media circus had subsided somewhat and the reporters, freelance writers, and other assorted groupies had had their say, the reviews that editors had invited from anthropologists (whether they had ever been to Samoa or not) began to appear. While the media response to the book had generally been quite supportive of Freeman, once the anthropologists began evaluating the book the tide took a definite turn.

The first reviews appeared late in March of 1983—long after every major newspaper had run a feature story on the book—with that by George Marcus of Rice University appearing in the *New York Times Book Review* (27 Mar. 1983) and that by Colin Turnbull of George Washington University appearing in *The New Republic* (28 Mar. 1983).

Marcus' review opened with the somewhat startling declaration: "This is a work of great mischief." The mischief to a large extent is described as involving Freeman's dual aims of "re-establishing the importance of biological factors in explanations of human behavior," and demolishing "the authority of Margaret Mead's knowledge of Samoan society and asserting his own in its stead." According to Marcus, Freeman's characterization of Frank Boas and Mead as "absolute cultural determinists" is a gross distortion, and he points out that "the Boasians—including Margaret Mead—were primarily concerned with the study of cultural variation, which they presumed took place within a context of general biological tendencies in human behavior." Although Freeman intimates that biology has been done a great injustice by anthropology, Marcus counters with the statement that this book does little to rectify the situation. He notes that it has nothing new to say about the relation of biology to culture, and that "Mr. Freeman's occasional efforts to bring biological factors into his account of Samoans are simply embarrassing compared to his masterful presentation of evidence by anecdote and historical example." This "masterful" presentation, however, involves such bad habits as being "quite selective in assembling quotes out of context," and "in the same paragraph combining quotes from works that are years, even decades apart."

Colin Turnbull's review is one of the most critical of the many published. He contends that the "myth" referred to in the book's title is of Freeman's own making, since the nature/nurture issue is not what Mead set out to investigate at all. Turnbull maintains that while Freeman takes great pains to characterize the young Mead as an idiotic, empty-headed, silly girl, without academic ability or perceptivity—and too naive to know that her adolescent informants were duping her—his own research procedures leave something to be desired. Turnbull writes, "Given his own dubious methodology, I doubt if Freeman's book is worth very much either as anthropology or biology. To my mind it deserves review only because it could do harm to anthropology, and particularly to the kind of humanistic anthropology that Margaret Mead preferred to petty academic rivalry."

In her review in the *Los Angeles Times Book Review* (10 Apr. 1983) Laura Nader (University of California, Berkeley) refers to Freeman's nit-picking efforts to discredit Mead as "historical tracking," noting that *Margaret Mead and Samoa* "is not a systematic restudy. Instead, Freeman uses history, early reports of Western missionaries and travelers, government and court records plus his and other people's observations to refute Mead." Although Freeman makes a great point of Mead's Boasian bias, which had the effect of causing her to overemphasize particular aspects of Samoan culture, Nader maintains that "he does what he accuses a 23-year-old inexperienced anthropologist of doing. He draws an extreme picture of the Samoans—the exact opposite of the one Mead drew. While she saw only the lighter side of Samoan life, he saw only the darker side. But if Mead is a cultural determinist, so too is Freeman, because the dispute is over cultural facts."

A review by Paula Brown Glick (SUNY, Stony Brook) in *Nature* (28 Apr. 1983) asks "Why has Freeman not written a monograph on Samoa describing his findings as a result of many years research rather than listing Margaret Mead's errors, one after the other. One can only surmise that his was personal preference for criticism over construction." But Glick also questions the validity of his criticism and points out that the data sources and evidence presented by Mead and Freeman are quite different. She writes, "While Freeman presents much evidence to contradict Mead's statements, he cannot claim to have reproduced her conditions of field work with adolescent girls in Manu'a in 1925. . . . Subsequent research among the same people— in this case an island group with a population of over 150,000—is likely to find differences attributable to local conditions, historical changes and interpretation of emphasis."

Marvin Harris (University of Florida), in "The Sleep-crawling Question," in *Psychology Today* (May 1983) sees Freeman's target as more than Mead and Boas: "He seems to be obsessed with the notion that to discredit Mead's Samoan material is to discredit any social scientist who holds that 'nurture' is a more important determinant of the differences and similarities in human social life than 'nature.' " While many reviewers of this book have found the chronicling of the nature/ nurture controversy one of the best sections, Harris maintains that Freeman is more confused about this controversy than Mead was confused about Samoa, since his characterization of the Boas position on the biological component in human behavior is so distorted.

Of the early formal reviews written by anthropologists the most negative of all is that by David Schneider (University of Chicago) in *Natural History* (June 1983). He opens his review with: "This is a bad book. It is also a dull book." And he maintains that it falls short of even the loosest standards of scholarship. Since the book, he feels, is more concerned with mounting an attack on Mead than dealing with scholarly questions, he concludes: "This is a commercial enterprise, not a contribution to knowledge." Just because it is published by a press that presents itself as scholarly, writes Schneider, does not necessarily make it a scholarly book. He notes in conclusion that "the current period seems to be one of those times when materialist, biologistic thinking is in some degree of ascendancy. Freeman's book fits into this climate very neatly. . . . It is a work that celebrates a particular political climate by denigrating another."

Like most of the anthropologists who have reviewed Freeman's *Margaret Mead and Samoa: The Making and Unmaking of an Anthropological Myth*, I am highly critical of the work and consider it not a scholarly analysis of a culture but a witch hunt whose target is not just Margaret Mead but Franz Boas and American anthropology in general. Some New Zealand and Australian anthropologists have already branded the opposition to this book "nationalistic" but one need not be an American to recognize the unscientific bias, the shoddy methodology, and the lack of professional ethics that characterize the Freeman attempt at refutation of Margaret Mead's work.

Some of my disenchantment with Freeman and his "scientific" refutation of Mead is derived from his statements to the media concerning what he accomplished in his book. An article by Jane Howard in *Smithsonian* records that Freeman believed that, due to his efforts, Margaret Mead's career might "do a 32" (32 feet per second per second being the rate at which falling bodies accelerate through space) and that he "may have written a book that will create the greatest donouement in the history of anthropology so far, not excepting Piltdown Man!" (Howard 1983:67).

Instead of making a contribution to anthropology and Samoan

ethnography, I believe that Freeman's enterprise is largely self-serving. Although Derek Freeman maintains that he is out to refute Mead's "negative instance" and thereby destroy the validity of the Boasian paradigm of "absolute cultural determinism," his attacks on Margaret Mead's writings often draw upon data from others (such as myself) who also follow the Boasian theoretical frame of reference. Why are my data (when they criticize Mead) so sound and Mead's so faulty? I also confirm the position that Ta'ū village adolescent behavior represents a "negative instance," but one does not acquire celebrity status by refuting *my* data!

Derek Freeman, on many occasions, has made the charge that I am a "decidedly suspect witness" because I was under pressure from my advisor, Melville J. Herskovits (a classmate of Mead's) to confirm the Mead/Boas paradigm. In correspondence with the editor of the *Anthropology Newsletter* in April 1984, Freeman wrote:

> In the controversy over my book, Professor Holmes, as a principal supporter of Mead's conclusions, is a decidedly suspect witness. In 1967, when I inquired of him how, given the fact of evidence in his PhD thesis markedly at variance with Mead, he could possibly claim that the "reliability" of Mead's account of Samoa was "remarkably high." Holmes replied that while he disagreed with Mead on "many points of interpretation," he did believe that "the majority of her facts were correct." He then went on, however, to state (these being his exact words of August 1, 1967): "I think it is quite true that Margaret finds pretty much what she wants to find. While I was quite critical of many of her ideas and observations I do not believe that a thesis is quite the place to expound them. I was forced by my faculty advisor to soften my criticism." To which he added: "The only tragedy about Mead is that she still refuses to accept the idea that she might have been wrong on her first field trip."

In reply to Freeman's letter (printed in the same issue) I stated:

> It is interesting how Derek Freeman, who is so quick to accuse the American anthropological community of unethical and unprofessional tactics, feels that it is perfectly proper to put his own self-serving interpretations on statements made by me in personal correspondence. . . . Since my letters to him were written on overseas aerograms, and I therefore have no copies of what I wrote, I can only assume that Dr. Freeman is a gentleman enough to have quoted me accurately. I am particularly upset by Freeman's accusation that my dissertation was censored by my mentor Melville J. Herskovits, who felt obligated to protect the

theoretical position of his teacher, Franz Boas. If one were to read my dissertation one would find numerous criticisms of Mead's Samoan research findings concerning ethos, but what is not found is a nit-picking inventory of every misspelled Samoan word and every observed discrepancy in ceremonial detail which marred the first draft of my dissertation. Herskovits maintained that I should deal with substantive issues of interpretation and not engage in witch-hunt tactics. I believe his recommendation was that I should be "icily objective." I will admit that in 1967 I might very well have written Derek Freeman that "she still refuses to accept the idea that she might have been wrong on her first field trip." My relationship with Margaret Mead was a very stormy one for several years after my restudy of her work. However, the statements I made about Mead "finding pretty much what she started out to find" was not in any way meant to imply that she falsified data. Ultimately Margaret Mead did admit that there might have been some errors in her interpretations of Samoan behavior. This was done in a chapter titled "Conclusions 1969," written for the second edition of her Bishop Museum monograph *Social Organization of Manua*(1969). Here she acknowledges a series of problems in reconciling her interpretations of Samoan ethos with those of later investigators (including Freeman and myself).

Derek Freeman was convinced that I was so intimidated by Mead's reputation and so much under the thumb of Herskovits that I didn't even attempt to challenge the "absolute cultural determinist" conclusions of Mead's Samoan study and instead spent my time doing a study of Samoan acculturation. In *Margaret Mead and Samoa*, Freeman writes:

> Lowell D. Holmes was working on a doctoral dissertation entitled "A Restudy of Manu'an Culture," which he was to submit in 1957 to the department of anthropology at Northwestern University. Holmes had gone to Samoa early in 1954, after preliminary training under Melville Herskovits, who was a follower of Boas, a friend of Mead, and a fervent cultural determinist. Because of the crucial role Mead's writings on Samoa had played in the establishment of the Boasian paradigm, there was, from a scientific point of view every reason to subject her conclusions to detailed testing by further investigations in the field. These conclusions had, however, become so well established in the anthropological departments of Northwestern and other universities as to seem eternally true, and Holmes made their systematic testing no part of his concern. Instead he devoted his energies to an "acculturation study" in

which his objectives were the description of contemporary Manu'an culture and the documentation of changes that had "taken place in the course of the history of European contact." [1983:103–10]

Beginning with the word "description," Freeman is quoting directly from the preface of my book *Ta'ū: Stability and Change in a Samoan Village*, which was published by the Polynesian Society in 1958. This was not my dissertation and this was not a critique of Mead's work. That effort, which Freeman says I did not make, is to be found in my 1957 doctoral dissertation entitled *A Restudy of Manu'an Culture: A Problem in Methodology* (available from University Microfilms International, Ann Arbor, Michigan). The major conclusions of that volume form the content of chapter 8 of this book, "Assessing Margaret Mead."

OBJECTIVITY IN FREEMAN'S STUDY

My restudy of Mead's Samoan research focused on reliability and validity and how these factors could be influenced by the personal equation. It is a quite natural extension that I am equally interested in Derek Freeman's methodological procedures and personal characteristics and the extent to which they meet the test in regard to accepted canons of objectivity and procedural ethics. The hallmark of science is objectivity. When I was a graduate student, I was taught that the ethnographic literature describing a given culture was valuable but not necessarily error-free. I was cautioned to go into the field with an open mind and to use cultural relativism both as a philosophical frame of reference and as a methodological tool. When I settled down in Ta'ū village I had no idea whether Margaret Mead was right or wrong in her pronouncements about Samoan culture and personality. It would have been to my professional advantage if I had been able to prove that this famous anthropologist had been in error on her first field trip, but that had nothing to do with the scientific mission I had accepted. Derek Freeman, from all the evidence I have seen, including his personal correspondence with me, was absolutely convinced that Margaret Mead was wrong and he set out to prove it. Since Freeman has stated, on many occasions, that he rejects cultural relativism as a methodological tool (which basically *demands* going to another culture with an open mind), perhaps he feels that it is also unscientific to approach the work of another investigator with an open mind.

From my correspondence with Freeman in 1966–67, it was obvious that his inquiries concerning my restudy of Mead were mostly di-

rected at finding out my criticisms of Mead. He persistently questioned my claim that Mead's research was remarkably reliable and
valid, and he discounted specific statements of mine that corroborated
Mead's ideas and concepts. When I told him of the personality testing
I had carried out and how I thought the results confirmed Mead's
conceptualization of Samoan character, he maintained that such tests
(California Test of Personality, Edwards Personality Preference Schedule, and Rogers Test of Personality Adjustment) probably did not have
cross-cultural validity. Freeman's letter of April 25, stated, for example:

> I am interested in your 'personality text material' which
> you are proposing to submit to computer analysis. I pre-
> sume that these are data derived from the tests given to
> students of the high school of American Samoa. My own
> training in psychology and my assessments of Samoan
> character lead me to have marked reservations about tests
> handled in this way. As you are probably aware, the Sa-
> moans (as a result of their experiences in childhood) are a
> highly repressed and defensive people, whose behavior is
> characterized by denial and deceptiveness to a high de-
> gree.

THE ISSUE OF RAPPORT

Despite the fact that he was a middle-aged man living with his wife in
a Western Samoan village more than 40 years after Mead worked in
the Manu'an village of Ta'ū in American Samoa, Freeman chooses to
believe that any discrepancies between his assessments and Mead's
are due only to her inability to use the language properly, her inexperience in field research, naivete, and cultural deterministic bias.
According to him, Margaret Mead was duped by her young informants. It is interesting to note that in an earlier debate with Melvin
Ember about Samoan culture, Freeman suggested that Ember's work
was incorrect because he was "an inexperienced ethnographer, lacking a command of the Samoan language and residing in a village for
only a few weeks or months" (1964:555). Also, in the *Anthropology
Newsletter* correspondence previously cited, he stated his standards
for quality research in Polynesia as "complete fluency in the local
language and intensive field research lasting for at least two years
continuously. These, I would note, are conditions that Holmes, in his
Samoan researches has never met" (Sept. 1984). Apparently some
three and one half years in the field over a period of thirty-two years
puts me at a disadvantage.

If one were to ask Derek Freeman why he was able to obtain the "truth" about Samoan culture from these people he characterizes as masters of duplicity, he would probably respond, as he has on numerous talk shows, that it is partly because he is a Samoan chief. He is not the first anthropologist, however, to be made a chief. My title, awarded in Ta'ū village in 1954, is Tuife'ai (King of Fierce Cannibals), but I have never considered this honor anything more than a friendly gesture (or perhaps a good joke) that is not to be taken seriously by anyone. Since holding a title involves both family responsibility and a certain amount of control over family property, including land, it is hardly something that Samoans grant foreigners *seriously*. Being known as the "King of Fierce Cannibals" has done little for me as an anthropologist other than give me access to *fono* (village council) deliberations.

Continuing with the issue of Freeman's rapport with his Samoan subjects, one must consider the quality of his survey of virginity among 67 females aged 14–19. In a society where the church is very restrictive and where young women, according to Freeman, are accomplished at distorting the truth (thereby completely "duping" Margaret Mead), one might question the extent to which an elderly white man and his wife could establish adequate rapport on such a sensitive subject. Exact knowledge could only be acquired through medical examinations, which as far as I know were not conducted.

I also have grave doubts about the research Freeman conducted on parent–child bonding. He states: "The primary bond between mother and child is very much a part of the biology of Samoans, as it is of all humans" (1983:203). He then goes on to describe how he and his wife tested the claim by Mead that "filial affection is diffused among a large group of relatives." The Freemans had the women of an extended family household walk away from an infant one at a time and recorded the child's response. Freeman maintains that an agitated reaction was forthcoming from the infant only when the separation involved the biological mother. This is pure ethological nonsense, and I have personally observed that adopted children showed no recognition of a biological mother when the two were temporarily reunited. Considering that Freeman condemns cultural explanations for behavior and calls for greater emphasis on biological interpretations in modern anthropology, it is interesting that this is one of the few places in Freeman's book where any kind of biological interpretation of Samoan behavior is presented.

CONTROLS IN RESTUDY LOCALITY

When one restudies the work of an earlier investigator, great care must be taken so that the data are comparable. Freeman's method of dealing with this problem is interesting. He begins by quoting George Turner (a 19th-century missionary) to the effect that the Samoans have but one dialect and have long maintained free communication from island to island (1961:279). He then cites a statement by Bradd Shore, that "culturally and linguistically, the entire Samoan archipelago reveals a remarkably unified identity and striking homogeneity," (1977:ix) and proceeds to attack Mead's observations of life on Ta'ū in 1925 with his own data drawn from Sa'anapu in the 1940s, 1966–67, and 1981. There are, however, just too many uncontrolled variables involved in Freeman's Ta'ū–Sa'anapu comparisons to make his case convincing.

It is perfectly correct that Samoans throughout the entire archipelago share a common culture; however, it is not true that Samoans behave in exactly the same way in all villages and on all islands. Just as the people of rural and small-town America, or Australia, think and behave differently in some respects from people in major metropolises, we can expect villages with varying degrees of isolation and with different political and economic histories to shape the lives of their residents in different ways.

When I was working in Ta'ū village in 1954 it was physically and culturally much as it had been when Mead was there, and many of the people with whom she had worked were still living. The village was different from others I have studied in subsequent years, and was quite different in its economy, history, and social organization from villages I have observed on the south coast of Upolu (where Sa'anapu is located). Keesing describes the Manu'a group, where Ta'ū is located, as islands which "have tended to retain their historic isolation; with the western end of Savai'i they form strongholds of conservatism" (1934:20).

In 1954 none of the Manu'a islands had a dock, and inter-island vessels called only about once a month. None of the islands had any vehicles, so one traveled between Ta'ū village and Fitiuta in exactly the way Mead had done, either by muddy mountain footpath or by long-boat. Ta'ū island provided only a handful of salaried jobs (teachers and nurses mostly), and almost everyone was engaged in subsistence agriculture. The only cash crop was copra (which provided a very small income). Schooling was available to the eighth grade; very few people had gone that far. Approximately 95 percent of the housing was of traditional architecture; there were no radios, no electricity, and no sanitary facilities.

Sa'anapu, on the other hand, is in Western Samoa, a country with a colonial history very different from that of Ta'ū. Gilson records that Manu'a took no part in the politics of the remainder of Samoa during the nineteenth century (1970:55). Although Sa'anapu is on the opposite side of the island of Upolu from Apia, in 1954 a daily bus was already providing communication with that port town, with its commercial establishments, theatres, nightclubs, libraries, and government buildings. Villagers on all parts of Upolu have for some time been heavily involved in working such cash crops as cocoa, bananas, copra, and coffee. People tired of working in agriculture could also find a fair number of jobs in Apia, which has been a cosmopolitan community with substantial numbers of European inhabitants for over a century. Gilson describes mid-nineteenth-century Apia as follows:

> Each side of the Vaisigano [the river bisecting Apia] also acquired its grog shops, boarding houses, billiard parlours and bowling alleys—'amenities' supported largely by transient trade. In addition, blacksmiths, coopers, mechanics and auctioneers set up at Apia Bay, some independently and others as employees or associates of the mercantile houses. The medical profession was also represented, with two 'surgeons' in practice during the 1850s. And contrary to the hope expressed earlier by the London Missionary Society, there was a large proportion of unskilled labourers among the immigrants. In 1856, about seventy-five foreigners were in more or less permanent residence at Apia Bay, and in 1860, more than one hundred; and these were often outnumbered by visitors and castaways. [1970:178]

Government census records for 1971 show 1,688 foreigners living in Apia and an additional 662 living in other parts of Upolu. Only 1,350 of the foreigners living on Upolu were Europeans, but in Ta'ū the only people of European ancestry who have ever been in even semipermanent residence have been a few U.S. Navy Pharmacist Mates, a handful of anthropologists and a few teachers (the latter only since the establishment of a high school approximately thirteen years ago). To maintain that these environmental differences have not differentially affected the behavioral patterns of the people of Sa'anapu and Ta'ū is incorrect.

There is also evidence that Sa'anapu has been for some time culturally more modern than most outlying villages in Western Samoa. J. W. Davidson, who resided in Western Samoa from 1947 to 1967, records the following about Sa'anapu and its village leadership:

> In Sa'anapu, for example, 'Anapu Solofa—the Leader of the Fono of Faipule—had allocated land definitively to the different branches of his *'aiga* and, like Va'ai Kolone, had abandoned many of his claims as a *matai*, in order to encourage his kinsmen to develop their own plantations.

In many villages, therefore, Samoans were reorganizing and expanding their agricultural activities and modifying, in varying degrees, the conventions of the Samoan social system. [1967:238]

TIME FRAMES

Not only must an anthropological restudy be made in the same locality as the original, but the time factor must be handled with great care. Although it was apparent to me in 1954 that Samoan culture was extremely conservative, my first consideration in the analysis and evaluation of Mead's materials was to control for the factor of change, reconstructing the culture of the mid-nineteenth century and the 1920–30 period. Freeman, on the other hand, states arbitrarily that

There is . . . no reason to suppose that Samoan society and behavior changed in any fundamental way during the fourteen years between 1926, the year of the completion of Mead's inquiries, and 1940, when I began my own observations of Samoan behavior. [1983:120]

Having established this dubious and undocumented premise, Derek Freeman goes on to state that he will "draw on the evidence of his own research in the 1940s, the years 1965 to 1968, and 1981" (1983: 120). He also uses historical sources, many going back to the late 1700s, as evidence against Mead's interpretations. I once wrote an article about the great stability of traditional Samoan culture (see Holmes 1980), but Freeman deals with the island group as though it has existed in an absolutely static condition despite its long history of contact with explorers, whalers, missionaries, colonial officials and bureaucrats, anthropologists and, more recently, educators with Western curricula and television networks.

USE OF GOVERNMENT DOCUMENTS

In *Margaret Mead and Samoa* Derek Freeman writes that his "researches were not completed until 1981, when I finally gained access to the archives of the High Court of American Samoa for the 1920s. Thus my refutation of Mead's depiction of Samoa appears some years after her death" (1983: xvi). It should be noted, however, that the bulk of the attack on Mead's work had already been formalized by 1968 (when Mead was still alive and well) in a privately distributed paper which

Freeman titled "On the believing of as many as six impossible things before breakfast; an analysis of the consequences of cathecting assumptions in cultural and social anthropology."

A seminar paper developed in 1978 entitled " 'Sweet Analytics, 'tis thou hast ravished me': a critical appreciation of the sexual values and behaviour of the Samoans of Western Polynesia" (sent out to select anthropologists—not me—with "confidential" stamped on the title page), carried many of the ideas which appear in Chapter 16 of *Margaret Mead and Samoa*.

Court records, which Freeman maintains were not open to him until 1981 (although I had complete access to them in 1954), reveal the fact that apparently in American Samoa some fourteen rapes per year occurred from 1975 to 1980. Freeman also states that court records from American Samoa show "numerous cases" of rape recorded for the first three decades of this century. He tells us nothing about where these rapes were committed nor even whether they were committed by Samoans. There has always been a sizeable population of Navy personnel or Department of Interior personnel in the American territory during this century. I know for a fact that there are no records of rapes occuring in Manu'a at the time of Mead's research and none for 1954 when I was doing my restudy of Mead. Rape and other violent crimes tend to be urban phenomena in the Pacific, and R. G. Crocombe has pointed out that "within Western Samoa, nearly 70 percent of the reported crime is said to be committed among the 18 percent of the population which lives in the capital" (1973:103). The same is true in American Samoa, where the area of Pago Pago Bay is the scene of the kind of crime that Derek Freeman makes so much of. And clearly this results from social disorganization brought on by cultural change and not a biological disposition toward aggression inherent in the Samoan make-up.

Felix Keesing quotes a government official in American Samoa concerning crime and juvenile delinquency in American Samoa in 1930 as follows:

> There are few crimes in the out districts other than acts of violence—assault with a knife, sex matters affecting the old native ideas of right and wrong such as those involving a chief's daughter—while civil cases cover such matters as straying pigs or trespass. Crimes such as breaking and entering, stealing, drunkenness and bootlegging are committed by people from villages around the naval station; nearly all crimes committed by boys and young men that come to our attention are likewise from these villages. [1934:240]

In regard to crimes in Western Samoa, Freeman maintains that government records reveal that in 1977 ten murders were committed which represents for the population of 150,000 a rate of 6.66 per 100,000. Cases of assault "causing bodily injury" that were reported to the police in the years 1964–66 showed a rate of 105.1 per 100,000 population (67 percent higher than the U.S. rate), and in the years 1964–66 the rate of common assault in Western Samoa was 773.35 per 100,000 of population, a rate 5 times that of the United States (1983:163–65). While many of these statistics may be correct, Vaiao and Fay Ala'ilima (noted authors and scholars of Samoan culture) at a conference at California State University, Fullerton in 1984 stated that they had searched the government records in Western Samoa at some length but had been unable to find much of the data which Freeman utilizes to establish that Samoans have an abnormally high incidence of murder, assault and other crimes of passion.

Derek Freeman pins much of his case against Mead's picture of Samoan temperament on government records from American Samoa to which he claims he did not have access until after Margaret Mead's death, but there is reason to question the validity of these data. It has been my experience that Samoans are not very careful record keepers, and I have found great discrepancies in government records. Apparently, others have also. Michael Hartmann, a United Nations demographer who was involved in the analysis of the 1976 census of Western Samoa, writes:

> The quality of vital registration is substandard because the registration of vital events is seen as a colonial remnant. After all, the registration of births and deaths in many parts of the underdeveloped world was introduced by colonial authorities. Another explanation may be that the reasons for vital registration are vague in the minds of politicians. In the case of Western Samoa it might prove more efficient to delegate the responsibility to the church organizations. [1980:309–310]

In American Samoa the quality of government records may be judged by their data on suicides for the year 1974. The Government of American Samoa Health Coordinating Council publication *American Samoa Plan for Health* (1978) records that "in 1974, there were 10 suicides in American Samoa for a rate of 34/100,000, an unacceptably high rate for an 'island paradise'" [1978:55–56] but the *Annual Report to the Secretary of the Interior* for the fiscal year 1975 records that in the previous year there were five suicides in American Samoa (1975:63). I spent several weeks going through government records both in 1954 and in 1962; in 1954 I discovered the startling fact that in that year the third most common cause of infant mortality was arteriosclerosis (15 deaths).

USE OF THE LITERATURE

Considering the fact that Freeman is often described as a brilliant researcher,[1] one might wonder at his methods for building a case from the anthropological literature. He uses literature selectively to support his position—a technique that is quite distinct from the way most anthropologists were taught to do research. He accepts the authors' statements he agrees with and ignores those he disagrees with and in some cases uses only portions of a quote if the total quote contains parts injurious to his position. While he cites or quotes my work twenty-six times in *Margaret Mead and Samoa* these are almost exclusively my critical statements concerning Mead's work. He either completely ignores or discounts my statements of corroboration. Nor is he particularly prudent in the selection of the sources he quotes. On one occasion he discusses how Mead's informants duped her by fabricating the information they told her in interviews, and the source he quotes, believe it or not, is Nicholas von Hoffman's and Gary Trudeau's book *Tales from the Margaret Mead Taproom* (1976:97) which is nothing but a spoof on anthropology, Margaret Mead, and Samoa, written almost entirely from "information" gathered in the bar of the Rainmaker Hotel in Pago Pago.

There are other examples of Derek Freeman's questionable use of the literature. He quotes Ronald Rose's assertions that Samoan mannerisms imply aggressive tendencies (which help to build his case against Mead), but completely ignores such statements by Rose as: "If a girl hasn't had a succession of lovers by the time she is seventeen or eighteen she feels she is 'on the shelf,' and becomes the laughing stock amongst her companions" (1959:161). This statement, of course, would hurt Freeman's case against Mead as would the following by Rose: "Mental disturbances, stresses and conflicts occur at puberty but, as might be expected, these are not quite as common as in our society where taboos associated with sex abound" (1959:164). He does not quote this either.

In *Margaret Mead and Samoa* Freeman states that "Campbell observed that with several of the broader aspects of Mead's account of Samoa, such as the lack of competitive spirit and the lack of crisis in human relations, Holmes's findings were in 'complete disagreement'" (1983:105). It should be pointed out that his reference to "complete disagreement" is taken out of context and thereby gives a faulty impression. What Donald Campbell actually was saying is conveyed in the following quote:

> As far as the great bulk of Mead's ethnology, Holmes confirms her findings, stating "the reliability of Mead's account is remarkably high." While he reports some differences in the description of traditional political systems and other matters, on matters of material culture and observable custom, there is general agreement. This extends also to the observed absence of an adolescent disturbance on the part of the girls, and the easy transition from childhood to adult life. But upon several of the broader aspects of ethos, his findings are in complete disagreement, for example, upon the lack of specialized feeling in human relations, the lack of competitive spirit, the lack of crisis in human relations, and the importance of "Mafaufau," or the gift of wise judgment. [1972:444]

It should be noted that Freeman did not mention that my disagreements with Mead were over matters of ethos, an area which Campbell believes is so much a matter of emotional response that "ethos may indeed be beyond the realm of scientific study" (Campbell 1961:340).

ON THE MATTER OF SAMOAN AGGRESSION

Much of the refutation of the anthropology of Margaret Mead is based on Freeman's divergent interpretations of Samoan aggression and Samoan sexuality, the two being related in some instances. In regard to Samoan "aggressiveness" and associated behavioral characteristics Freeman makes the following assertions:

1. Samoans are aggressive;
2. Samoans have strong passions;
3. Samoan authoritarianism results in emotional stress and psychopathological behavior;
4. Samoan personality is characterized by ambivalence toward authority figures;

1. *Samoans are aggressive:* Freeman's Chapter 11, titled "Aggressive behavior and warfare," is a detailed challenge to Mead's position that Samoans are unaggressive and "one of the most amiable, least contentious, and most peaceful peoples in the world" (Freeman 1983:157). His first example of their overly aggressive nature pertains to the La Pérouse massacre, wherein Samoans on the island of Tutuila

attacked and killed a number of the explorer's crew. On the surface
this is impressive evidence, but Newton Rowe (who did research in
Western Samoa at about the same time as Mead was in Manu'a)
presents a different picture. He writes: "To those who know their
character it is inconceivable that the Samoans attacked without
provocation" (1930:16). Rowe then proceeds to explain that the attack
was provoked when French crew members hung a Samoan from the
top of a long-boat mast by his thumbs. After presenting the La
Pérouse example, Freeman states: "It was not, however, until the early
1830s that the bellicosity of the Samoans became firmly established
through the observations and inquiries of the pioneer missionary and
explorer John Williams" (1983:158). While Williams encountered a
certain amount of strife associated with the despotic reign and subsequent assassination of the powerful chief Tamafaiga, he described his
departure from the islands after his first visit as follows:

> Many hundred also of the natives crowded round us, by all
> of whom we were treated with the greatest possible re-
> spect, and these rent the air with their affectionate saluta-
> tions, exclaiming O le alofi i le ali'i, "Great is our affection
> for you English Chiefs." [1839:302]

It is difficult to undertstand how an investigator seriously studying
Samoan character with the aid of historical sources would not include
the statement made by the first European explorer actually to make
contact (in 1722) with the people of Ta'ū. After observing them for two
hours on board his ship, Commodore Jacob Roggeveen commented:

> They appeared to be good people, lively in their manner of
> conversing, gentle in their deportment towards each other,
> and in their manners nothing was perceived of the sav-
> age. . . . It must be acknowledged that this was the nation
> the most civilized and honest of any that we had seen
> among the Islands of the South Sea. They were charmed
> with our arrival amongst them, and received us as di-
> vinities. And when they saw us preparing to depart, they
> testified much regret. [Burney 1816:576]

The above would not make good reading in a chapter on the
aggressive nature of Samoans and obviously was not included for that
reason; perhaps Dr. Freeman is not familiar with much of the Samoan
literature.

It is true that the early literature, particularly that produced by
explorers, often referred to the hostile nature of Samoan islanders,
but R. P. Gilson records in *Samoa 1830 to 1900* that, in the early 1840s,
"Lafond de Lurcy, a shipwrecked mariner travelling aboard the vessel

[Lloyd], was convinced that the Samoans' bad reputation was a myth kept alive by ships' captains to discourage desertions" (1970:66). Gilson also notes that George Bass, the man who supplied provisions for Botany Bay, might have given one of the more favorable accounts concerning the temperament of Samoans, "for in 1803 he visited Tutuila to trade for fruit and vegetables and found the Samoans he encountered friendly and receptive. Moreover, he found an Englishman there, a man who claimed to have drifted to the island from Tonga several years before and who, when offered his passage back to civilization, elected to remain where he was" (ibid.:67).

Maintaining that "their society is conducive to aggressive behavior" (1983:163), Freeman describes a series of conflicts between villages, districts, and royal factions in Samoan history and prehistory, which leaves the impression that this was characteristically a warlike, violent society. However, I do not believe that martial conflicts were either as frequent or as brutal as Freeman would have us believe. Missionaries Brown and Turner both tell us that when groups of opposing warriors met they would exchange kava roots and speeches and make plans about the time that battles would begin. John Williams records that impending war took up considerable time in aboriginal Samoa. Meetings were held in a large guest house or on the village green *(malae)* and often went on for ten or twelve months before hostilities commenced (LMS Microfilm:1832). He further maintains that although wars were frequent, they were not very bloody. Five or six deaths were an average. Turner, however, says that the death rate in a war could be anywhere from two to fifty (1861:301). Newton Rowe describes Samoan warfare as involving "a few skirmishes in ambush by land, or at respectable distances in their war-canoes at sea," and that the contest was decided "without much loss of life, until some fresh occasion brought about a similar scene" (1930:70–71).

Ellison maintains that "frequent struggles between rivals for the kingship [of Western Samoa] were not uncommon. Such conflicts took place before the advent of the missionaries in 1830 and again in 1845 and 1869. These wars were not very destructive and often were looked upon as a pleasant diversion, a sort of game, with the prospect of gaining military distinction for the number of heads taken." Whatever predisposition Samoans might have had for engaging in such conflicts was, according to Ellison, greatly exacerbated by the machinations of Europeans. He writes, "The injection of intrigue and domination by the white man increased the susceptability of the native Samoan to the disease of war. First, there was the land question. The natives bitterly resented the loss of their best lands to the foreigners, especially the Germans, whom they accused of acquiring their planta-

tion land through trickery" (Ellison 1953:96). Testimony to this allegation is to be found in *The Story of Lauli'i* wherein Lauli'i Willis records,
"What has been the cause of the natives parting with their lands? For
purposes of gain, white men in business in Samoa have encouraged
and fostered the disputes between the tribes, and then liberally supplied them with arms and ammunition, charging exorbitant prices,
and taking in payment the most fertile lands in the country" (Willis
1889:37).

Robert Louis Stevenson, whose sojourn in Samoa from 1890 to 1894
was marred by the dangers of intrasocietal warfare, described the
people's "warlike" behavior as follows:

> The religious sentiment of the people is indeed for peace at
> any price; no pastor can bear arms; and even the layman
> who does so is denied the sacraments. In the last war the
> college of Malua, where the picked youth are prepared for
> the ministry, lost but a single student; the rest, in the
> bosom of a bleeding country and deaf to the voices of
> vanity and honour, peacefully pursued their studies. But if
> the church looks askance on war, the warrior in no ex-
> tremity of need or passion forgets his consideration for the
> church. The houses and gardens of her ministers stand
> safe in the midst of armies; a way is reserved for them-
> selves along the beach, where they may be seen in their
> white kilts and jackets openly passing the lines, while not a
> hundred yards behind the skirmishers will be exchanging
> the useless volleys of barbaric warfare. Women are also
> respected; they are not fired upon; and they are suffered to
> pass between the hostile camps, exchanging gossip,
> spreading rumours, and divulging to either army the se-
> cret councils of the other. This is plainly no savage war; it
> has all the punctilio of the barbarian, and all his parade;
> feasts precede battles, fine dresses and songs decorate and
> enliven the field; and the young soldier comes to camp
> burning (on the one hand) to distinguish himself by acts of
> valour, and (on the other) to display his acquaintance with
> field etiquette. [1892:147–148]

The above, strangely enough, was written by the man who Freeman quotes numerous times in *Margaret Mead and Samoa* and who he
describes as "incomparable." This is also the man who in *A Footnote to
History* characterized Samoans as "easy, merry, and pleasure loving;
the gayest, though by far from either the most capable or the most
beautiful of Polynesians" (1892:148). Equally impressed was his step-
son Lloyd Osbourne, who described Samoans as "extraordinarily
good-looking, with gracious manners and an innate love of what for

lack of a better term I will call 'good form.' To fail in any of the little courtesies of life is to write oneself down a boor" (1930:xiv). Yet another testimony on Samoan manners and demeanor is to be found in a letter by one "Dr. Wood," which is reproduced in Willis' book *The Story of Lauli'i*. This European resident of Western Samoa records that

> the Samoans are hospitable, affectionate, honest and cour-
> teous, and have well been described as a nation of gen-
> tlemen. Towards strangers they display a liberality which
> contrasts greatly with the cruel and blood-thirty customs of
> the Papuan tribes. The Fijians, for example, do all in their
> power to repel strangers from their shores, either driving
> them off, or killing and eating them. The Samoans, on the
> contrary, welcome strangers, allot to them their best
> houses, give them the best food and make them feel that
> they are honored guests.
>
> Courtesy is, among the Samoans reckoned as one of the
> duties of life. . . . The earlier voyagers have all been struck
> with the gentle demeanor, perfect honesty, scrupulous
> cleanliness, graceful costume and polished manner of the
> Samoans. [1889:180]

2. *Samoans have strong passions:* In *Margaret Mead and Samoa* we are told that "central to Mead's depiction of Samoan character is her claim that among Samoans there are 'no strong emotions.' 'Love, hate, jealousy and revenge, sorrow and bereavement,' we are told, are all matters of weeks; a 'lack of deep feeling' has been 'conventionalized' by Samoans 'until it is the very framework of all their attitudes to life' " . . . (1983:212).

My own observations of behavior in Ta'ū village were that residents seemed to go to extremes to avoid conflict and to arrive at compromises. Village council decisions always had to be unanimous, and council meetings often dragged on for days while the assembled chiefs made minor concessions until everyone was satisfied with the collective decision. Breaches of acceptable conduct or the moral code often involved elaborate ceremonies of apology, called *ifoga*, during which persons, families, or even entire villages publicly humbled themselves, sitting cross-legged with mats over their bowed heads, until forgiven by the offended party. Even murder and manslaughter were handled this way if government authorities permitted it. This nonviolent tradition has long been observed, as George Brown, a nineteenth-century missionary testifies:

> gossiping, tale-bearing, were universally condemned. It is
> rather singular, by the way, that the term used for backbit-
> ing *(tuāupua)* literally means "wordy behind the back." The

aged were reverenced, and there are probably no people in the world more polite than the Samoans. Any person acting otherwise is called *utafanua* or *faalevao*, i.e. a man from inland or a bushman. [1910:264]

Derek Freeman alleges that Samoan temperament results in people being jealous, harboring grudges and acting on impulse, often with violence, but the following events reported by United Press International in 1982 and by *Pacific Islands Monthly* in 1971 present a very different picture of Samoan response to crisis situations.

2 WITNESSES FORGIVE KILLER OF RELATIVE
United Press International

HONOLULU—Two relatives of a murder victim have observed the American Samoan tradition of forgiveness— "ifoga"—which allowed the slayer to plead guilty to a lesser charge of manslaughter.

The two relatives lived by the principle, set in the criminal code of American Samoa, and refused to testify against the defendant. They were the two key witnesses for the prosecution.

Thus, defendant Tonny Williams was allowed to plead guilty to the manslaughter charge last week after a plea bargain with the prosecution.

The relatives were living by the practice of "ifoga" in which a family seeks forgiveness from the aggrieved family so that both may continue to live in harmony.

Williams had been charged with murder in the June 1981 fatal stabbing of Anosau Foutuua in Hawaii.

In the court statement, Williams said he got into a fight with the victim and, "although I do not exactly remember if I stabbed Anosau Foutuua, the evidence indicates that I did."

Rick Reed, administrative assistant to Prosecutor Charles Marsland, said the problem with the case was that there were no witnesses willing to testify.

According to Reed, the two witnesses said "they would go to jail before testifying because it was over (as a result of at least two 'ifogas'). They fully forgave Williams."

Rather than lose the case, the prosecutor's office was forced to accept Williams' offer to plead guilty to manslaughter, Reed said. [5/31/82]

DRINK AND FA'A SAMOA

Centuries-old Samoan custom and modern United States justice confronted each other in the High Court in Pago Pago towards the end of June. It was a kind of legalistic tug-of-war and the prize—a man's freedom. The man, an Australian navyman, went to gaol.

But there was give and take with honour satisfied on both sides. Only the man, and a woman, lost in the end and, because of *Fa'a Samoa* (in the Samoan way), he is due out of gaol in August. He could have been inside for five years.

It all happened this way.

The Royal Australian Navy destroyer *Queenborough* sailed into Pago harbour on June 21 for a routine goodwill visit during a training cruise. There were official visits, the traditional cocktail party on board for the local VIPS, and shore leave for the ship's company.

Franz Habenschuss, young, thin, tattooed, a career sailor with three years of faultless service and a wife and infant son in Australia, went ashore in the first group.

After a few beers in a local bar, he and four other ratings set off to see more of the island of Tutuila than the bars of the Pago Bay area. Franz drove a rented car towards the western side of the island. . . . And they drank more beer at village stores. That night the car, with Franz at the wheel, knocked down and killed Mrs. Fa'afouina Faimalie Moeivanu, who was walking along the road in the village of Futiga.

There were stories that Franz and a shipmate were beaten by villagers. The local police took over and Franz was locked up. The following afternoon he pleaded guilty in the High Court to a charge of driving while drunk and causing a woman's death.

It was then that *Fa'a Samoa* took over. Commander Donald Weil, the destroyer captain, and some of his officers went to Futiga along with High Chief Sonoma Unutoa, deputy secretary of the Office of Samoan Affairs. With them they carried $250, collected by *Queenborough's* crew for the Moeivanu family, plus a pile of traditional fine mats, one of the basic symbols of Samoan ceremonial.

The money and mats were presented and Chief Unutoa voiced the apologies of Commander Weil and the ship's company on Franz' behalf. Futiga High Chief Ulufale and other village leaders responded. Custom, Samoan custom, which has settled disputes for centuries was satisfied. Franz was forgiven. The matter was closed.

It was—*Fa'a Samoa*, but there was still American legal justice to satisfy. The High Court resumed the following morning and the Samoan judges heard about the ceremony, were satisfied that *Fa'a Samoa* had been followed and voted for a lengthy sentence which would be immediately suspended, allowing Franz to rejoin the *Queenborough*.

Then American justice spoke through Associate Justice
Goss. . . . He overruled the Samoan judges, and imposed
a sentence of 200 days subject to parole, which could mean
Franz' release in 64 days. . . . The *Queenborough* sailed and
Franz went to gaol. But, once again, *Fa'a Samoa* prevailed.
The gaol warden, Chief Fele Falasuamaile, who was a relative of the dead woman, had heard that during the anxious
hours of the hearing, Franz couldn't eat. Chief Fele took
him to a hotel, bought him a meal and tried to persuade
him to eat. . . . The gaol authorities, bending over back-
wards to help, are currently allowing Franz to leave gaol for
visits in local homes. [1971:31]

While I became aware, during my restudy in 1954, that individual
passions could be aroused even to the point of assault, murder, or
suicide, and while I differ somewhat from Mead in my interpretation
of the placid nature of Samoans, I differ very strongly with the
Freeman position that Samoans are characteristically violent, aggressive, and strong passioned. Freeman cites a case where a chief
who arrived late at a Sa'anapu village council meeting *(fono)* demanded another kava ceremony since he missed the the one that
traditionally opens such meetings. When his demand was refused he
and another chief ended up fighting furiously just outside the *fono*
house. Such behavior would not be tolerated in the village of Ta'ū;
chiefs have far too much respect for the village council. While Freeman might have observed this behavior, such a grossly abnormal
incident has no bearing on Samoan cultural norms or Samoan personality. It is merely a description of deviant behavior, something that is
becoming more and more frequent as Samoa modernizes and secu-
larizes.

3. *Samoan authoritarianism results in emotional stress and psychopathological behavior:* Freeman's chapter on "Samoan Character" states:

Mead also claimed in *Coming of Age in Samoa* that among
Samoans there was an "absence of psychological malad-
justment," and a "lack of neuroses." Those who grow up
and live within the highly authoritarian Samoan society are
frequently subjected to emotional and mental stress, and
this experience sometimes results in psychopathological
states, suicides and other violent acts (1983:216) . . . This
tension also occasionally finds expression in outbursts of
uncontrollable anger (Ibid.:218). . . . Yet another expression of these tensions is a form of hysterical dissocia-
tion known as *ma'i aitu*, or ghost sickness. [ibid.:222]

Other observers of the Samoan scene, however, do not corroborate
Freeman's claim regarding the oppressiveness, authoritativeness, and

lack of flexibility of the Samoan social system. Grattan, for example, comments on the democratic nature of the society.

This is the society that without the horrors of revolution or even a general election has achieved the social miracle that knows neither poverty nor the stigma of illegitimacy; whose warm laws of courtesy and hospitality embrace even the unheralded stranger within its gates; a system that, in the present disordered state of world society, is, with all its faults, something that is rare and rather wonderful. [1948:158]

And in regard to matters of social and political rank he writes:

There is a mutual interdependence and recognition of titled and untitled people, and each group has its recognised and respected place in the community. Social groups in Samoa are therefore complementary: on the one hand, respect, obedience and service with the hope of a later improvement in status, and on the other, a prudent appreciation of the essential contribution of the untitled members of society. Where social inferiors feel dissatisfaction at treatment received they are at liberty to withdraw their support and attach themselves to some other branch of their family connections in another part of the country, and thus a large measure of social equilibrium and social justice is maintained. [ibid.:14]

R. P. Gilson also comments on the somewhat complex nature of the Samoan family system that on the surface appears authoritarian but upon closer scrutiny reveals itself as remarkably flexible. While the family head (*matai*) controls the recruitment of household members and has it within his power to expel any who refuse to submit to his authority (thereby threatening the unity of the group) "a member of a household—an adult member, at any rate—will always have several alternative places in which he may reside; if conditions in one become unsatisfactory, he may choose to go elsewhere" (Gilson 1970:15).

This flexibility and respect for the individual, regardless of status, that marks Samoan social relations finds expression in many aspects of life including the centuries-old kava ceremony. Here "respect and recognition are the motivating factors that influence the order of distribution, and the elasticity of Samoan custom, which is evidenced here as elsewhere, allows for a nice and discriminating judgment to be exercised by the orator directing that part of the ceremony" (Grattan 1948:49).

While Grattan's observations pertain to a period some years after Mead had documented the Samoan scene, the following quote by

George Brown, a missionary who worked in Samoa from 1860 to 1874, describes an equally comfortable social environment—certainly not one which would promote mental illness.

> With regard to the Samoan youth, it may be said that, judging from our standards, the life of the young people was on the whole a very happy one. They have of late years had to attend school, but this has never been regarded as a very serious matter by the Samoan boys and girls. As a rule, they went because they wished to go, and stayed away when they pleased to do so without any fear of punishment. [1910:59]

Even at the level of village politics the authority of the chiefs has always been limited and social participation was not only permitted but encouraged. John Williams recorded in 1832 that the chiefs had no power to compel their people, that decisions were reached at meetings on the village green *(malae)* where men, women, and children might all speak, except in the case of declaring war when women and children were not allowed to be present (LMS Microfilm 1832).

4. *Samoan personality is characterized by ambivalence toward authority figures:* The Samoans are, in Freeman's view, "a proud, punctilious, and complex God-fearing people, whose orators delight in extolling the beauty of mornings that dawn with the sanctity and dignity of their ancient polities serenely intact. Yet, as we shall see, such are the rigors of the Samoan rank system and so intense is the emotional ambivalence generated by omnipresent authority that this goal is all too frequently not attained; . . . for as anyone who has grown up within a Samoan polity well knows, 'the Samoan way is difficult indeed' " (1983:130).

Throughout the 32 years I have been researching Manu'an culture, I have observed that teenage and young adult males are given a great deal of personal freedom. Members of the *aumaga* (society of untitled men), some of whom are teen-agers, often sleep together in the home of one of the village families, and frequently sit up until wee hours strumming guitars, joking, and playing cards. If these young people are repressed, they are also adept at hiding it. Young women are perhaps more restricted and given more household responsibility than men. But they also seem relaxed in family interactions. By adolescence, Samoans have learned to regulate their own personal conduct, and there is practically no testing of the limits of sanctioned behavior.

Nor do I believe that Samoan authority was any more oppressive in 1925–26 than when I observed the culture. William Green, a government school principal in American Samoa who was in residence when Mead was there, wrote:

> Personal combats and first fights are rather rare today. I believe there has been no murder case in American Samoa since our flag was raised in 1900. Natives will suffer indignities for a long time before resorting to a fight but they remain good fighters. Boxing contests are held occasionally. . . . Respect for elders and magistrates has, I suppose, tended to discourage frequent combats. Life is easy, and one's habitual tendencies and desires are seldom blocked. [1924:134]

In other words, Green sees Samoan young people as neither aggressive nor ambivalent in their attitude toward authority. Finally, I believe that there is probably no better example of a lack of ambivalence toward authority in Samoan (or any other) history than the case of Fa'ase'e Fa'agase, a person hanged for murder in Western Samoa. The incident is described by Chief Justice C. C. Marsack of Western Samoa:

> There had been a large number of convictions for murder, but in all other cases the sentence of death had been commuted by the Governor-General of New Zealand to imprisonment for life. In Fa'ase'e's case the Governor-General did not intervene. . . . The execution was carried out in secret at Vaimea gaol: but the Sheriff had agreed that there should be a Samoan representation in the presence of two of the Samoan judges. The senior judge gave me a full report the next day.
> "Just before Fa'ase'e had to go up the steps I asked him if he wished to say anything, and if he wanted to give a message to Samoa. He said, 'It is right that I should die. I killed a man, and though he forgave me before he died it is not right that I should live when he is dead. And there is another reason: the Chief Judge said that I should be hanged, and whatever the Chief Judge says should be obeyed. I am very happy that this ceremony is so dignified. . . . Tell the people of Samoa that I have no complaint to make, and that not many men can die in such a dignified way as I am going to die now.' " [1961:23]

SAMOAN SEXUAL BEHAVIOR

Derek Freeman begins his chapter "Sexual Mores and Behavior" with the suggestion that the reason "*Coming of Age in Samoa* so rapidly attracted popular attention was due more than anything else to Mead's alluring portrayal of Samoa as a paradise of adolescent free love" (1983:226). However, Mead maintained that some young women of rank—village *taupou*—who were often the daughters of paramount chiefs, were not permitted to partake of the "free and easy experimentations" enjoyed by other young females. While Margaret Mead observed that occasionally even a *taupou* had to falsify evidence of virginity at her defloration ceremony which preceded her marriage to a bridegroom of rank, there was definitely a "cult of virginity" which had to be observed by a few young women of high status. Freeman, however, believes that Samoan sexual norms were extremely puritanical and he sees the "cult of virginity" as having a blanketing effect on all courtship behavior and he believes that Mead's research has done the Samoan people a grave injustice. He writes:

> According to the elders of Ta'ū who, when I interviewed them, well recollected the state of their culture in the mid 1920s, the requirement that sexually mature adolescent girls should remain chaste was at that time, very much the ideal of their strict protestant society. [1983:238]

Virginity, according to Freeman, is still a prized condition and one that is demanded by a harsh, inflexible society; he provides as his proof his investigation of virginity (the methodology is not described) among adolescent girls in Western Samoa. He states:

> In 1967 I was able to complete a detailed survey of the incidence of virginity in adolescent girls by making, with the assistance of my wife, a census of all the young females of a village on the south coast of Upolu born within the period 1945–55. This gave a sample of sixty-seven individuals varying in age from 12 to 22. [ibid.:238–239]

According to Freeman's survey, seventy-three percent (30 out of 41) of the girls between the ages of 14 and 19 claimed to be virgins. Although Freeman tells us nothing of why he believes that adolescents would tell him and his wife the truth about such a delicate matter, he obviously believes that his data on adolescent sexuality are better than that collected by Margaret Mead, and states that this proves that "after the mid-nineteenth century, when a puritanical Christian sexual morality was added to an existing traditional cult of virginity, Samoa became a society in which chastity was . . . the ideal for all women before marriage and in which this religiously and culturally sanctioned ideal strongly influenced the actual behavior of adolescent girls" (1983:239).

Every culture projects ideal behavior in its ceremonies and its descriptions of itself to foreigners and real behavior in its homes and day-to-day social interactions. Freeman shifts back and forth between these, always to the advantage of his theories. When, for example, he is out to impress the reader with the restrictive nature of the Samoan sexual code, he points to the defloration ceremony (which was mainly performed on girls of high rank, such as *taupou*) or to the fact that village councils *(fono)* fined family heads *(matai)* when teenaged members of their households became pregnant out of wedlock. On the other hand, he ignores real behavior that indicates Samoans take a rather natural attitude toward sex before and outside of marriage. While young people in Samoa are not promiscuous, as Mead suggested, neither are they models of chastity, as Freeman would have us believe. I recall a pastor once remarking during a sermon in the Ta'ū village church, in 1954, that some Manu'an villages had reported record crops of breadfruit and bananas, but that, as usual, Ta'ū had its record crop of *tama o le po* (literally, "children of the night"—illegitimate, in other words). This, of course, was an exaggeration, but it attests that sexual experience was far from nonexistent among Ta'ū village young people.

Since Derek Freeman is prone to call upon the early literature to document his arguments on any number of subjects, let us also utilize accounts of nineteenth century as well as modern authors in assessing the quality of the Freeman statements concerning Samoan sexuality. Missionary-scholar George Brown records:

> Unchastity in either sex before marriage was not considered a very serious offence against morality, but adultery was always condemned. Unnatural crimes were abhorred. They were not common. . . . There were few cases of rape. These were not much thought of except in the case of some person of rank or by the relatives of the family. [1910:265]

Almost all observers of the nineteenth century scene indicate that they sensed that the people, while not promiscuous, were at least quite sexually active. All agreed, however, that chief's daughters (primarily those who were *taupou*) were carefully guarded in order to protect their chastity. These precautions were taken, however, not because the Samoans placed such a high moral value upon chastity but rather because a virgin bride who was also the daughter of a high chief could command a very high price in the marriage market.

The fact that the taboo on premarital sex primarily applied to the *taupou* but not the other girls of the village is substantiated by London Missionary Society reports written in 1836 by John Williams. Williams maintains that

> Young women can be deflorated by chiefs at any time in
> public ceremony. This is considered honorable and does
> not change her chances to marry. In fact—often she is
> given a special honorable name by the chief. [LMS Micro-
> film 1836]

Williams goes on to speculate that this was done because the girls
did not want to remain virgins and needed a respectable way to avoid
it. His journal also states that shortly before his arrival in the islands
that Malietoa's son had in a short space of time deflowered six girls.
These occasions, he maintains were marked by dancing, merriment,
and feasting. The fact that this sort of thing took place has never been
recorded by later missionaries. This suggests that the earliest Christian influence was such that the practice was discarded during the
early years of mission contact. It also suggests that the base line of
Samoan behavior in regard to chastity as proposed by Mead in *Coming
of Age in Samoa* is one which was established after mission contact, not
with the true aboriginal behavior. This is reasonable because without
Williams' account there has been no reason to believe that the culture
provided any flexibility in regard to the matter of chastity. However, it
does change the picture in regard to sex behavior as it is described and
evaluated by Mead and Freeman.

Margaret Mead says

> Aboriginal Samoa was harder on the girl sex delinquent
> than is present day Samoa. . . . Deviations from chastity
> were formerly punished in the case of girls by a very severe
> beating and a stigmatizing shaving of the head. Mission-
> aries have discouraged the beating and the head shaving,
> but failed to substitute as forceful an inducement to cir-
> cumspect conduct. The girls whose activities are frowned
> upon by her family is in far better position than that of her
> great grandmother. [1928:273–274]

It is true that the *taupou* who was found not to be a virgin was
beaten, but if we use Williams' information about the defloration of
girls in the village being an acceptable procedure this would indicate
that the aboriginal customs were set up so as to provide a sanctioned
departure from chastity for most girls. The *taupou* was a special case.

Now the question remains, in spite of the passing of the *taupou*
system, has the Christian church been able to extend the "cult of
virginity" to all women regardless of rank? Modern observers (other
than Freeman) seem to think not. Ronald Rose, a parapsychologist
who worked in Western Samoa about the time that I was restudying
Mead in Ta'ū writes

Sex adventures begin at an early age. Although virginity is prized, it is insisted on only with the *taupou*, who formerly was required on marriage to submit publicly to the groom's orator and exhibit the signs of virginity. . . . The *taupou* is a sort of scapegoat; she is heavily chaperoned; she symbolizes the high value placed on virginity. But the Samoans reckon that one to a village is enough!

A girl's first experience is usually with a married man, and a boy's with a married woman. Virgins, male and female, are thought of as prizes in the sex game, but a permanent adulterous relationship between the mature and the immature is frowned on. Adultery is, however, as Margaret Mead says, "exceedingly frequent." [1959:161]

And Robert Maxwell, whose studies of extroversion in American Samoa led him to investigate sexual matters, wrote:

The most frequent pattern seems to be that, at about the time of puberty, boys and girls are segregated by sex into two play groups. But they are beginning to notice members of the opposite sex. Flirtation between boys and girls is common and, apparently, sporadic sexual encounters occur. It is during this period, shortly after puberty, that many young people lose their virginity. This is by no means a universal experience, however. Some of the boys are shy, others take the rules of the church against fornication quite seriously. [1969:173]

Maxwell discovered, as did I, that sexual behavior is a very difficult area of inquiry with many pitfalls for the unwary investigator. He recalls:

I began questioning informants about their sexual activities and received, in reply, a series of fantastic distortions and exaggerations and outright falsifications. Such lies—often in these cases concerning *moetotolos*, the sneaky sexual intruders of the night, made so famous by Margaret Mead—both benefit the teller, if he is the hero, by boosting his reputation as a lover, and are presumed by the informant to entertain and please the listener. I recorded, in my field notes, as accurately as possible one story told by an informant of his crawling into his girl friend's house, having intercourse, and then being discovered and chased away by the father. A few days later I learned that the entire tale was a fabrication. [1969:180]

While I personally did not feel that Manu'a islanders were as sexually active as Margaret Mead portrayed them, neither did I find them puritanical. My own observations of Samoan sexuality are probably most compatible with those of Judge C. C. Marsack, a Chief Justice of Western Samoa for over 15 years, and an authority that Derek Freeman cites on numerous occasions in his critique of Margaret Mead. Marsack observes,

> The Samoans take a very realistic view of the subject of sex. Their outlook is healthy and no interest would be evoked if they were to see the scribblings on the walls of public latrines in the more enlightened countries. Sex is a natural fact and is to be treated as such. . . . Sex is not, in his view, a suitable topic for whispered conversations between men in the corner of a hotel bar. It is not that the female sex has no physical interest for him. On the contrary, very definitely. It is merely that the relations between the sexes constitute just one very important factor among the sum total of the factors which together make up the life of mankind. [1961:89]

The Samoan attitude toward sex is complex. There is a tradition of public tests of virginity (of high-ranking girls) and village regulations requiring the chief's council to fine the *matai* (and thereby the family) of an unwed pregnant family member on the one hand, and on the other, there is the fact that such indiscretions are easily forgiven and quickly forgotten. While perhaps no more sexually active than young people in the United States there is hardly a cult of virginity in Samoa in spite of church and village pressures. As Ronald Rose writes for Western Samoa, in Ta'ū village, "there is little, if any, stigma attached to pre-marital pregnancies. Children are always welcome in the Samoan household" (1959:162).

Derek Freeman, however, finds difficulty in reconciling the ideological and situational factors and rejects Mead's descriptions as contradictory and feasibly improbable.

> Mead's depiction of Samoan culture, as I have shown, is marked by major errors, and her account of the sexual behavior of Samoans by a mind-boggling contradiction, for she asserts that the Samoans have a culture in which female virginity is very highly valued, with a virginity-testing ceremony being "theoretically observed at weddings of all ranks," while at the same time adolescence among females is regarded as a period "appropriate for love-making," with promiscuity before marriage being permitted and "expected". . . . Something, it becomes plain at this juncture, is emphatically amiss, for surely no human population could be so cognitively disoriented as to conduct their lives in such a schizophrenic way. [1983:289]

What appears to be mind-boggling in this incidence is Freeman's lack of knowledge of the basic anthropological literature. In Robert Lowie's most famous and acclaimed monograph, *The Crow Indians*, he describes a society which, like the Samoan, contains apparently contradictory sexual themes. He writes that young Crow were extremely active sexually and that "after nightfall the young men were wont to roam about camp, blowing flutes for the amusement of their mistresses. Some venture to pull up the pegs outside the part of the tipi where a particular young woman slept and tried to touch her genitalia—a custom known as bī'arusace" (1935:50).

According to Lowie's account

> Sexual behavior was largely dominated by a double standard, which, however, was rather different from that of the Victorian era. That is to say, women were admired for immaculate purity, but they did not become outcasts by departing from the ideal.
>
> During the Sun Dance the honorific office of tree-notcher was conferred on a married woman of irreproachable fidelity, and in the same ceremony the leader of the firewood expedition was expected to be equally chaste. Even minor positions of religious character were held inconsistent with looseness. When I quoted a certain old woman's claim that she had filled such a post, my informant scoffed at the idea: Why, the Crow would never dream of choosing someone who was always running around with men. However, even a wanton was never ostracized, she simply lost prestige. [ibid.:47]

Before closing discussion on the issue of Samoan sexuality one additional matter needs to be addressed. That is the matter of rape. In *Margaret Mead and Samoa* Derek Freeman quotes statistics for Western Samoa which indicate a per annum rape rate of 160 per 100,000 females.[2] These figures, he writes, "indicate that rape is unusually common in Samoa; the Samoan rape rate is certainly one of the highest to be found anywhere in the world. . . . There is every indication that this high incidence of rape has long been characteristic of Samoan society. Cases are reported by the early missionaries, as by Pratt in 1845" (1983:249).

My own perusal of the literature does not confirm this allegation, however. George Brown found that in the 1860s and 1870s that "there were few cases of rape," (1910:265) and Newton Rowe, who worked in Western Samoa at the same time Mead was in Manu'a wrote:

> A circumstance which created a considerable sensation about the end of 1922, and ruffled a period of calm, was

that one of the white sisters [nurses] from the hospital was raped by a Samoan on the lonely stretch of up-hill road between Vailima and the Government resthouse at Malololelei. It was an occurrence, I think, entirely unprecedented in Samoa. [1930:133]

SUMMING UP

The reader now has three slightly different accounts of the culture of the Samoans who live on the island of Ta'ū in American Samoa. One account—Freeman's—has been described as emphasizing the "dark" side of Samoan life, while Mead's had been described as favoring the "light" side of life. But life in any culture is not all "dark" or "light," and I believe that my restudy of Manu'an culture falls somewhere in between.

I did not go to Samoa to refute the findings of Margaret Mead as Derek Freeman admits he did (1983:xii, xvii); I went to Ta'ū village to evaluate what Mead had written a generation earlier. I approached my task as objectively as possible. I had no axe to grind; I had no favors to repay. I did not feel compelled to support any body of theory— Mead's, Boas' or Herskovits'. I believed that it was important for the discipline of anthropology to undersand the role of the personal equation in the collection and interpretation of data.

I found that Margaret Mead, because she was young in a society that venerates age and a woman in a society where the major political and ceremonial roles are in the hands of men, was at a great disadvantage in documenting certain formal aspects of Samoan life. In the study of young Samoan women, however, I believe she was able to establish excellent rapport because of her age and gender. I do not believe that Margaret Mead was "duped" by her young informants, because I believe she was too much aware of scientific controls and the need for data verfication to be lead astray by a group of teenage girls. I also do not believe that Samoans lie to people they have developed a close relationship with just for sport.

I am convinced that Margaret often over-generalized and was given to exaggeration but I also realize that she was on her first field trip with only twenty-three years of life to season her and only three years of exposure to anthropology to prepare her for her scientific adventure in the South Seas. During those three years she had been in close association with Ruth Benedict, whose configurational approach to culture emphasized dominant themes or major ethos sets and often overlooked individual atypical behavior.

While Margaret Mead discovered what she hoped to find in

Samoa—that storm and stress in adolescence is not a universal phenomenon related to human biological nature but one related to particular cultural systems, I believe her findings were correct, that her
approach was objective, and that her methodological skills in observation were exceptionally good for one of her age and experience. She
has demonstrated the force of culture within people's lives without
insisting that culture is the only determining factor in human behavior. Mead went to Samoa a young woman in a young science. She
wrote a book that has had a major impact on anthropology and the
way that behavioral scientists in general view the human animal.
When I went to Manu'a to restudy the work of Margaret Mead I will
admit that I would have liked to play the role of a "giant killer," and I
believe that my mentor, Melville J. Herskovits, might have relished
being associated with such an accomplishment. While I found interpretations which I could not totally support in Mead's writings, I
found her to be more than an adequate recorder of facts and an
insightful interpreter of those data. The "giant" was indeed a "giant."
I have returned to Samoa for study in 1962–63, 1974, and 1976–77 and
I still believe that Margaret Mead was essentially correct in her characterization and conclusions about coming of age in Samoa. And I still
am impressed with the quality of her investigation.

On the other hand, I am not impressed with the quality of the
Freeman research and I believe that this "refutation" effort has contributed little to anthropology or Samoan studies. There are some
fundamental flaws in Freeman's investigative procedures that greatly
reduce the credibility of his findings. There is, for example, a lack of
sensitivity to regional differences in behavior and an apparent disregard for time differences and evidence of cultural change. This is to
say, Sa'anapu, Western Samoa is not Ta'ū village, American Samoa
and 1925–26 is not 1942, 1967, or 1981. There should have been
careful, pains-taking control exercised to render these different places
and different times comparable. This was not done. In addition to
this, Freeman failed to meet a basic requirement of science—that
generalizations be documented with testable evidence. David
Schneider maintains that one of the canons of science "is that evidence be presented for statements of fact and that the method of
obtaining that evidence be fully explained. Freeman holds Mead's
work of 1925 to standards that he, in 1983, does not live up to in his
own work." (1983b:6).

I also believe that Derek Freeman, through selective use of the
anthropological literature on Samoa, has built a case that is far from
accurate. In regard to the documentation in Freeman's book, Colin
Turnbull writes

His random collection of quotations, as unscrupulously
selective as ever, comes largely from early travelers and
missionaries, writers and poets, with no anthropological
training. [1983:34]

One of Derek Freeman's major criticisms of Mead is that she had to
depend to a great extent on acquiring information from informants
(Freeman 1983:288) rather than through personal observation and that
some of these informants deceived Mead just for sport. But one
cannot criticize Margaret for believing the sexual accounts of young
Samoan girls, many of them about her age, and then expect the
scientific community to believe that the investigations of an elderly
white male among girls of adolescent age could be reliable and valid
on such a delicate subject as virginity (Freeman 1983:238–40).

One of the more serious flaws of Freeman's anthropology is his
inability or refusal to grasp the theoretical position of Boasian anthropology. Concerning this misconception, Marvin Harris writes:

By showing that Mead was mistaken about Samoa Freeman
presumes to right the balance between the extreme heredi-
tarian and cultural viewpoints. . . . He portrays himself as
a veritable paragon of scientific objectivity and common
sense. But his portrayal is a sham, for in order to counter-
balance these two extremes—the absolute biological determinism of Galton and the absolute cultural determinism of
Boas—Freeman erects his own fable of Boasian anthropology. [1983:20]

The fable, of course, describes Boas and his students as "absolute
cultural determinists" who held a *tabula rasa* view of human nature in
which biological considerations could be disregarded. This position
never characterized Boasian anthropology.

Although Freeman calls for a theory of human behavior which
would give greater weight to biological explanations and less to
cultural ones, a critical review of *Margaret Mead and Samoa* by anthropologist Jerry Gold in the *Samoa News* (26 Aug. 1983) notes that
"Freeman hardly ever opposes Mead's environmental, or cultural
determinist position by arguing from a biological position. Rather, he
opposes her by arguing from his own stances to wit, that his knowledge of Samoan culture is superior to hers." Gold also suggests that if
Freeman has access to evidence of a biological sort that the "nurture"
school has suppressed, then he should bring it forward. In a similar
vein Paul Shankman suggests that "the adequacy of his new paradigm
is a moot point because he is not able to determine precisely how
culture and biology interact to produce Samoan behavior, and because
he employs cultural and not biological explanations of Samoan behavior" (1983:22).

Marvin Harris also has searched in vain for biological data in Freeman's book. He writes

> Freeman's book ends without any discussion of how sleep crawling, status rivalry, the virginity cult, or any other aspect of Samoan adolescence can be better understood by invoking human nature more than Mead did, when she asserted that there is one human nature that allows for unlimited cultural diversity. [1983:21]

I am not certain whether the Mead/Freeman controversy has been a good thing or a bad thing for the science of anthropology. It has brought charges that anthropology is a "soft science," and Freeman's book has given comfort to supporters of what David Schneider has referred to as a political philosophy marked by "materialist, biologistic thinking." However, it has also forced anthropologists to re-examine issues like nature/nurture, proper field methodology, scientific objectivity, and professional ethics.

It is unfortunate that Margaret Mead was not alive when the Freeman book was published so that she might have entered the fray. It would have been a colorful battle and one from which we all would have profited. It is also unfortunate that Derek Freeman, who has spent some six years living in Samoa, who speaks the language fluently and, who, because he is a chief, claims better rapport with the people than other Samoan specialists, did not choose to write a comprehensive treatise on Samoa rather than a refutation of the work of a single investigator. Imagine the value of work which would have honestly evaluated all of the ethnographic literature on Samoa and would have posed various hypotheses (not only his own) about Samoan behavior for future investigators to test. A body of scientific, anthropological data is something that many people contribute to and amend in the search for better explanations and greater predictability of human behavior. It should not be something that attempts to close the door on all further investigation and purges alternative interpretations. This is the effect of *Margaret Mead and Samoa, the Making and Unmaking of an Anthropological Myth*. It could have been a great contribution.

POSTSCRIPT

The Problems of Youth in Contemporary Samoa

Eleanor Leacock
THE CITY COLLEGE, CUNY

In the spring of 1985 I went to Samoa to inquire into the problems of youth and to find out what influence Derek Freeman's book might be having on the professionals who were working with them. I am now pleased indeed to have been invited to add a postscript on my research to Lowell Holmes' critique of Freeman's work.[1]

Freeman's book on Samoan culture and the media coverage it received trouble me for much the same reasons it troubled Holmes and the other reviewers he discusses. From general reading in Samoan and Polynesian ethnography, I could not accept the extremity of Freeman's harsh portrayal, too negative to be sufficiently mitigated by his closing reference to some of Samoa's "shining virtues" (1983:278). I was also critical of his failure to deal seriously with the complexities of recent social-historical change. Although this failure has characterized much anthropological analysis of the past, it is surprising to find it in a contemporary book that specifically purports to advance scientific method. In addition, I was astonished by Freeman's misinformed presentation of Franz Boas as a scientist who ignored the importance of biology in human affairs. After all, it was the work of Boas, a physical as well as social anthropologist, that laid the basis for the "new physical anthropology" which, in the United States, has stressed the intricate relations between the physical and the cultural in relation to human evolution itself, and to such matters as fertility, nutrition, and health.[2]

The issue raised by Freeman's book that made me decide to go to Samoa, however, pertains to its implications for understanding and dealing with problems of adolescents and young people in Samoa today. Elsewhere in the world, delinquency, suicide, and other escalating problems of Third World youth are seen as arising from new social and economic conflicts, and from the malaise and hopelessness associated with such difficulties as school failure, unemployment, and loss of cultural identity. By contrast, the proposition that is central to Freeman's argument with Mead is that the problems of Samoan youth in recent decades are nothing new. To Freeman, high rates of delinquency, suicide, and other expressions of psychological disorder are indications of difficulties that are old in Samoan society. Freeman asks us to believe that the culprit is not new forms of social disorganization, but instead Samoan culture itself. In this respect, I would argue that it is he, not Mead, who would make Samoa out to be a unique case.

I have not been a Pacific scholar, but research on colonization and education and their relations to social conflicts in other parts of the world made it impossible for me to accept Freeman's proposition.[3] Consider, for example, the problem of youth unemployment. The phenomenon had no counterpart in societies based on subsistence farming, where the economic future of young people was assured. In 1970 I was studying schooling in urban and rural Zambia, and I noted the considerable attention that was being given to what was a relatively new problem in that and other sub-Saharan African countries—the lack of jobs for young people who had completed secondary school. Youth unemployment is of course older in industrialized countries than in countries where, in their pre-colonial and independent past, urban centers were more integrated with and less disruptive of village farming life. Everywhere, however, youth unemployment is on the increase, and everywhere with deleterious psychological effects. As stated in a UNESCO report of five conferences on youth held in different parts of the world between 1977 and 1981, youth unemployment "gives rise to other very serious problems, producing a sense of guilt, frustration, loss of identity and social rejection which may drive young people to self-ruination (drug abuse) or delinquency" (UNESCO 1985:42).

Freeman makes no mention of youth unemployment and its possible harmful effects in Samoa. Nor, as Holmes indicates, does he examine the distribution of the figures he gives on delinquency among youth in relation to distinctions between hinterland villages and those next to or part of the harbor centers of Pago Pago in American Samoa and Apia in Western Samoa. Instead he simply closes his chapter on delinquency with a vague reference to biology (Freeman 1983:268).

Freeman likewise gives no consideration to conflicts of young people that can be associated with schooling. Generally speaking, these are of two kinds: those associated with school failure and the consequent threat to self esteem; and those associated with disjunctions between school and home social relations and values, and the consequent threat to cultural identity. "Modern" schooling, as a learning process whereby children are thrown into sharp competition with their peers, and at which they can fail, contrasts with traditional forms of learning in non-capitalist societies, where everyone learns basic skills in the course of cooperatively structured daily activity, and where there is leeway for individuals to concentrate on activities they may excel at or find particularly satisfying. Sutter (1980) has documented this clash in a Western Samoan primary school. Writing about Latin America some time ago, Illich referred to the depressing effects of school failure on young people, and of the new "inferiority of the school dropout who is held personally responsible for his failure." Illich stated, "The higher the dose of schooling an individual has received, the more depressing his experience of withdrawal. The seventh grade dropout feels his inferiority much more acutely than the dropout from the third grade . . ." (Illich 1969:32). Reimer, an associate of Illich's, emphasized that "a dropout from a general school system . . . has learned that the good things of his society are not for him—and probably also that *he does not deserve them*" (Reimer n.d.:4, italics in the original).

In my study of Zambian schooling, I was impressed with the commitment of teachers, parents, and students, and with the amount that had been accomplished in building a national school system in a short period of time. However, curriculum planning was still dominated by the entirely incorrect assumption that there was nothing in the children's "traditional" home experience on which to build a scientifically oriented "modern" educational program (Leacock 1973). Superficial aspects of Zambian culture, such as names and places, were present in grade school texts, but the themes pervading the materials, as well as those sections of the curriculum relevant for future employment, were basically Western and constituted a serious challenge to a young person's sense of identity. With reference to this problem, the above-mentioned UNESCO report stated that "at the African meeting, the participants were highly critical of the educational system inherited from the colonial period . . . [for] rejecting all their values and 'importing' undesirable features such as elitism and individualism." The need was strongly expressed to establish a new system on the basis of "solid values underlying the African approach to education—mainly solidarity, continuity and the unity of theory and practice" (UNESCO 1985: 44).

A firm knowledge of their history is particularly critical for young people who must make their life choices in the context of the present clash between tradition and a form of "modernity" that is "highly ambivalent" in that it "negates and undermines the authentic values" of their past (UNESCO 1985: 45). Firm knowledge of the past choices made by their forbears and of constraints upon these choices imposed from the outside, and understanding of changes and continuities in their culture over time, are enormously important if young people are to maintain a sure sense of identity as they face the difficult constraints and choices of the present. In Africa, reconstruction of the myriad culture histories that have unfolded on that continent is understood to be essential both for pride and self-respect, and is the basis for making informed choices about social programs and policies. I myself have contributed to the ethnohistorical analysis of the cultural changes that were taking place in native North American societies from the sixteenth century on (Leacock 1980; Leacock and Lurie 1971). Such analysis offers a parallel example of scholarly effort which furnishes a valuable resource for people who have to choose among different possible strategies for dealing with the many practical problems that confront them.

In Samoa I met some of the people who share this view of how important it is for a people to reconstruct its culture history. Lafi A. Sanerivi, General Secretary of the YMCA of Western Samoa, addressing a leadership training workshop, spoke in part as follows:

> The fact that our nations were colonized is not a new concept. We were victims of the Western "dare sport" of exploration and domination of the then called "dark and uncivilized lands." In school we studied of the "mighty ships" that braved the unknown seas that came back to England with riches and tales of vast stretches of lands . . .
>
> They came with their education and we got educated. Their way. We learnt their language, but they did not learn ours. If we did have a history, we were told to forget it because it is a history of savages. Their manners and ways of living became a model . . . Suddenly, we open our eyes and see . . . And ironically enough, we realize that we have actually learnt of how our countries were exploited, our ancestors murdered and enslaved, our values discarded,

our cultures vanishing . . . We open our eyes and come to
our senses and find ourselves in the Third World . . . We
are the poor. We are the under-developed. We are the
"have-nots" . . .

Now we try and sift through the mess to identify what is
really ours and what isn't. We grapple with issues and
concerns of which we were a part in their making either
directly or indirectly . . . These are Asia-Pacific realities . . . We are weak, poor and lost. Our present
awareness attempts to build a people from non-entities,
build a nation from a colony . . . (Sanerivi 1985:1–2).

Lafi Sanerivi was one of the approximately forty professionals I
interviewed in American and Western Samoa who were concerned in
one way or another with the problems of youth. These included
school principals, teachers, and counsellors, as well as social workers,
public health workers, psychologists, administrators, and pastors. I
also attended workshops on the difficulties confronting young people, a week-long workshop held by the YMCA in Western Samoa,
and a day-long session with high school students in American Samoa.
Thanks to the cordiality and hospitality of which Samoans are justly
proud, I talked with young as well as older people in various informal
settings, visited Samoan homes, and attended weddings, church
services, and public festivities. In order to probe more deeply into the
changing nature of youth in the culture history of Samoa, I have since
begun ethnohistorical inquiry into missionaries' accounts of their
activities in nineteenth century Samoa.[4]

Shankman (1983:52) has written that "the current economic and
political troubles of Western Samoa weigh heavily on younger Samoans, who are excluded from the political system and are on the
margins of an economy that cannot fulfill their rising expectations,"
and that "these pressures and others may have contributed to an
increase in juvenile delinquency and alcohol abuse in the Apia area."
Further, he suggests that the explanation for the overall increase in
suicide, especially among youth, between 1970 and 1982, may lie "in
the modernization of Western Samoa and its interaction with traditional Samoan culture." My interview materials, in conjunction with
administrative and other reports, and with the information on youth
available in ethnographic studies of Samoan village life, tallied with
this general position and that taken by Holmes. When coupled with
historical writings and archival materials, all indications are that adolescence has indeed changed from being a period of relatively little
stress, as Holmes argues, to being highly charged with the stress
manifested by the delinquency and suicide figures given by Freeman.

Freeman (1983:205–6, 222–5) argues that it is the authoritarianism and parental severity of Samoan culture that are responsible for the psychological disturbances and other difficulties of youth. Moreover, he sees these traits as "integral to the pagan culture of Samoa," and merely reinforced, rather than qualitatively altered, by church teachings on the beating of children. Thus

> Samoans, as children, adolescents, and adults, live within an authority system the stresses of which regularly result in psychological disturbances ranging from compulsive behaviors and musu states to hysterical illnesses and suicide (Freeman 1983:225).

As discussed above, serious youth problems are simply traditional in Freeman's view; by implication they are insoluble without major changes in Samoan culture itself.

To be sure, the immediate source of stress for many young people is a perceived lack of empathy and concern on the part of stern and demanding parents, while parents and elders who become angry over the perceived lack of proper respect on the part of the young may be excessively abusive—unfortunately an all too familiar pattern in today's world. In relation to the problem, youth workers in both American and Western Samoa feel it is critical to educate parents about the changing needs of youth in a changing society and the importance of intergenerational communication and mutual respect. Significantly, historical materials indicate that such respect was an old feature of Samoan society. In this regard, Samoa was no different from those other societies around the world where competition over rank and status had not undercut the strong value placed on cooperative work relations, hospitality, and sharing. Respect for parents was apparently so firmly built into the structure of work groups in Samoa, as in other such societies, that parents felt comfortable allowing their children considerable leeway. In turn, youth made their contribution according to their age and, to some extent, their status, knowing their future was assured.[5] In speaking about how much he enjoyed this period in his life, one elder said, "and then my time of serving was ending up in being served—that is the other side of the picture."

Missionaries to Samoa in the 1840s construed parental permissiveness as "lack of control" and repeatedly complained about it in their letters.[6] "It may be safely affirmed that a parent has no means of compelling his refractory child of seven years of age to obey him," wrote the missionary Bullen in 1847, and continued, with respect to keeping a child at school,

> He may use entreaties and threaten punishment, but the child having made up his mind to leave, and who knows

full well from experience the issue of such contests, will perhaps run off to some of her family relations, who will readily undertake to confirm her in disobedience to parental authority. Would the parents continue in a resolute discipline till the child should be completely subdued, the evil would be greatly remedied but alas! they know nothing of such discipline and seem utterly unable to learn it. After once or twice correcting the child, I have heard them say *in her hearing,* "Well, if this do not suffice, I suppose she must have her own way" (Bullen 1847, underlining in the original letter).

One might wish to argue that the parent in this incident was perhaps not that interested in keeping the child in school in the first place. However, consider another account, one of a little boy who was undeniably going against his parents' wishes. After attending the mission school, the missionary reported, the boy determined to take no further part in "the heathenish practices of his people."

After forming this resolution, one evening his father and mother were going to attend the night-dance in their village, and they called him to accompany them. He told them that he did not wish to go, but would rather remain in the house. This request was complied with after some little rebuke from his father. The next night, his parents again prepared for the dance, and desired their son to go with them. Again he refused . . .

This time the boy's friends became angry and argued with him but to no avail. The next day the parents took the boy to the teacher, related the preceding events, and asked the teacher to take the boy under his care (Ella 1851).

With respect to parental severity, Freeman (1983:205) cites the missionary Stair who wrote that at one time children "were indulged in every wish, at another severely beaten for the most trivial offense." Freeman does not cite the rest of the sentence. Stair (1987:178) goes on to say, "and then shortly after an oven of food was prepared, as a peace-offering to appease their offended dignity." Such ritualization suggests that such beating was hardly a common occurrence and was by no means as capricious as Stair assumed, and also that, in keeping with Samoan mores, it was shame, not physical pain, that was the more cogent sanction. In any case, the whole picture from the mid-nineteenth century given by missionaries who, with their wives, were in daily contact with their parishioners, contrasts sharply with that of recent times, where beating can be serious and where, in American Samoa at least, actual child abuse is beginning to be acknowledged as a social problem. The typical case reported to the Mental Health

Department of the LBJ Hospital in American Samoa, as told to me, like contemporary intergenerational conflict concerning older youth, has a familiar ring: a drinking father, probably battering his wife, and a frustrated mother taking it out on her children, in a family with from five to nine children living in too small a house. The trend towards a nuclear family unit and European-style housing means that social forms of control have become largely inoperative in such cases; economic problems have become a major source of frustration for parents; and compulsory schooling has robbed mothers of their former baby-tenders during a good part of the day.

Youth suicide has also become a recognized social problem in Samoa, especially in Western Samoa. In the late sixties suicide began to grow from a rare event into a virtual epidemic, reaching a high point of forty-nine known deaths from suicide in 1981. By comparison with the usual pattern recorded for industrialized countries, where suicide rates increase with age, suicides were heavily concentrated among young people from fifteen to twenty-four, especially young men. Perhaps in part due to the reduced availability of paraquat, the herbicide responsible for nearly four-fifths of the 1981 deaths (Bowles 1985:19), and in part due to a public information campaign through the press, the radio and meetings, known suicide deaths dropped to thirty-five in 1982, twenty-five in 1983, and lower again in 1984 (Oliver 1985; The Lifeline Team 1984). The rate of attempted suicide among youth continues to be high, however. Young people may take paraquat into their mouths and spit it out without swallowing any, or take other herbicides that are not quite as deadly. A "Lifeline Team" for suicide prevention has been established to work with these young people and their families.

A conference on suicide in the South Pacific was held at the East-West Center in Hawaii in 1984, and papers by Rubinstein (1985) on Micronesia and Macpherson and Macpherson (1985) on Western Samoa explore the blockages to youth aspirations that lie behind the phenomenon. Like Western Samoa, Micronesia has experienced a tragic epidemic of youth suicide, the rate climbing from eight per hundred thousand in 1960–63 to forty-eight in 1980–83. Suicides are almost entirely young men; the ratio to women is twelve to one. Although rebuffs from parents, lovers, schools, or other sources trigger suicides, deep socio-cultural conflicts produce the malaise that has caused a sudden rise in the number of youth who respond to rebuff or punishment with this ultimate act of rage and despair.

The developments that are responsible for the rise in suicide in Micronesia follow from the extreme rapidity of the changes associated with the post-World War II "modernization" of this area (plus, I would add, the stepped up colonial exploitation), and sharp discontinuities in experiences and expectations of parents raised before the war and their children raised in the post-war period. As I understand Rubinstein's interpretation, the change from a largely subsistence economy with its cooperative work groups, to a market economy and its requirement for individualized economic activity, has thrown young people into greater dependency on their parents, and has substituted specifically parental authority for the more diffuse authority of village or lineage leaders. Further, children who have grown up in the post-war world expect and need a different kind of behavior from their parents than these parents think necessary or appropriate. Finally, at the same time as young men are developing new aspirations that most of them cannot achieve, they are losing old sources of satisfaction in the social relations of the lineage meeting houses where they used to sleep (these have all but disappeared), and in the gratification of working on large, important lineage activities. Interestingly, the highest rates for suicide are neither in the towns, where there are new social outlets for young men, nor in remote villages, where life has changed less, but in intermediate villages where the gratifications of the subsistence economy have disappeared while means for achieving new goals are blocked.

There are, of course, many differences between Micronesia and Samoa, and for that matter, within Micronesia itself, but similarities with respect to the general pattern of dilemmas for young men are striking. Like Rubinstein, the Macphersons (1985:59) propose a "blocked opportunity model" for the social stress Samoan young men have been experiencing. New *matai* titles were created after independence (in order to distribute votes evenly across districts), but further increase disallowed, and access has been further restricted by increasing longevity. Increasing longevity and no enforced retirement has also restricted the opportunity of those aspiring to become pastors. Economic difficulties have limited expansion of the job market which cannot accommodate school graduates, and the over supply of labor has depressed wages. Meanwhile, and most important, the New Zealand economy slowed, and American Samoa made it more difficult to enter and go on to the United States, which cut off the option of working for a while overseas that used to be taken for granted. The Macphersons (1985:56) write, "It is significant that the decline coincides with the increase in the rate of suicide . . ."

Dennis Oliver (1985) looked at the distribution of suicide in different villages and found a strong correlation between suicide-prone villages and a high *matai*-to-commoner ratio that at first blush might seem to contradict the Macphersons on blocked opportunity. The four villages with the highest suicide rates had particularly high *matai*-to-commoner ratios—1:1.6 by comparison with the national average of 1:24 in 1961 and 1:12 in 1981. However, although from a long-term point of view there would be more openings for youth, from an adolescent's immediate viewpoint, in a changing and difficult situation, the virtual lack of any mature untitled men in the *aumaga* could create a greater sense of distance and powerlessness. Further, the tendency of many matai to become involved in extra-village business and political affairs can lead to a breakdown in the traditional coupling of authority with responsibility, and of the face-to-face contact that allowed traditional balancing mechanisms to function, such as the license allowed the young to criticize their elders in humorous song. Oliver (1985:76) writes that in one village with a high suicide rate and a relatively high *matai*-to-commoner ratio, he was told the *matai* were trying to "imitate Hitler," and that "there was continual friction and conflict between the top *matai*." In Lockwood's (1971:104) 1965–66 study of four villages ranging from a largely subsistence to a largely market economy, in the village at the market end of the continuum the *matai* "were too involved with politics and other matters beyond the village boundaries to give their full attention to the village itself." Such circumstances would add powerfully to the anger and frustrations of youth whose traditional avenues for gratification are quickly eroding and whose new aspirations are being blocked.

In sum, then, it is a serious misrepresentation of the situation to say that youth difficulties simply follow from the authoritarianism of the Samoan past. Instead they follow from the fact that the nature of youth as a life period has been transformed in many ways. With respect to Mead, I met few people who had read her book on Samoan adolescence. However, two of the people I came to know best in Western Samoa had read it, and both said it rang true to them in the light of their own youth. One had visited Manu'a in the thirties when he was a teen-ager. This is not to say Mead's account is without faults. On one point in particular I agree with Freeman, and I see Holmes does as well. This is with respect to Mead's ethnocentric ascription of "shallow feelings" to Samoans. Other anthropologists working in the personality and culture tradition have also assumed that the dispersed parenting so common in village-based societies leads to a shallowness of feelings. The assumption is unjustified and one I have always questioned.

Reports on the sexuality of teen-age girls and young women in the recent past, mostly given by women, ranged from formal statements about well-guarded virgins, through statements that this might be a goal but not necessarily adhered to, to criticisms of church teachings on chastity as imposing unnecessary stress on young women. In the end it seemed that discretion, rather than actual chastity, was usually the more cogent issue—a common enough state of affairs. Further, the elite or well-to-do families were in general more concerned than others, and rumors would be circulated about their sending their daughters off to Hawaii for abortions—again a familiar-sounding story. At the same time, the ceremonial defloration of the *taupou* remains an important cultural theme, and a blood-stained sheet on the wedding night is a source of family pride.

Variable concern with virginity today does not mean it was expected of an unmarried woman in the past. On the contrary, missionary descriptions and complaints concerning night dancing plus what some people said about its latter-day forms makes the sexual freedom of adolescents, with the exception of the *taupou*, undeniable in my view. This is not too surprising. After all, despite Victorian ideology, it was not so long ago that a goodly proportion of children were born "out of wedlock" in England, and this was hardly thought a matter for comment, as long as the inheritance of property or title was not involved. Unfortunately, however, the fact that teenage sexuality has been widely accepted, indeed expected, in societies around the world[7] does not help a young woman who is caught in changing and ambivalent standards. In Samoa, where adolescent behavior reflects strongly on family honor, fear of shame and disapproval concerning a sexual relation can today be a precipitating factor in a young woman's suicide attempt.

The difficulty of rendering traditionally expected service and meeting the requirements of school or job is another source of tension for a young woman whose parents have not modified their demands upon her. Furthermore, the fact that the service of young women may often today be rendered in the privacy of a nuclear family household has changed its nature. Gerber's study of family relationships in a large American Samoan village describes how vulnerable a girl may be to parental demands and how sensitive to parental disapproval (Gerber 1975:38–54). Anxiety over whether she will be reproved by her parents, or perhaps will be commended by her father in the evening family prayer is altogether different from the assurance of public recognition a girl traditionally received for her service and especially for the completion of her first fine mat. Although mat-making was time-consuming and even onerous, it was accorded the highest public value.

In closing, I want to say a few words about my personal reactions to Samoa. I have been focusing on problems but do not want to give the wrong impression. Most young people are handling them well, and I was constantly impressed with their buoyancy and creativity. I photographed the elegant dancing at school festivities and the fine paintings on exhibit at a high school, and I would have liked the time to record more of the marvelous singing I kept hearing.

I was also impressed with the understanding and concern of people working with youth, the men as well as the women. Of the people I interviewed, none were simply holding a job, though there are those in Samoa as everywhere. I was particularly impressed with the ease and assurance with which the women I met dealt with authority—not only older women—a retired mayor, a *matai*, a high-titled school principal—but young women who had successfully battled discrimination with respect to good jobs and were managing both work and family. Unlike Western women, Samoan women are not uncomfortable handling authority; by contrast with Western women they have behind them a long tradition of their own publicly recognized organizations and responsibilities.

With respect to the influence Freeman's book may have had on people working with youth in Samoa, I found it to be at best indirect. In American Samoa the only person I met who had read the book, an educator from the United States, was very critical, and, interestingly enough, the newspaper interview that informed most people about the work made no mention of any negatives in Freeman's portrayal. Freeman cites supporters of his work in Western Samoa but opinions were clearly mixed. The few people I talked with who had read the book were unfavorable, and I was told of the angry criticism Freeman had received on the occasion of a public lecture.

All told, far more relevant than Freeman's work to the problems of young people in Samoa today is the approach expressed by Lafi Sanerivi (1985:2) in his closing sentence to the passage cited above, "Our present awareness attempts to . . . build a vision of hope, equality and a just society from the aftermath of colonization."

NOTES

Chapter 1

[1] See Freeman's *Margaret Mead and Samoa* (1983), pp. 46, 57, 75, 78, 81, 94, 281–82, 295, 297, 301.

[2] Freeman leveled such an accusation in personal correspondence with me (October 10, 1967).

Chapter 2

[1] On April 25, 1967, Freeman wrote: "The conclusions I have reached (based on my researches in anthropology, evolutionary biology, ethology, history and psycho-analysis) have little in common with those of Mead and her avowal of the doctrine of 'absolute cultural determinism,' and I am now interested in the critical scrutiny of a whole trend in anthropology associated with the doctrines of Boas, Benedict, Mead, and others. The re-examination of *Coming of Age* and Mead's other early writings is one of my starting points." And on May 25, 1967 Freeman wrote: "I have read [chapters X and XI of your doctoral thesis] with interest and I am in agreement with all of your criticism of Margaret Mead's account of Manu'a. What puzzles me, however, is that having made these substantial criticisms you should go on to say in your summary conclusions (p. 232) that "the reliability of Mead's account is remarkably high." Freeman's October 10, 1967 letter stated: "You will also know, I take it, that Margaret Mead's name is execrated in Manu'a (as elsewhere in Samoa), for her writing and expecially *Coming of Age in Samoa* are regarded as *luma fai tele*, a defamatory libel. Indeed, the people of Ta'ū told me that if she ever dared return they would tie her up and throw her to the sharks."

Let me say that when Margaret Mead returned to Ta'ū in 1971 to dedicate a power plant, she was welcomed with open arms and showered with gifts and honors.

[2] "I would merely comment that as we look back on Mead's Samoan researches we are able to appreciate anew the wisdom of Karl Popper's admonition that in both science and scholarship it is, above all

189

else, indefatigable rational criticism of our suppositions that is of decisive importance, for such criticism by 'bringing out our mistakes . . . makes us understand the difficulties of the problem we are trying to solve,' and so saves us from the allure of the 'obvious truth' of received doctrine" (Freeman 1983: 292–93).

[3]For Mead's depiction of Samoan character, see Freeman (1983: 82–94). For Freeman's counter-claims in the same volume, see p. 290 (sex), p. 161 (aggression), and p. 142 (competitiveness).

[4]It is amusing to note that Derek Freeman (1984: 404) implied that Herskovits censored my material so that Mead's finding would not be damaged in any way. What Freeman apparently did not realize is that although Mead and Herskovits were fellow graduate students at Columbia and both were students and admirers of Boas, there was little affection between them. In fact, Herskovits would have been delighted if I had returned with evidence that the work of Mead in Samoa was substandard. But such was not the case.

[5]It is true that in Tutuila a few women hold titles, but this is not permitted in Manu'a.

[6]Informants are often so anxious to please that they hesitate to contradict the erroneous perceptions of an investigator.

Chapter 3

[1]By the first century A.D. the Samoan islands had been settled by emigrants from eastern Melanesia. The diffusion of dark-skinned people into the islands of eastern Melanesia did not take place until fairly late in time. Archeological evidence suggests that negroid-type people (probably from New Guinea) did not arrive in the Fiji islands until about 1000 A.D. Physical anthropologist W. W. Howells (1933: 335) suggests that since Fijians differ in physical type from Samoans only in their slightly shorter faces, somewhat darker pigmentation, and broader, flatter noses, the introduction of negroid physical traits into the originally Samoan-Tongan-type population of Fiji did not occur until as late as the eleventh century A.D.

Chapter 4

[1]Chief with a capital 'C' indicates an executive chief; Talking Chief indicates an orator chief.

Chapter 5

[1]See Brown 1910:227; Turner 1861: 238–240, 244–255; Wright and Fry 1936: 217.

[2]During the middle and late 1830s missionaries devised a written

form of the Samoan language, printed religious tracts—usually portions of the Bible—and began forming classes to teach the people to
read and study the truths of the Christian theology. Charles Wilkes
estimated that in 1839 there were approximately 10,000 literate Samoans. The ability to read was a prerequisite for church membership.

Chapter 6

[1] Most corporal punishment is administered by biological parents
but extended-family surrogates have the right to do so.

[2] The *taupou* was the only girl required to remain a virgin. Today,
taupous only function on ceremonial occasions and often are married
women.

Chapter 7

No notes.

Chapter 8

[1] See note 4 below regarding these "high stakes."

[2] When I mentioned this problem to Mead in personal conversation
she maintained that she had combined "typical" Samoan activities
into a "typical" day. She said she had never observed some of the
activities first-hand, but had had them described to her in interviews.

[3] This difference might very well be the result of Mead's flair for the
dramatic as evidenced by her stylized description of a "day in Samoa,"
or it may merely be the result of generational changes in references to
amorous activities.

[4] Evidence of cases of suicide do not necessarily provide proof that
such behavior was characteristic of Samoans but it does perhaps
suggest that there was some deviation within the society and that
Samoan character might well have been more complex than presented
by Mead.

[5] "And Hezekiah spoke encouragingly to all of the Levites who
showed good skill (*mafaufau*) in the service of the Lord." Some Bible
editions use "understanding" in place of "skill."

Chapter 9

No notes.

Chapter 10

[1] *Time* magazaine, in its article "Bursting the South Sea Bubble,"
described Freeman as "an extraordinarily careful scholar," a "sound
researcher," and "brilliant" (Feb. 14, 1983, p. 69).

[2] This figure is arrived at by combining actual reported rape cases with cases of surreptitious rape, or indecent assault reported to the police.

Postscript

[1] I can only skim the surface of my material in the brief pages here allotted me, but I am writing them up for full publication elsewhere. I am indebted to the American Association of University Women, whose Founders Fellowship made my field work possible, and to the Faculty Research Award Program of the Professional Staff Congress, City University of New York. I travelled to Samoa with Ruby Rohrlich and we shared ideas and information although we each worked separately on our own projects. I am grateful to the many people who extended their help and hospitality in Samoa, but I want to extend particular thanks to Meripa Weir for her friendship, her information, and her translation of tapes from a workshop on youth. I also want to thank the anthropologist-photographer Frederic Sutter for putting me in touch with some of his friends in Samoa.

[2] It was the simplistic explanation of complex social behaviors in terms of simple genetic determinants that Boas eschewed.

[3] Specifically, my long-term ethnohistorical research on North American Indian societies, my study of schooling in Zambia, Africa, and my investigation of women's changing roles under the impact of colonialism.

[4] I am grateful to the Centre National de la Recherche Scientifique of France for inviting me to spend time at the Laboratoire d'Anthropologie Sociale, thereby making it possible for me to work in the archives of the London Missionary Society at the School of Oriental and African Studies, University of London, and in the Archives de la France-d'Outre-Mer. I also wish to thank my sister, Elspeth Hart, for her generous and able assistance in the LMS archives.

[5] The parallel with African societies is brought out by the following discussion by Boubaker Ly of the University of Dakar on youth in "traditional" society:

> Education was in general diffuse, informal, pragmatic and functional. Vocational training formed no small part of it: in traditional African society it was one of the dimensions of human kind, for it was part of life. Training was progressive, in step with the acquisition of maturity in life. Vocational training was concerned *inter alia* to reproduce the position of the father, mother or other person in charge of the child . . . The reproduction of the position of the 'authorities' in charge of the young person was facilitated by family tradition . . . society suggested to young people that their

place in society was prestigious because it was that of the founding ancestors and all their descendants from time immemorial.

In such a context work of whatever kind carried prestige. Young people accepted and loved their trades. They were in a hurry solely and only to finish their training and take their place in the family production structures, which society skillfully portrayed as imbued with both honour and prestige . . .

Society as such was never challenged . . . indeed, young people aimed rather to integrate themselves into society by becoming more responsible and playing a part in perpetuating it. The act of freedom lay in the will to play a part in perpetuating society . . . (Ly 1981:155–56).

[6]E.g., in the London Missionary Society archives, School of Oriental and African Studies, University of London, South Seas Correspondence, letters from Harbutt (Mar. 16, 1842, Box 15, Folio 5, Jacket B, and Oct. 15, 1847, B 20, F 6, J A); Hardie (Nov. 12, 1842, B 15, F 5, J D); Mills (Mar. 19, 1844, B 17, F 6, J B and Jul. 1, 1852, B 24, F 10, J B); Stallworthy (Dec. 31, 1851, B 24, F 5, J d).

[7]For a recent entry into Human Relations Area Files data on adolescent sexuality, see Barry and Schlegel 1986.

BIBLIOGRAPHY

American Samoa, Government of. 1975. *Annual Report to the Secretary of the Interior.* Pago Pago: Government Printing Office.

———. 1978. *American Samoa Plan for Health.* American Samoa Health Coordinating Council. Pago Pago: Government Printing Office.

Angier, Natalie. 1983. Coming of Age in Anthropology. *Discover,* April:26–30.

Anthropology Newsletter. 1984. April:2.

Barnouw, Victor. 1983. Coming to Print in Samoa: Mead and Freeman. *Journal of Psychoanalytic Anthropology* 6:425–432.

Barry III, Herbert and Alice Schlegel. 1986. Cultural Customs that Influence Sexual Freedom in Adolescence. *Ethnology,* XXV(2), 151–162.

Blazer, Leland K. 1968. Samoan Character as Revealed by Three Tests of Personality. M.A. thesis, Wichita State University.

Boas, Franz. 1910. Psychological Problems in Anthropology. *American Journal of Psychology* 21:371–384.

———. 1911. *The Mind of Primitive Man.* New York: Macmillan.

———. 1914. *Kultur und Rasse.* Leipzig: Veit and Company.

Bowles, John R. 1985. Suicide and Attempted Suicide in Contemporary Western Samoa. In Hezel, Francis X., Donald H. Rubinstein, and Geoffrey M. White eds. *Culture, Youth and Suicide in the Pacific: Papers from an East-West Center Conference.* Honolulu: Center for Asian and Pacific Studies, University of Hawaii at Manoa. pp. 15–35.

Brown, George. 1910. *Melanesians and Polynesians.* London: Macmillan.

Buck, Peter. 1930. *Samoan Material Culture.* Honolulu: Bishop Museum (Bull. no. 75).

Bullen, T. 1847. Letter Jun. 12. London Missionary Society Correspondence, South Seas, Box 20, Folio 5, Jacket C.

Burney, James. 1816. *A Chronological History of the Voyages and Discoveries in the South Seas or Pacific Ocean.* London: Luke Hansard and Sons.

Campbell, Donald T. 1972. The Mutual Methodological Relevance of Anthropology and Psychology. In F. L. K. Hsu (ed.), *Psychological Anthropology.* Cambridge, Mass.: Schenkman Publ. Co., pp. 435–63.

Cassidy, Robert. 1982. *Margaret Mead, A Voice for the Century.* New York: Universe Books.

Code of American Samoa. 1949. Pago Pago: Government of American Samoa.

Copp, John D. 1950. *The Samoan Dance of Life.* Boston: Beacon Press.

Churchill, William. n.d. Fa'alupega i Manu'a. Manuscript.

Crocombe, R. G. 1973. *The New South Pacific.* Canberra: Australian National University Press.

Davidson, J. W. 1967. *Samoa mo Samoa.* Melbourne: Oxford University Press.

Downs, Evelyn. 1942. *Everyday Samoan: Grammar Elucidated from Conversations in the Language.* Apia:Western Samoa Mail Office.

Ella, Samuel. 1851. Letter, Nov. 10. London Missionary Society Correspondence, South Seas, Box 24, Folio 5, Jacket C.

Ellison, Jos. 1953. *Tusitala of the South Seas.* New York: Hastings House.

Emeneau, M. B. 1935. Toda Culture Thirty-Five Years After: An Acculturation Study. *Annals of the Bhandakar Oriental Research Institute* 19:101–121.

———. 1937. Toda Marriage Regulations and Taboos. *American Anthropologist* 39:103–112.

Fields, Cheryl. 1983. Controversial Book Spurs Scholars' Defense of the Legacy of Margaret Mead. *Chronicle of Higher Education* 26(11):27–28.

Folsom, Joseph K. 1934. *The Family: Its Sociology and Psychiatry.* New York: J. Wiley and Sons.

Fox, James W., and K. B. Cumberland. 1962. *Western Samoa: Land, Life and Agriculture in Tropical Polynesia.* Christchurch: Whitcombe and Tombs.

Freeman, Derek. 1962. Review of *Trance in Bali* by Jane Belo. *Journal of the Polynesian Society* 71:270–73.

———. 1964. Kinship and Political Authority in Samoa. *American Anthropologist* 66:553–568.

———. 1965. Anthroplogy and Psychiatry and the Doctrine of Cultural Relativism. *Man* 65:65–67.

———. 1981. The Anthropology of Choice. *Canberra Anthropology* 4(1):82–100.

———. 1983. *Margaret Mead and Samoa: The Making and Unmaking of an Anthropological Myth.* Cambridge, Mass.: Harvard University Press.

———. 1984. O Rose thou art sick. A Rejoinder to Weiner, Schwartz, Holmes, Shore and Silverman. *American Anthropologist* 86:400–404.

Gardner, Louise C. 1965. *Gautavai: A Study of Samoan Values.* M. A. thesis, University of Hawaii.

Garsee, Jarrell W. 1965. A Study of Samoan Interpersonal Values. M. A. thesis, University of Oklahoma.

———. 1967. Samoan Interpersonal Values. *Jounal of Social Psychology* 72:45–60.

Gerber, Eleanor Ruth. 1975. *The Cultural Patterning of Emotions in Samoa,* Ph.D. dissertation, University of California, San Diego.

Gilson, R. P. 1970. *Samoa 1830 to 1900: The Politics of a Multi-Cultural Community.* Melbourne: Oxford University Press.

Glick, Paula B. 1983. Brouhaha Among the Breadfruit. *Nature* 302:758–759.

Gold, Jerry. 1983. Is Freeman Wrong about Mead? *Samoa News,* August 26, p. 14.

Goodsell, Willystine. 1928. *Problems of the Family.* New York: Century Company.

Grattan, F. J. H. 1948. *An Introduction to Samoan Custom.* Apia: Samoa Printing and Publishing Co.

Gray, J. A. C. 1960. *Amerika Samoa*. Annapolis, Maryland: United States Naval Institute.

Green, Roger. 1966. Linguistic Subgrouping within Polynesia. *Journal of the Polynesian Society* 75:6–38.

Green, William M. 1924. Social Traits of Samoans. *Journal of Applied Sociology* 9:129–135.

Hall, G. Stanley. 1904. *Adolescence: Its Psychology and its Relations to Physiology, Anthropology, Sociology, Sex, Crime, Religion, and Education*. New York: D. Appleton and Company.

Harris, Marvin. 1968. *The Rise of Anthropological Theory*. New York: Thomas Y. Crowell Company.

———. 1983a. The Sleep-crawling Question. *Psychology Today*, May:24–27.

———. 1983b. Margaret and the Giant-Killer. *The Sciences* 23(4):18–21.

Hartmann, Michael. 1980. Census Experiences in the Pacific 1976–79. *Sartryck ur Statistisk Tidskrift* 4:307–316.

Herskovits, M. J. 1949. *Man and His Works*. New York: Knopf.

———. 1953. *Franz Boas*. New York: Charles Scribner's Sons.

Holmes, Lowell D. 1957. A Restudy of Manu'an Culture: A Problem in Methodology. Ph.D. dissertation, Northwestern University.

———. 1958. *Ta'u: Stability and Change in a Samoan Village*. Wellington, New Zealand: Polynesian Society (Reprint no. 7). (Orig. 1957. *Polynesian Society Journal* 66:301–38, 398–435).

———. 1965. Decision-making in a Samoan Village. *Anthropologica* 7:229–238.

———. 1967. *The Story of Samoa*. Cincinnati: McCormick-Mathers.

———.1969. Samoan Oratory. *Journal of American Folklore* 82:342–345.

———. 1971. Samoa: Custom vs. Productivity. In R. Crocombe (ed.), *Land Tenure in the Pacific*. Melbourne: Oxford University Press.

———. 1974. *Samoan Village*. New York: Holt, Rinehart and Winston.

———. 1980. Factors Contributing to the Cultural Stability of Samoa. *Anthropological Quarterly* 53:188–197.

Holmes, Lowell D., Gary Tallman, and Vernon Jantz. 1978. Samoan Personality. *Journal of Psychological Anthropology* 1:453–472.

Holmes, Lowell D., and Wayne Parris. 1981. *Anthropology: An Introduction*. New York: Wiley and Sons.

Holmes, Susan. 1951. *Report on a Qualitative Nutrition Study in Western Samoa*. Noumea: South Pacific Commission.

Howard, Jane. 1983. Angry Storm Over the South Seas of Margaret Mead. *Smithsonian* 14(1):66–75.

———. 1984. *Margaret Mead: A Life*. New York: Simon and Schuster.

Howells, W. W. 1967. *Mankind in the Making*, Rev. ed. Garden City: Doubleday.

Hsu, Francis L. K. 1972. *Psychological Anthropology*. Cambridge, Mass.: Schenkman Publ. Co.

Illich, Ivan. 1969. Outwitting the 'Developed' Countries. *New York Review of Books*, Nov. 6.

Irwin, George. 1965. *Samoa—A Teacher's Tale*. London: Cassell.

Johnson, R. T. 1962. Observations of Western Samoan Culture and Education.

Unpublished manuscript. Minneapolis: University of Minnesota, Bureau of Educational Research.

Keesing, Felix. 1934. *Modern Samoa: Its Government and Changing Life*. London: George Allen and Unwin.

Keesing, Felix, and Marie Keesing. 1956. *Elite Communication in Samoa*. Palo Alto, CA: Stanford University Press.

Kluckhohn, Florence, and F. L. Strodtbeck. 1961. *Variations in Value Orientations*. Evanston, IL: Row Peterson.

Kramer, Augustin. 1941. *The Samoan Islands* (trans. from the German). 2 vol. in 9. Rarotonga.

Kroeber, A. L. 1931. *Report on the Seri*. Los Angeles Southwest Museum Papers, 6.

Leacock, Eleanor. 1973. *Primary Schooling in Zambia; Final Report*. Bethesda: ERIC Document Reproduction Service.

————. 1980. Montagnais Women and the Jesuit Program for Colonization. In Mona Etienne and Eleanor Leacock, eds. *Women and Colonization, Anthropological Perspectives*. New York: Praeger in association with Bergin & Garvey Publishers. pp. 25–42.

Leacock, Eleanor and Nancy Lurie, eds. 1971. *North American Indians in Historical Perspective*. New York: Random House.

Lesser, Alexander. 1968. Franz Boas. *International Encyclopedia of the Social Sciences* 2:99–108. New York: Macmillan.

Lewis, Oscar. 1951. *Life in a Mexican Village: Tepoztlan Restudied*. Urbana: University of Illinois Press.

Li An-Che. 1937. Zuni: Some Observations and Querries. *American Anthropologist* 39:62–76.

Lockwood, Brian. 1971. *Samoan Village Economy*. Melbourne: Oxford University Press.

Lowie, Robert. 1935. *The Crow Indians*. New York: Holt, Rinehart and Winston.

Ly, Boubaker. 1981. African Youth between Tradition and Modernity. In the UNESCO Press, *Youth in the 1980s*. Paris: UNESCO. pp. 154–186.

Macpherson, Cluny and La/avasa Macpherson. 1985. Suicide in Western Samoa, A Sociological Perspective. In Hezel, Francis K., Donald H. Rubinstein, and Geoffrey M. White, eds. *Culture, Youth and Suicide in the Pacific: Papers from an East-West Center Conference*. Honolulu: Center for Asian and Pacific Studies, University of Hawaii at Manoa. pp. 36–73.

Marcus, George. 1983. One Man's Mead. *New York Times Book Review*, March 27:2–3, 22–23.

Marsack, C. C. 1961. *Samoan Medley*. London: Robert Hale Ltd.

Maxwell, Robert J. 1969. *Samoan Temperament*. Ph.D. dissertation, Cornell University.

Mead, Margaret. 1928a. *Coming of Age in Samoa*. New York: William Morrow.

————. 1928b. The Role of the Individual in Samoan Culture. *Journal of the Royal Anthropological Institute* 58:481–495.

————. 1930. *Social Organization of Manua*. Honolulu: Bernice P. Bishop Museum (Bull. 76).

———. 1937. *Cooperation and Competition Among Primitive People*. New York: McGraw-Hill.

———. 1949. *The Mountain Arapesh. V. The Record of Unabelin with Rorschach Analysis*. Anthropological Papers of the American Museum of Natural History 41, pt. 3. New York.

———. 1952. The Training of the Cultural Anthropologist. *American Anthropologist* 54:343–346.

———. 1961. Review of *Ta'u: Stability and Change in a Samoan Village* by Lowell Holmes. *American Anthropologist* 63:428–30.

———. 1965. *Anthropologists and What They Do*. New York: Franklin Watts.

———. 1969. *Social Organization of Manua*. Honolulu: Bishop Museum (Reprint of Bull. 76).

———. 1972. *Blackberry Winter*. New York: William Morrow.

———. 1977. *Letters from the Field 1925–1975*. New York: Harper and Row.

Milner, G. B. 1966. *Samoan Dictionary*. London: Oxford Press.

Nader, Laura. 1983. A Historic Friction in the Field of Anthropology. *Los Angeles Times Book Review*, April 10:2.

New York Times. 1983. New Samoa Book Challenges Margaret Mead's Conclusions. January 31.

Oliver, Dennis. 1985. Reducing Suicide in Western Samoa. In Hezel, Francis K., Donald H. Rubinstein, and Geoffrey M. White, eds. *Culture, Youth and Suicide in the Pacific: Papers from an East-West Center Conference*. Honolulu: Center for Asian and Pacific Studies, University of Hawaii at Manoa. pp. 74–87.

Oliver, Douglas L. 1951. *The Pacific Islands*. Cambridge, Mass.: Harvard University Press.

Osbourne, Lloyd. 1930. Introduction to *Samoa Under the Sailing Gods* by N. A. Rowe. New York: Putnam.

Pastore, Nicholas. 1949. *The Nature–Nurture Controversy*. New York: King's Crown Press, Columbia University.

Popper, Karl. 1959. *The Logic of Scientific Discovery*. New York: Basic Books.

Powell, T. A., and G. Pratt. 1891. Some Folk-songs and Myths from Samoa. *Proceedings of the Royal Society of New South Wales* 24: 195–217.

Pratt, G. 1862. *Grammar and Dictionary of the Samoan Language*. Samoa: London Missionary Society.

Radin, Paul. 1933. *The Method and Theory of Ethnology*. New York:McGraw-Hill.

Redfield, Robert. 1929. Review of *Coming of Age in Samoa* by Margaret Mead. *American Journal of Sociology* 34(4):728–730.

Reimer, Everett. n.d. *Second Annual Report of the Seminar on Alternatives in Education*. Cuernavaca: Centro Intercultural de Documentacion, Document 69.

Rose, Ronald. 1959. *South Seas Magic*. London: Hale.

Rowe, Newton A. 1930. *Samoa Under the Sailing Gods*. New York: Putnam.

Rubinstein, Donald H. 1985. Suicide in Micronesia. In Hezel, Francis K., Donald H. Rubinstein, and Geoffrey M. White, eds. *Culture, Youth and Suicide in the Pacific: Papers from an East-West Center Conference*. Honolulu:

Center for Asian and Pacific Studies, University of Hawaii at Manoa. pp. 88–111.

Sanerivi, Lafi A. 1985. Development vs. Social Realities. In *Report of Leadership Training in Upolu and Savaii, 1985*. Young Mens Christian Association of Western Samoa. (Mimeographed as translated from the Samoan).

Schneider, David. 1983a. The Coming of a Sage to Samoa. *Natural History* 92(6):4–10.

———. 1983b. David M. Schneider replies. *Natural History* 92(12):4–6.

Shankman, Paul. 1973. Remittances and Underdevelopment in Western Samoa. Ph.D. dissertation, Harvard.

———. 1983. The Samoan Conundrum. Typescript. Boulder: Department of Anthropology, University of Colorado. Later revised for publication in *Canberra Anthropology* 6(1):38–57.

Shore, Bradd. 1977. A Samoan Theory of Action: Social Control and Social Order in a Polynesian Paradox. Ph.D. dissertation, University of Chicago.

———. 1982. *Sala'ilua, A Samoan Mystery*. New York: Columbia University Press.

Stair, J. B. 1897. *Old Samoa*. London: Religious Tract Society.

Stanner, W. E. H. 1953. *The South Seas in Transition*. Sydney: Australasian Publishing Co.

Stevenson, R. L. 1892. *Vailima Papers* and *A Footnote to History*. New York: Charles Scribner's Sons.

Swanton, J. R. 1930. Franz Boas. *Science* 73:146–148.

Sutter, Frederic Koehler. 1980. *Communal vs Individual Socialization at Home and in School in Rural and Urban Western Samoa*. Ph.D. dissertation, University of Hawaii.

The Lifeline Team. 1984. *Annual Summary of Activities and Narrative Report*. Western Samoa: Suicide Prevention Program, Catholic Relief Services. (Mimeographed).

Time Magazine. 1983. Bursting the South Sea Bubble. February 14:68–70.

Torrance, E. Paul. 1962. Cultural Discontinuities and the Development of Originality of Thinking. *Exceptional Children*, September:2–13.

Turnbull, Colin. 1983. Trouble in Paradise. *New Republic* 188(12): 32–34.

Turner, George, 1861. *Nineteen Years in Polynesia*. London: Snow.

———. 1884. *Samoa a Hundred Years Ago and Long Before*. London: Macmillan.

UNESCO. 1985. *Towards International Youth Year, Round Table on Youth in the 1980s*. Paris: UNESCO.

Vinacke, William E. 1968. *Samoan Personality*. Typescript.

Von Hoffman, Nicholas, and Garry B. Trudeau. 1976. *Tales from the Margaret Mead Taproom*. Kansas City: Sheed and Ward.

Wendt, Albert. 1983. Three Faces of Samoa: Mead's, Freeman's, and Wendt's. *Pacific Islands Monthly*, April: 10–12, 14, 69.

Williams, John. 1832. *South Sea Journals*. London Missionary Society Records (on microfilm).

———. 1839. *A Narrative of Missionary Enterprises in the South Seas*. London: Snow.

Williamson, R. W. 1924. *Social and Political Systems of Central Polynesia.* Cambridge: Cambridge University Press.

———. 1933. *Religious and Cosmic Beliefs of Central Polynesia.* Cambridge: Cambridge University Press.

Willis, Lauli'i. 1889. *The Story of Lauli'i.* San Francisco: Jos. Winterham.

Wright, Louis B. and Mary Fry. 1936. *Puritans in the South Seas.* New York: Henry Holt.

Index

"Absolute cultural determinism," 13, 126, 144
Adolescence (1904), 4
Adolescence, 75–76, 111; in Samoa, 104–107; in U.S. (1925–26), 107–108
Afoa, Mulima, quoted, 137
Agriculture, 32
Ala'ilima, Vaiao and Fay, 153
Amerika Samoa (1960), 58
Angier, Natalie, quoted, 13
Anthropology as a discipline (Boas' influence), 2
Apology ceremony *(Ifoga)*, 159, 160, 161
Appell, George N., 123
Aualuma (unmarried women), 42–43, 77–78, 83, 96, 97
Aumaga (untitled men), 32, 42–43, 44, 48, 76–77, 101, 109, 117, 118, 185
Authority, Samoan attitude toward, 164–165, 182

Bagley, William, 3
Barnouw, Victor, quoted, 6
Barry, H., and A. Schlegel, 193n
Bateson, Gregory, ix
Benedict, Ruth, 5, 17, 172
Blazer, Lee, 132–33
Boas Franz, vii, viii, ix, 1, 2, 3, 4, 5, 6, 7, 8, 13, 15, 16, 139, 144, 145, 172, 174,
    177, 190n; quoted, 1–2, 7
Bowles, John R., 184
Brother-sister respect patterns, 40
Brown, George, 56, 157; quoted, 56, 159–160, 164, 167, 171, 190n
Buck, Sir Peter, 14, 94, 100, 124; quoted, 92–93
Bullen, T., quoted, 182–183

California Test of Personality, 132–133, 147
Campbell, Donald, 127; quoted, 155

Other Books of Interest from *Bergin & Garvey*

Women's Work
Development & the Division of Labor by Gender
ELEANOR LEACOCK, HELEN I. SAFA & CONTRIBUTORS
This vibrant survey of women's work analyzes reproduction and production in industrial capitalism, nonindustrial societies, the Third World, and Socialist societies.
304 Pages   Illustrations

Women & Change in Latin America
New Directions in Sex and Class
JUNE NASH, HELEN I. SAFA, & CONTRIBUTORS
"When women's issues are made paramount then we must question development goals that emphasize production for profit rather than concern for quality of life."
—FROM THE INTRODUCTION

384 Pages   Illustrations

In Her Prime
A New View of Middle-Aged Women
JUDITH BROWN, VIRGINIA KERNS, & CONTRIBUTORS
"These ethnographies are fascinating, heartening, and provocative."
—WOMEN'S REVIEW OF BOOKS

240 Pages   Illustration

Nicaragua—*The People Speak*
ALVIN LEVIE
Introduction by Richard Streb
"Outstanding . . . For everyone questioning Nicaraguan self-determination."
—ED ASNER, ACTOR

224 Pages   Illustrations

Beyond Revolution
A New Theory of Social Movements
DANIEL FOSS & RALPH LARKIN
Introduction by Stanley Aronowitz
256 Pages

The Politics of Education
Culture, Power & Liberation
PAULO FREIRE
"Here speaks a teacher who lives life, a revolutionary with hope."
—CHANGE
240 Pages   Illustrations

Applied Anthropology
An Introduction
JOHN VAN WILLIGEN
320 Pages   Illustrations

Now in Paper!
Spiritualist Healers in Mexico
KAJA FINKLER
Foreword by Arthur Kleinman
272 Pages

Crisis in the Philippines
The Making of a Revolution
E. SAN JUAN
288 Pages   Illustrations

Recalling the Good Fight
An Autobiography of the Spanish Civil War
JOHN TISA
265 Pages   Illustrations

Now in Paper!
Transnationals & the Third World
The Struggle for Culture
ARMAND MATTELART
192 Pages

The Struggle for Rural Mexico
GUSTAVO ESTEVA
320 Pages

Sex & Class in Latin America
JUNE NASH, HELEN SAFA & CONTRIBUTORS
352 Pages   Illustrations

Women and Colonization
MONA ETIENNE, ELEANOR LEACOCK & CONTRIBUTORS
352 Pages   Illustrations

Political Anthropology
An Introduction
TED LEWELLEN
Foreword by Victor Turner
160 Pages   Illustrations

The Nicaraguan Revolution in Health
From Somoza to the Sandinistas
JOHN DONAHUE
188 Pages   Illustrations

Women & Nutrition in Third World Countries
SAHNI HAMILTON & CONTRIBUTORS
160 Pages